D1451806

FISH OF THE WORLD

H. Aramata

FISH
OF THE WORLD

A Collection of
19th-Century Paintings

Portland House
New York

The illustrations in this book are from the Aramata Collection
Scientific consultation for the international edition
by Andrea Marconato and Mariella Rasotto
Texts by Ettore Grimaldi
Chapter introductions by Lorenzo Colombo

Copyright © 1990 by Fenice 2000 s.r.l., Milan
(for the international edition)

Copyright © 1989 by Hiroshi Aramata

Copyright © 1989 by Heibonsha, Tokyo

All rights reserved. No part of this book may be
reproduced or transmitted in any form or by
any means, electronic or mechanical, including
photocopying, recording, or by any information
storage and retrieval system, without
permission in writing from the publisher.

This 1990 edition published by Portland House,
a division of dilithium Press, Ltd.
distributed by Outlet Book Company, Inc.,
a Random House Company,
225 Park Avenue South, New York, New York 10003

Printed and bound in Italy

ISBN 0-517-03048-9

87654321

Contents

TRANSPARENCIES THAT DECEIVE

Fishes, ichthyologists, artists:
searching for an elusive reality

NEPTUNE'S GIFT

Picture Books of Fish in Japan and in the West

The Europeans who visited Japan at the end of the sixteenth century were unanimous in their admiration for the extreme vividness with which the Japanese portrayed fish. Even in paintings on the established Oriental theme of carp swimming up a waterfall, the fish leaped with striking animation.

Many folktales in Japan tell of painted fish that steal out of their paintings every evening and play in ponds, swimming at their leisure. In the West, such tales are quite rare.

What surprised Europeans even more was that the fish painted by the Japanese actually looked delicious. Fresh, lustrous, and plump, these fish look as if they would, without doubt, taste good broiled.

In Europe too, needless to say, from earliest times there have been paintings of fish, and even superb picture books. Representative of these are the eighteenth-century works Poissons, Ecrevisses et Crabes, by Louis Renard, and Ichthyologie, by M. E. Bloch, and the nineteenth-century works Histoire Naturelle des Poissons, by G. Cuvier and A. Valenciennes, and Atlas Ichthyologique des Indes Orientales, by P. Bleeker. For some reason, however, specimen fish-plate pictures are common among Western fish paintings, and half of them look like dried fish. They are not paintings that stimulate the appetite.

Why did the Japanese paint such lifelike and delicious-looking fish? In all likelihood, the reason is due to the Oriental view of life. Since before the Edo Period, owing to the influence of Buddhism, the Japanese have customarily had an aversion to taking life, and for that reason meat-eating was ostensibly abandoned in Japan. Accordingly, killing living beings even to obtain scientific specimens was abhorred.

In addition, it was believed that people who made a practice of saving living beings that were about to be killed or that were injured would, in the afterlife, go to heaven. The folktales of Urashima Taro, beloved of the Japanese, symbolize this belief. Therefore, when Japanese painted pictures of fish, they did not paint dead fish, because such paintings would not be blessed. Or, rather, the more lifelike the fish paintings were, the more desirable they were thought to be, much as Western painters judge paintings according to how realistic they are.

Consequently, fish in Japanese fish paintings look fresh and delicious. In that respect, these picture books of fish rendered in beautiful colors are the greatest legacy Japanese natural history may pride itself on having given the world. From the twin points of quality and quantity, since the Edo Period and on through the Meiji and Taisho periods, no other area in the world has produced fish pictures to equal those of Japan.

By way of experiment, let us compare the history of picture books of fish of the Indian and Pacific oceans in Japan and Europe. About four hundred fish are depicted in the first collection of colored fish illustrations in the world, Poissons, Ecrevisses et Crabes (1718-19), by Louis Renard in Holland. In Boch's monumental Ichthyologie (1785-89), completed about seventy years later, the number exceeds five hundred, and in the definitive work by Cuvier and Valenciennes, Histoire Naturelle des Poissons (1828-49), it approaches seven hundred, which surpasses the number for the Atlantic Ocean. If we look at Fische der Südsee (1873-1910), by A. Garrett and A. Günther, called the last masterpiece of Western picture books of fish, the number of fish illustrations in its one hundred and eighty color lithographs reaches three hundred.

By contrast, even Shurin-zu ("Pictures of a Multitude of Scales," 1760, final edition), ordered by a lord of Shikoku and the first book of color pictures of fish in Japan, easily surpasses Bloch's monumental work of the same period: almost six hundred kinds of fish are depicted in the four volumes of this beautifully copied folding book.

However, Shurin-zu, an outstanding masterpiece that in at least this one respect excels all Western books of fish illustrations, is almost unknown nowadays, even to naturalists professing to be lovers of fish or of natural history paintings. This unfortunate circumstance is not limited to this book, but applies to all books of fish illustrations in Japan. The reason is that these books were never printed, as was customary in Europe and America, and existed only as handmade copies.

Looking closely at the detailed figures in this picture book, one is immediately struck by the creation of three-dimensionality. For example, the swelling ventral side of a flatfish glitters, giving the sense of a spherical surface. This kind of depiction, of course, tends to create a three-dimensional sensation, but what is awesome is the ingenuity with which the paper has been used. In fact, this illustration is not done on one sheet of paper. Lacquer has been applied to paper cut out in the shape of the fish, and protuberances have been attached to make the scales seem real. It was then beautifully colored and pasted into the folding book.

In other words, Shurin-zu is not a book of paintings but a collection of paper models. It should be called a specimen collection made of paper. It is the only picture book in the world in which the contours of fish can be understood by touching the page.

It is interesting to know the circumstances that went into making Shurin-zu. This deluxe picture book was made by order of the Takamatsu lord, Matsudaira Yorichika, and, it is assumed, was produced in Edo (present-day Tokyo) or more probably in both Edo and Takamatsu. It was probably made around the tenth year of Horeki (1760). Because it was done by order of a lord, it goes without saying that in form and content it is both accurate and elaborate. It is necessary, though, to suppose the existence of a director, guiding the project from behind the scenes to create a thoroughgoing view of natural history that, from the first, adhered scrupulously to three-dimensionality.

This director was Hiraga Gennai, the most brilliant and gifted natural historian in Japan during the Edo Period. Hiraga Gennai spread Western picture books of natural history throughout Japan and by means of those paintings also contrived the modernization of nihonga, of Japanese-style painting. At the same time he was in the service of Lord Yorichika of Takamatsu. While accompanying the lord during a journey up to Edo for an alternate year of residence there, he visited all the natural history collections they passed along the way. Lord Yorichika had Gennai collect plans for a picture book of fish and put him in charge of identifying most of the fish.

The originator of the "three-dimensional model" picture book of fish, the first of its kind in the world, was in all likelihood Hiraga Gennai. He visited his friend Soh Shiseki (Kusumoto Setsukei), who had returned to Edo after studying drawing in Nagasaki, then began the work of choosing a painter for producing the book. Selected at that time was Miki Bunryu, one of Setsukei's pupils in Edo. It seems most likely that Bunryu visited the fish markets in Nihonbashi and other places and then, in the space of about two years, finished painting a prototype.

This prototype went back and forth between Takamatsu and Edo again and again, and with the paintings added by Bunryu or other painters seems to have reached the form it has now as seen in Takamatsu. If we look at the folding book, we see there are blank pages, too. In other words, the book is a kind of file of paintings to which additions could be made whenever rare fish were offered as presents.

Another famous maker of picture books of fish was the Edo naturalist called Kurimoto Tansyu. A high-ranking priest in the late Edo Period, Kurimoto Tansyu (1756-1834), whose real name was Rissi, was born the second son of Tamura Genyu, the master of Hiraga Gennai. He was adopted into the medical family of Kurimoto, studied medicine, and while having access to the shogunate herbal garden, devoted his energies for more than twenty years to the study of the natural history of insects and fish. Only one of his books, Mr. Ritsu's Fish Album (Ritsu *means* "Kurimoto"), was printed, but the twenty-two volumes of fish albums, done in his own hand, which he left have provided an invaluable resource to scholars of later generations. Okukura Tatsuyuki, Takagi Shunzan, and other makers of fish albums who appeared during the closing days of the Tokugawa shogunate all relied on Tansyu's fish albums.

When Philipp Siebold came to Edo, he met Tansyu and received many natural history illustrations from this feudal doctor. Siebold then sent them to Holland and used them as references for the illustrations in his Fauna Japonica. *It was then that Kurimoto Tanshu became known in the West.*

Since Tansyu was the son of Tamura Genyu, a man who can be called one of the original Edo natural historians, it can be assumed that he was, as a matter of course, exposed to salons where natural historians gathered to exchange thoughts with like-minded people. Out of such experiences evolved the **Shaben-kai** ("Red Whip Society"), a group of natural historians formed at the very end of the shogunate. Much of the legacy of Kurimoto Tansyu, in fact, was handed down through the Shaben-kai.

As mentioned above, the first Western book of color fish pictures printed in Europe was Louis Renard's Poissons, Ecrevisses et Crabes. *The first printing was done in Amsterdam from 1718 to 1719. Today, only about fifty copies of this rare book exist.*

This first book of illustrations is composed of paintings of tropical fish in their natural environment done by Samuel Fallours, a painter living in the Molucca Islands. These "live" fish are painted in brilliant colors as realistically as possible, but to contemporary eyes the finished products look more like surrealist paintings or the illustrations in children's picture books. In fact, Westerners who saw these paintings did not believe that such fish actually existed. However, when professional ichthyologists are shown these apparently fanciful paintings, they are able to identify correctly about 70 percent of the fish. As Fallours, the painter, asserted, these are definitely illustrations of live fish painted realistically. Indeed, Fallours said in his preface that these paintings were mere pale copies and that the actual fish have even more fantastic colors and shapes. That is to say, the actual wonder of the fish is nothing like this. That illustrated books of natural history were destined to be executed realistically is clearly shown by the difference between the Westerners' reaction and the painter's explanation.

The most significant feature of Renard's book is that living fish are rendered in detail in their actual environment. Because the colors of live fish and dead fish are totally different, it is impossible to imagine from the fish arranged in rows at a fish shop what those fish actually look like swimming in the ocean. But in ordinary illustrated books of fish, dead fish are painted as if they were living fish. Fallours, however, showed Westerners living tropical fish painted in an unexpectedly realistic style. The finished works could not but become surrealistic, fantastic paintings, largely divorced from a Westerner's sense of realism and far beyond the recognition of a fish shop owner.

In other words, the more realistically natural history paintings are done, the more likely they are to suffer the ironic destiny of becoming fantasy paintings. Conversely, if one wished to paint not fantastic but realistic fish paintings, one would paint the fish in a fish shop. That is to say, a dead fish presents an unreal image far remote from the actual image of a live fish, but such images are accepted as realistic by most people. It makes sense then that Takahashi Yuichi, who had decided to bring realism to Japanese contemporary oil painting, painted not live salmon but slightly salted ones, for a paintng of the dead body of a fish certifies the reality of fish as they appear on land (fish in a fish shop) for those who live on land. In which case, realism is actually a vague notion.

To Europeans, surrounded by cold currents, the

fantastically colored fish of the Indian Ocean seemed sinful. The ichthyologist Bennett, whose study of fish was supported by the British East Indian Company, in 1830 encountered the same disbelief that Renard had met a hundred years before. When Bennett showed the illustrations he had done of live tokara-bera (wall wrasse), which he had collected on the beach, to one of the prominent figures of English colonial society, that person did not think the illustrations were of real fish and highly praised Bennett's wonderful powers of imagination. Incensed, Bennett went the next morning to the beach eight hundred meters from his residence, collected some live tokara-bera, took them in a glass bowl to the table of the prominent figure, and announced, "There! These are the models for the fanciful paintings I showed you yesterday." Shown the real thing, the prominent figure is said to have been horrified.

Dealing with creatures from an unknown world, ichthyologists had first of all to fight people's disbelief.

Unlike the Japanese, the Europeans were not familiar with the fish found in the warm currents of the Pacific Ocean, so it is understandable that, living in a region of cold currents, they would not believe in the actual existence of the beautiful fish of the Pacific Ocean. Those fish were originally believed to be creatures from another world.

The history of the relationship between humans and fish begins with people realizing that the inhabitants of the watery world were edible. From this discovery, human awareness of fish proceeded along the lines of an evolution similar to that of plants, which went from being used as medicinal herbs to becoming the object of the science of botany. Plants were first classified as "drugs" according to their efficacy and mode of application, and that knowledge eventually gave way to the science. Thus, if the science of plants began with the investigation of drugs, that of fish began wih food. Undaunted by hives and other adverse reactions, those ancient people who discovered that fish could be eaten were the founders of ichthyology.

The subsequent story of humans and their relation with fish is natural history. The roles of the main fishy characters in the story were determined according to their value as food. Fish that could not be eaten had no role; therefore, they were not included among fish. But fish are different in one respect from plants and land animals: they are creatures that live in water. For humans, the world of water is nothing less than another world, and the creatures that live in that other world, like ghosts and goblins, were originally invisible beings. The nameless sensation that attacks the heart of a fisherman, when terrified at not knowing what being from that other world he has caught, recalls the primeval image of fish held by ancient peoples. Fish were once mysterious creatures.

Accordingly, it appears that fish were not originally recognized by color or shape. The difficulty of holding eel, the strong pull of carp and sea bream, the panicky struggles of gray mullet when held in two hands, the discordant cry of croaker — these were the actual sensations fish transmitted, and there is no doubt that they were a code for identifying kinds of fish. Heat, an absolute shared response that cancels other subtle sensations between birds and mammals, can also be said to make a decisive difference. The cold skin of a fish awakens abruptly our instinctive bodily sensations. It can also be said that birds and mammals, excepting those that smell bad or have strange cries, were rationally recognized as living beings solely through the sense of sight.

The only way to actually see fish as they are is to transfer them into water. But the body color of many delicate species of fish changes drastically just on being transferred from the ocean to an aquarium. The blue devil, a beautiful fish, is a shining cobalt blue, but if caught and transferred to an aquarium, it changes color to a purplish-black and becomes a totally dull-looking fish, as breeders well know.

Consequently, the image of fish fixed in the human mind, to put it simply, cannot help being that given by a fish shop. Proof of this is the image we have, for example, of bonito. We usually think of bonito as having a characteristic pattern of stripes, but that striped pattern appears almost not at all in living bonito. Fish leave their real images in that other world.

Beginning in the 1700s, when colored illustrations of live fish were finally produced in Europe, it is no wonder that ordinary people, who knew only the fish in a fish shop, exclaimed that they had never seen such fish and expressed disbelief and wonder when viewing those pictures.

There is a body of knowledge about fish assembled through the wisdom of East and West, and if we make a careful comparative study we can point to several topics of great interest to natural history. One of these is eels.

Eastern and Western perceptions of eels could be termed contradictory, divided as they are into two extreme opinions. One sees eels as useful; the other sees them as frightening and weird. Whether emphasis is put on the objective view of a nourishing edible fish or on that fish's peculiar external appearance, resembling a snake, is a problem that clearly divides opinions of eels.

For example, Buffon, in his Histoire Naturelle, général et particulière, claims the Romans did not much like eels because they resembled snakes. Proof of that is the following poem by Juvenal (circa 50-131): "For you there is the eel, a snake raised in a ditch."

In support of his claims, Buffon goes on to stress the similarities between snakes and eels. At night these fish come onto land and crawl to meadows, but this is no mere migration; it is for the purpose of eating snails.

Roman and Italian views on eels are not uniform. The Romans, who are supposed to have disliked eels, called them the queen of the banquet. Later Italians do not seem to have liked eels. In Walton's The Complete Angler the following words appear as a remark often used by pitiless Italians. "Give an eel to your enemy, but only the eel, without any liquid." The natural historian Aldrovandi explains, however, that in the typical view of a sixteenth-century Italian eels were not a food but a necessary medicine.

Because it is written in Chapter 11 of the Book of Leviticus that fish without scales are detestable, Jews will absolutely not touch eels. Although England, Walton's homeland, recognizes countless ways of eating eels, doctors believed the fish a harmful food.

In comparison, many places extol eels as wonderful fish. In ancient Greece eels were such a superior edible fish that from old the Greeks had tried cultivating them. Although he did not write about the method in detail, even Aristotle made observations about eel cultivation. According to him, because eels have small gills, if their water is not clean they will suffocate. To cultivate them, therefore, it is vital either that water be kept flowing over a flat stone sheet or that the bucket the eels are put in be coated with whitewash so that the water does not become muddy.

In China, eels are peerless fish, capable of creating many mixed breeds and making different animals give birth, not to mention being autogenous. In Chinese Materia Medica, eels are described as able to make not only snakeheads but also catfish and snakes give birth.

It is in Japan, however, that the disparity of opinions regarding eels reaches its acme. In Japan, eels are considered manifestations of different kinds of beings. For example, from old there was a popular belief that taro change shape and turn into eels. In the late Muromachi dictionary, Zinten-nôzin-shô, it says that snakes turn into eels and that taro turn into eels too. In the Wakan Sansai Zue is the belief that taro that are wetted for a long time turn into eels, a notion that presupposes that inanimate objects can turn into animate beings, but there were still examples of doubt and disbelief that all taro could change in like manner. Be it taro or eels, this view that only a small number of "strange" individuals is able to effect such a transformation conforms to an old belief that a being that had lived for a long time possessed exceptional power, like those of a goblin cat. This belief, called "ninety-nine gods," was widespread.

In Japan eels are an edible fish rich in nutrition. The smoke that results from broiling them is used as an insect repellent. The smoke issuing from a broiled-eel shop not only attracts customers but also serves as a substitute for naphthol. In the Chinese Materia Medica, too, it says that if mosquitoes are touched by the scent, they transform into water, and if the rugs and bamboo wood in a house are scented with it, insects go away. It also says that if eel bones are put in clothing chests, there will be no insects. According to the Teijo-Zakki, if goods made of straw are fumigated in the smoke of broiled eel before they are put in the storehouse, they will be safe from insects.

Again, in the Kishu Fish Album, it is said that eating the uncooked heart of an eel is popularly believed to cure bed-wetting. Eels are said to be efficacious because they are rich in vitamin A.

There is also a deep-rooted belief that broiled eels is good medicine for a long life. According to the botanist Dr. Makino Tomitaro, as the body advances in age it gets weaker, but eating broiled eel every day will increase one's lifespan by ten years.

The above is just part of the natural history of eels, but it includes matters of ample interest to contemporary people. This information is taken from a Japanese natural-history magazine, and it is regrettable that such magazines are not translated. For that reason, topics of great interest concerning fish other than eels have not been introduced to foreign readers, and the wonderful illustrations in the Japanese fish picture books shown here should be a novel experience for Europeans.

Besides the Japanese fish picture books in this book, famous works have been assembled from Renard, at the top of the list, as well as from Bloch's famed Ichthyologie, E. Donovan's Natural History of British Fishes, Bennett's A Selection from the most Remarkable and Interesting Fishes found on the Coast of Ceylon, A. Garrett and A. Günter's Fishe der Südsee, and F. Day's The Fishes of Malabar, among others. In addition, numerous plates from the beautiful records produced by nineteenth-century French natural-history voyages, such as the Astrolabe, the Coquille, and the Venus, have been reproduced here.

I believe this is the only book, past or present, that contains so many fish illustrations from around the world. I hope this book, which presents the point of view of the residents of "a half-hidden region," will be exciting to Western readers.

— Hiroshi Aramata

CAPTAIN NEMO AND ALEXANDER'S BELL

"Suddenly there was light at the sides of the room, through two oblong openings. The liquid masses were brightly lit by an electric effect. Two crystal plates separated us from the sea." Professor Pierre Aronnax of the Muséum d'Histoire Naturelle of Paris, a brilliant marine biologist, author of the much appreciated book Mystères des grands fonds sous-marins *("Mysteries of the great undersea depths"), Conseil, the generous and faithful servant who accompanies all 18th-century "heroes" in the most unusual of circumstances, and the Canadian Nel Land, the whaleman who never misses when throwing his harpoon, had never seen nor imagined anything of the sort: when the black bathypelagic waters were illuminated (or better "it was no longer luminous water, but liquid light") the gorgeous, bizarre, astonishing marine life was revealed ("What a spectacle! what pen could describe it?"). The episode is well known; it is one of Jules Verne's novels* (Twenty Thousand Leagues under the Sea); *the story takes place in 1867, the book was written in 1869. The futuristic submarine* Nautilus *astonishes us not so much because of its navigational performance and the high technological level of its navigational equipment as because of the exorbitant Victorian luxury of its accommodation: a hall after Second Empire luxury hotels in Paris, a library after the castles of the British nobility, a dining room after a New York financier's dwelling overlooking Central Park, even an organ which Captain Nemo "used to play with great skill, but only at night, in the middle of the most secret darkness, when the* Nautilus *was asleep in the ocean waste."*

When, barely sixty years later, real men, and not characters created by fancy, were able to observe for the first time, for scientific purposes, sea waters and marine creatures from behind a glass, they were certainly dreaming of the large oval windows with the small spiral columns and the soft sofas of the Nautilus *that Verne's words and, even more, De Neuville's drawings, had printed in the childish memory of two or three*

generations. William Beebe and Otis Barton reached a depth of one thousand meters (1934) in the coastal waters of New Nonsuch Island (Bermuda) inside a steel sphere hanging from a wire. The biologist William Beebe was the director of the department for tropical research of the New York Zoological Society, Otis Barton had designed the thing that had been baptized "bathysphere." It had an interior cavity of 1.37 m, corresponding more or less to 54 inches or to two seats in the subway, but mostly occupied by oxygen cylinders, bowls for chemical solutions for the air change, a telephone, electric batteries and a floodlight to light up the waters, still cameras and movie cameras, a few scientific instruments. Crouching against the round steel wall, they were looking out through three twenty cm wide round windows blocked by fused quartz crystals 76 mm thick. The entrance was a 35 cm round hole onto which a door weighing about two hundred kilos was fastened by ten bolts; to get in and out of the bathysphere required accurate acrobatics and a very thin body. Gloria Hollister, with earphones on her head and a stenographer's pad in her hands, onboard the pontoon Ready, *from which the batysphere was lowered into the Atlantic waters, carefully took down Beebe's words in the course of the plunges and could not help writing down at the end: "Bolts and doors are removed; Beebe and Barton emerge, stiffened and tired."*

Though fragmentary, the dry remarks of the American biologist in Miss Hollister's transcription convey the feeling of the increase in progress of naturalistic knowledge and the taste for human adventure:

"690 m.: Never seen such obscurity, it is the darkest place in the world.
710 m.: Small forms, like independent sparks, with the consistency of a network; could it be the luminous fluid tissue that crustaceans emit in the water?
853 m.: Here is a fish with telescope eyes; all around, marvelous lights... water full of lights...
884 m.: Extremely cold in here; hands freeze if we touch the window's edge...

774 m.: I saw a fish with hundreds of lights, about twenty centimeters, the whole body from head to tail sprinkled with tiny lights; lights of a pale lemon color" (plunge of August 15, 1934; from William Beebe, Half Mile Down).

Ocean museums sunk in the waters of coral reefs where free-swimming fish crowd in front of the windows of the boxes containing spellbound tourists, boats with glass bottoms gliding over tropical seabeds and their multicolored creatures, natural marine parks where fishes do not swim away when interested and inquisitive visitors with masks and flippers swim at their side — has all this and all the rest of new, detailed information dulled our emotions in front of the "oblong openings" of the Nautilus or of the small crystals of fused quartz of Beebe's bathysphere? Perhaps.

Actually, both things — Nautilus and bathysphere — are for the great majority fruits of fancy. Or "provocations" that, together with others in the universal world of images, have attracted again man's interest toward the multiform charm of that part of aquatic life that corresponds to the biological definition of fish.

The following pages create a sort of counterproof: their illustrations, by means of techniques that closely resemble art — or, even if this may sound a little exaggerated, that accurately follow the history of taste (besides of course the history of ichthyological science) — depict all the astonishing variations that enrich our idea of a fish: hydrodynamic shapes of functional purity; colors, iridescence, transparency created by nature's unequalled imagination; prodigiously bizarre features (lights in the abysses, wings to glide over the oceans, stings and venoms, electric fields to "monitor" the environment); sudden darts, patient ambushes, anatomic, biological, behavioristic "cunning" to create often impossible forms of life, innumerable sources of surprise that gave vent to legends and inspired men with the desire to know more. Above of all was the surprise, the amazement of aquatic life itself, of that world whose

refraction and transparency are so highly metaphysical.

A man who like professor Aronnax had the good luck to observe the creatures living in the ocean depths and that like professor Beebe descended into them hanging from a wire (as European miniatures of the Middle Ages and Indian miniatures of the 16th century describe) was the extraordinary Alexander the Great. Or at least this is proclaimed by almost all of the many versions — Greek, Latin, French, Italian, German, even Scandinavian, Bohemian and Russian as well as Syrian, Persian, Ethioipian, Turkish, Indian, and Malaysian — of his legendary exploits. This originated from a tale attributed to Callisthenes, a relative of Alexander's, who was also a philosopher and one of Alexander's companions during his great conquering adventures, but it had been written instead about five hundred years after Alexander of Macedon's death, in the second or third century of our age, and this legend, following a traditional line picked up Christian religious elements and edifying motifs. In the Ethiopian version, contained in a manuscript brought to Great Britain after Sir Robert Napier's expedition against emperor Theodore II (1868), Alexander is called the "two-horned one" (figuring him perhaps as Jupiter Ammonius adorned with the horns of a ram, in memory of his visit, historical this time, to the oracle of the Egyptian god Amon in the Siwa oasis in the Libyan desert); he reaches the sea that stretches "beyond the earth and the sky and which no ship has ever sailed" and is lowered into the waters inside a glass bell "covered with a donkey skin" hanging from chains. The hero wants to know what divine creations "exist in the sea," and an angel arrives who "looks after the sea and the animals it contains": he orders the monsters to go by "as swift as lightning" in front of the glass cage; it takes three days and three nights for "the back parts and the tail" of one of the creatures to become visible.

The image of the Conqueror can well support the allegory of the desire for knowledge. Ichthyology is more interested in Aristotle, who was the teacher of the historical Alexander. The ancient scholar describes 115 species of fishes, almost all of them of the Aegean Sea, without any seventy-two-hour-long monster. Also for Oppianus, a Greek from Cilicia who dedicated to Emperor Marcus Aurelius (Alieuticae) a poem on the art of fishing, the species of fishes are 115. Over one thousand years later, Pierre Belon, a French doctor who visited the East with an embassy from King Frances I, describes 110 of them in his De Aquatilibus (Paris, 1533). Ippolito Salviani from Città di Castello, Pope Julius III's archaitrist, enumerates only ninety-nine, but for each of them he suggests how to fish and cook it (Aquatilium animalium historia, Rome, 1558).

This book brings us back to the glorious age of the historical development of naturalistic knowledge: from the 19th-century ichthyological books listed on page 261 it selects roughly 950 species, a record number as to iconographic presentations. At the time, the known species were about 7,000; this is their number in Albert Günther's classic Catalogue of the fishes in the British Museum (1859-70).

And today? We rely on estimates. However odd it may appear outside the halls of universities, much has still to be discovered in the waters. A few decades ago some authoritative assumptions suggested numbers varying from fifteen thousand to forty thousand living species; twenty years ago a final conclusion emerged that specifies the number to be around twenty-eight thousand.

The problem of classification of the largest group of vertebrates (the number of species is estimated to correspond to 42 percent of those known, the rest corresponds to mammals, reptiles, amphibians, and birds) is a specialistic matter; it is sufficient to mention here the fundamental subdivision of the cephalochordata groups (amphioxi), of cyclostomes (lampreys and myxines), of cartilaginous fishes (sharks, rays, chimaeras), and of osseous fishes (the "perfect" fishes, if you prefer; this last group includes almost all of the above-mentioned twenty-eight thousand species, instead

of the scarcely over five hundred species of the third group and the about fifty species of the first and second groups together).

We may add one curious remark: as there are fishes both in the Andean waters of Lake Titicaca, at an altitude of 5,000 meters, and in the ocean trenches, over 11,000 meters below the surface, what we call "vertical extension" is much higher for fish than the vertical extension of any other vertebrate.

Let's go back for a moment to Verne. When his more learned companions (Conseil, the servant, had absorbed science by looking after the professor) involve him in a discussion about fish classification, good Ned Land bursts out: "Fish are classified as those that we can eat and those that we cannot eat."

Verne uses this gag to make his ichthyological lecture more amusing, a lecture he delivers in those pages according to the 19th-century optimistic belief in instructing and amusing at the same time. Now it is time to terminate this invitation to follow Alexander's, Beebe's, and professor Aronnax's example and inform the reader that here fishes have been subdivided into three chapters: in the first one we have grouped cyclostomes and cartilaginous fishes, in the other two groups we have subdivided the orders of osseous fishes according to the prevailing presence of sea fishes and fresh-water fishes (and the word "prevailing" demonstrates how empirical this subdivision is).

Should we like to put the two last chapters under the protective sign of a poet, the above-mentioned Oppianus, with his didactic Greek verse, would be appropriate for sea fishes, whereas Decimus Magnus Ausonius from Burdigala (Bordeaux) would be appropriate for the other: he was the teacher of Emperor Gratianus (4th century) and in his short Latin poem Mosella, meant for the celebration of Treviri, the emperor's preferred residence, he enumerates fourteen fresh-water fish species mostly unknown to former writers. A name to remember for people who like to throw a fishing-line from a riverbank.

Sharks, rays, chimaeras

In one of the first books dedicated exclusively to fish, published in Lyons in 1554 by the naturalist Guillaume Rondelet under the title Libris de piscibus marinis in quibus verae piscium effigies expressae sunt, 244 ichthyological species are described and elegantly illustrated. Two centuries later, in his work Sistema naturae, Carolus Linnaeus listed 414 species of fish.

How hard the taxonomic work of later ichthyologists has been is demonstrated by the fact that Joseph S. Nelson, in his work Fishes of the World published in 1976, records a number of no fewer than 18,818 living recognizable species. However, it seems likely that this number will increase about 50 percent because at least 28,000 species are believed to exist.

In fact, even in a rather limited systematic group, supposedly well known, such as sharks, the number of species has risen from 250 to 344 in the period from 1970 to today. Very likely, therefore, fishes are even more numerous than the other large group of vertebrates, the tetrapods, which includes amphibians, reptiles, birds, and mammals, groups that number 21,450 known species, a figure that is probably close to the real number.

Fishes occupy a central position in the long evolutionary history of vertebrates and are important not so much for the total number of their species, which is much higher in other zoological groups, as for the fact that they have originated the largest, most mobile, and most voracious species of the whole animal kingdom. Yet, according to the most credible reconstructions of that remote past of over 500 million years ago, the ancestors of today's giants were tiny, inconspicuous sea creatures, sessile or static, that fed simply by filtering microscopic organisms suspended in the water. These ancestral creatures have been extinct for ages, but from them, in addition to vertebrates, a parallel evolutionary line has developed, the Cephalochordata, with several primitive characteristics. This line has survived to these days, with a meager group of 20 surviving species, grouped in the genera Branchiostoma and Asynnetron (pages 22-23) and called collectively amphioxi. They are cosmopolitan sea animals of small size (up to 9 cm), with elongated lanceolate bodies with no paired fins, without a skeleton but supported by a rigid axial cellular cord, called the notochord, that allows the amphioxi to bend laterally without losing shape. It takes advantage of this characteristic to sink in sand or in the small pebbles of shallows.

The quiet way of life of the amphioxi, based on their habit of sinking in the sand and their pharyngeal filtering, can also be found in the larval forms, called ammocoetes, of the most primitive vertebrates, agnates or cyclostomes, so-called after their more or less circular mouth, not articulated into mandible and jaw, that therefore cannot be closed. The stage of ammocoetes is typical to Petromyzoniforms, otherwise called lampreys. Ammocoetes have an eel-shaped body, without paired fins, supported, like in the adult individual, by a notochord strengthened by vaguely vertebra-shaped cartilaginous elements. At the moment of their metamorphosis, they cease feeding on microorganisms. According to the different species, after their metamorphosis, the individuals reproduce and then die within a short time, or else change into ectoparasites that suck the blood of teleostean fishes through their suctorial mouth, which produces an anticoagulant secretion, as in the case of Petromyzon marinus and Lampetra fluviatilis (page 22).

Unlike lampreys, which are mostly fresh-water fishes (32 species out of 41), myxines, which belong to the second group of Agnates and with their 32 species compose the order of Myxiniforms, are essentially sea fishes. Myxines are very viscid animals with an elongated body and no paired fins, that live in schools on muddy bottoms at a depth of several hundred meters. They are the only vertebrates with circulating fluids made of a saline composition somewhat resembling sea water and appeared earlier than 400 million years ago. Both Petromyoniforms and Gnatostomes seem instead to have evolved from Agnates already suited to life in fresh water or at least in estuarine environments: their internal fluids contain saline concentrations lower than sea-water concentrations.

Gnatostomes, which correspond to fishes and tetrapods, have mouths with jaws and mandibles, originally deriving from the skeletal structure of the first branchial arch, which make catching and swallowing large prey possible. Together with greater mobility, thanks to the development of paired fins or limbs, and stronger structure, thanks to the evolution of the notochord into a real spinal column in adult individuals, this capacity can account for the evolutionary success of this group in comparison with the Agnates.

As to fishes, two phylogenetic lines have reached the present time: Chondroichthyes, or cartilaginous fishes, and Osteoichthyes, or osseous fishes, both of which appeared in the Devonian period (from 400 to 350 million years ago) starting from the primitive Gnatostomes that lived in the internal waters of the three continents existing at the time.

Chondroichthyes have a calcified cartilaginous skeleton, and, as they lack a swim bladder with which to control their hydrostatic balance, they are compelled to swim continuously in order not to sink, unless they live on the bottom. The present forms live almost exclusively in sea water, and though their body fluids have a saline concentration of about half the concentration of sea water, they run no risk of dehydration through osmosis, as they acquire a condition of hypertronicity by accumulating in their blood over 1 percent of urea and trimethylamine oxide.

At a systematic level, the Chondroichthyes class can be divided into two subclasses: Elasmobranchs, with about 700 species, and Olocephala, with 30. Elasmobranchs include two superorders: Selachii or sharks, and Bathoides, including rays, electric rays, and saw-fishes.

Selachii have a tapering body of a not very bright color, a pointed snout, and a lower jaw with several rows of sharp teeth that are continually replaced. They have 5 to 7 lateral branchial openings. Body sizes can be remarkable, up to the 18 m of the whale shark, Rhincodon typus (page 23), the largest living fish, and the 14 m of the elephant shark, Cetorhinus maximus. Both of them feed on plankton. Excluding these gentle giants, sharks are efficient carnivorous predators, provided with unsuspected intelligence and a high sensorial sharpness. In addition to their excellent sense of smell, they have the ability of detecting, better than any other animal, extremely weak electric fields that can reach as little as 5 manovolts/cm (25 million times less than the minimum field a man can perceive) thanks to head electrosensors called Lorenzini's ampullae. So they can detect their prey from the electric activity of their muscles, or orient themselves following the earth's magnetic field.

Bathoides had differentiated from shark-shaped ancestors in the late Jurassic period (about 150 million years ago), to become suited to benthonic life. Their body is flattened in the dorsal-ventral direction, it is rather elongate in the case of saw-fishes, or it widens in front into a round-shaped disk in the case of electric rays, or else it is subrhomboidal as in rays, stingrays, and devilfishes. In spite of their harmless appearance, some Bathoides can be dangerous because of poisonous glands located at the foot of a caudal sting, as in stingrays, Dasyatis pastinaca (page 28), or because of electric organs capable of emitting discharges ranging from 3-6 kw to 200 volts, as in electric rays.

The small order of Chimeriforms is the only surviving order belonging to the subclass of Olocephala, which were very numerous in the Mesozoic period (from 230 to 65 million years ago). These fishes have a rather unusual appearance, which can be compared to a mosaic of heterogeneous parts, hence their name. Their most generally known representative, Chimaera monstrosa (page 30), about 1 m long, lives an abyssal life (down to a depth of 1,800 m), except in the mating season, when it swims near the coasts.

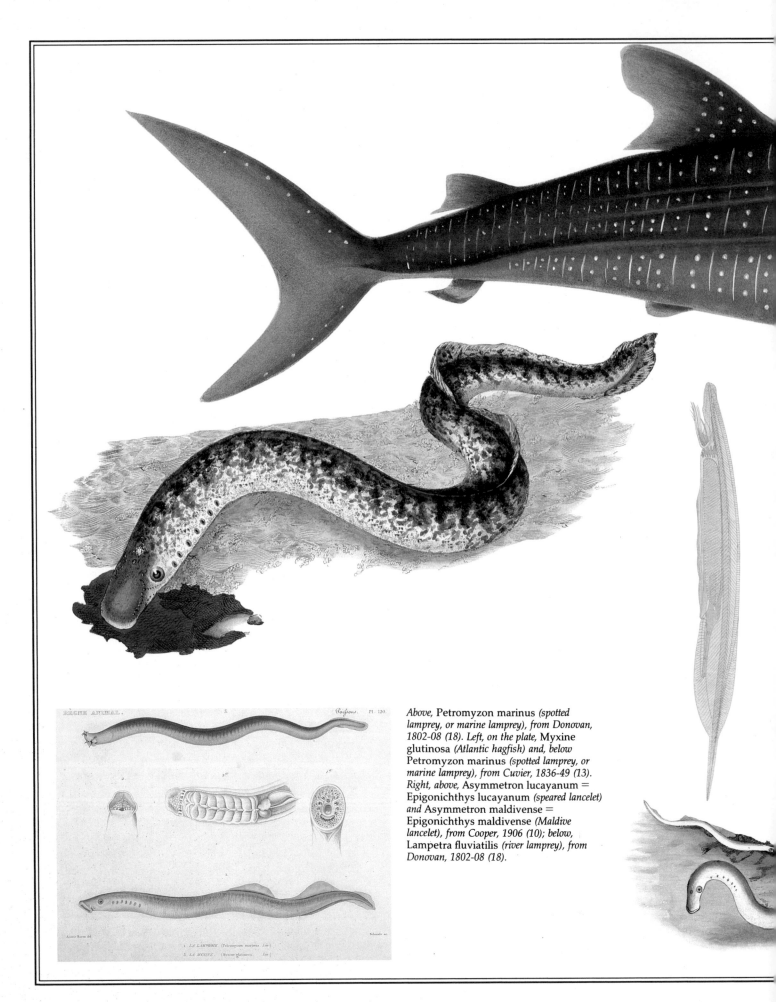

Above, Petromyzon marinus *(spotted lamprey, or marine lamprey), from Donovan, 1802-08 (18). Left, on the plate,* Myxine glutinosa *(Atlantic hagfish) and, below* Petromyzon marinus *(spotted lamprey, or marine lamprey), from Cuvier, 1836-49 (13). Right, above,* Asymmetron lucayanum = Epigonichthys lucayanum *(speared lancelet) and* Asymmetron maldivense = Epigonichthys maldivense *(Maldive lancelet), from Cooper, 1906 (10); below,* Lampetra fluviatilis *(river lamprey), from Donovan, 1802-08 (18).*

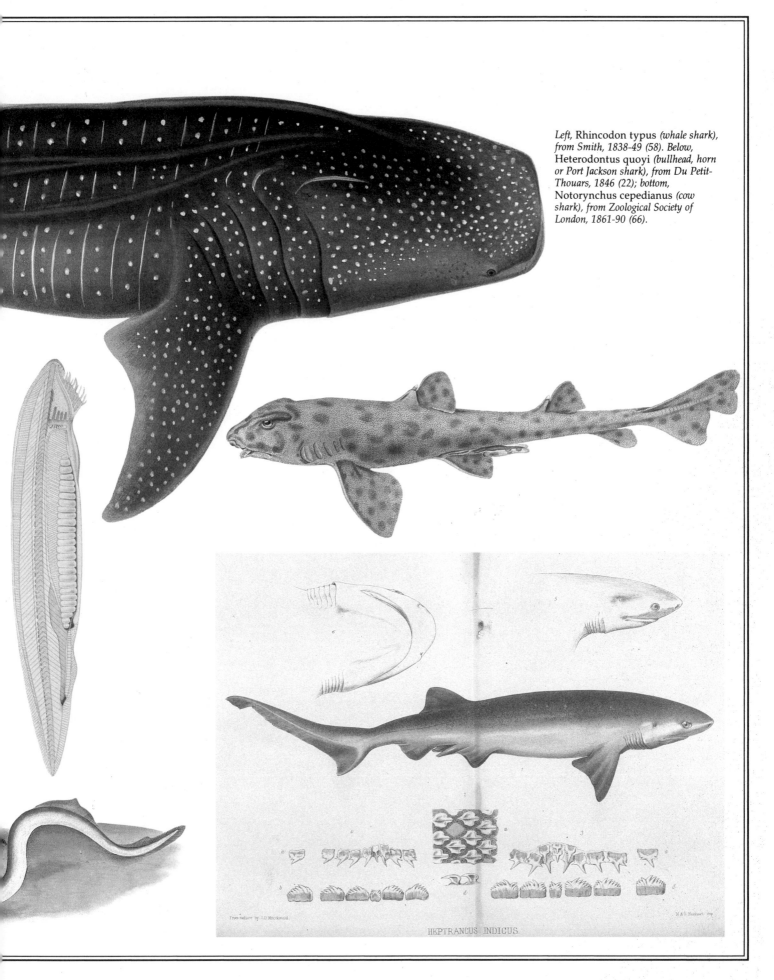

Left, Rhincodon typus *(whale shark), from Smith, 1838-49 (58)*. Below, Heterodontus quoyi *(bullhead, horn or Port Jackson shark), from Du Petit-Thouars, 1846 (22); bottom,* Notorynchus cepedianus *(cow shark), from Zoological Society of London, 1861-90 (66)*.

From nature by J.D. Macdonald.

M. & N. Hanhart. imp.

HEPTRANCUS INDICUS.

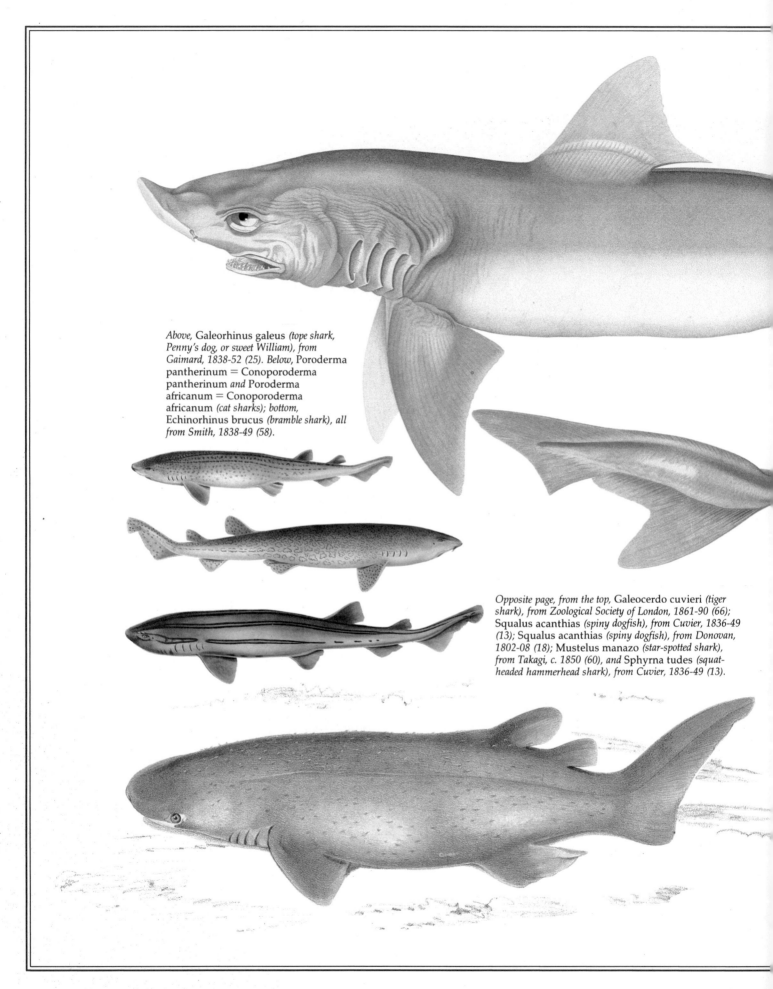

Above, Galeorhinus galeus *(tope shark, Penny's dog, or sweet William), from Gaimard, 1838-52 (25). Below,* Poroderma pantherinum = Conoporoderma pantherinum *and* Poroderma africanum = Conoporoderma africanum *(cat sharks); bottom,* Echinorhinus brucus *(bramble shark), all from Smith, 1838-49 (58).*

Opposite page, from the top, Galeocerdo cuvieri *(tiger shark), from Zoological Society of London, 1861-90 (66);* Squalus acanthias *(spiny dogfish), from Cuvier, 1836-49 (13);* Squalus acanthias *(spiny dogfish), from Donovan, 1802-08 (18);* Mustelus manazo *(star-spotted shark), from Takagi, c. 1850 (60), and* Sphyrna tudes *(squat-headed hammerhead shark), from Cuvier, 1836-49 (13).*

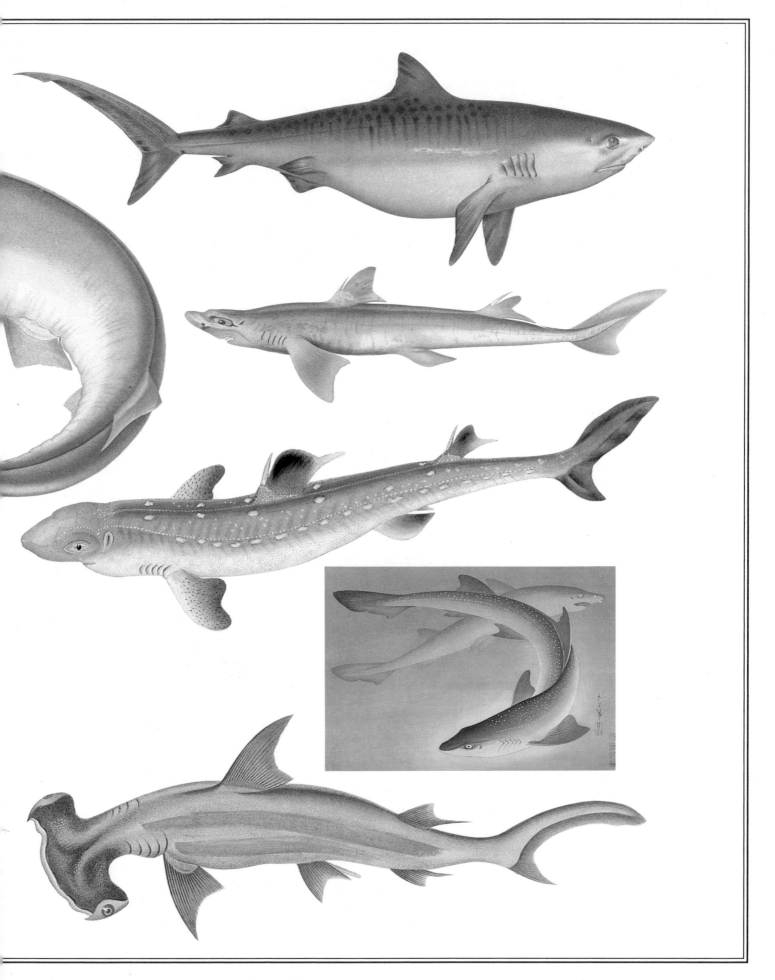

Above, Carcharhinus melanopterus *(black-tipped shark), from Cuvier, 1836-49 (13). Right,* Pristiphorus nudipinis *(saw shark), from Donovan, 1823-27 (19).*

Below left, Lamna nasus *(porbeagle), from Donovan, 1802-08 (18); right,* Pteromylaeus bovinus *(eagle ray), from Hamilton, 1843 (30).*

Squatina squatina *(angel shark), from Donovan, 1802-08 (18).*

The Eagle Ray

Above, Rhinobatos annulatus *(guitarfish); left,* Carcharodon carcharias *(great white shark), both from Smith, 1838-49 (58).*

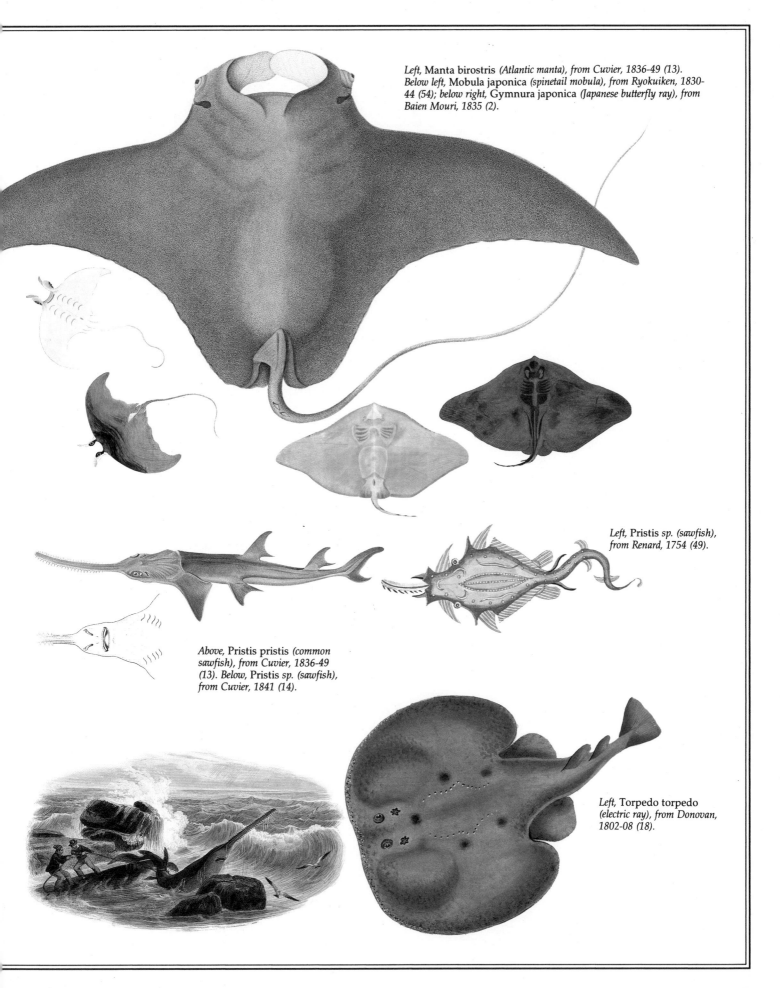

Left, Manta birostris *(Atlantic manta), from Cuvier, 1836-49 (13). Below left,* Mobula japonica *(spinetail mobula), from Ryokuiken, 1830-44 (54); below right,* Gymnura japonica *(Japanese butterfly ray), from Baien Mouri, 1835 (2).*

Left, Pristis sp. *(sawfish), from Renard, 1754 (49).*

Above, Pristis pristis *(common sawfish), from Cuvier, 1836-49 (13). Below,* Pristis sp. *(sawfish), from Cuvier, 1841 (14).*

Left, Torpedo torpedo *(electric ray), from Donovan, 1802-08 (18).*

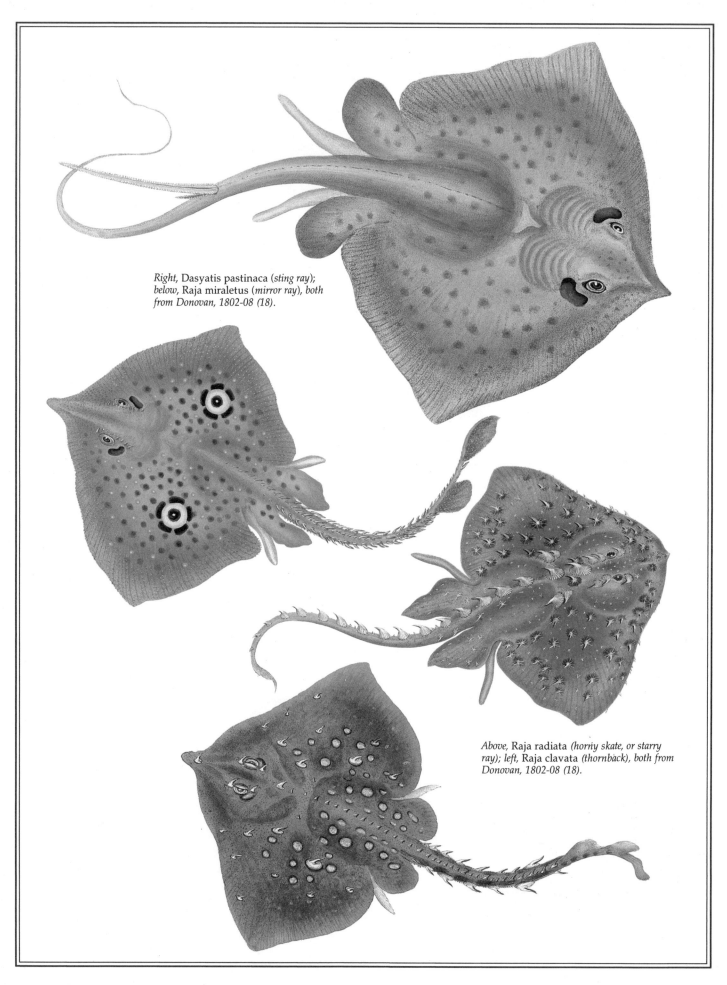

Right, Dasyatis pastinaca (*sting ray*); *below*, Raja miraletus (*mirror ray*), *both from Donovan, 1802-08 (18)*.

Above, Raja radiata (*horny skate, or starry ray*); *left*, Raja clavata (*thornback*), *both from Donovan, 1802-08 (18)*.

28

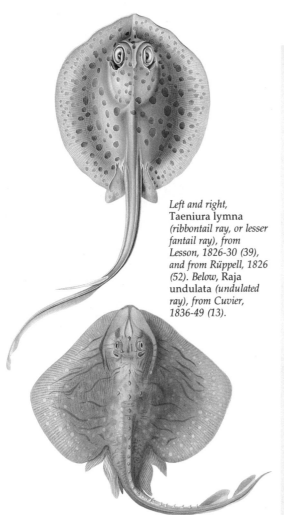

Left and right,
Taeniura lymna
*(ribbontail ray, or lesser
fantail ray), from
Lesson, 1826-30 (39),
and from Rüppell, 1826
(52). Below,* Raja
undulata *(undulated
ray), from Cuvier,
1836-49 (13).*

Dasyatis akajei *(Japanese sting ray, or whip
ray), from Ohno, 1937-44 (46).*

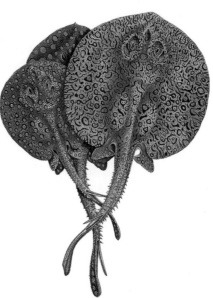

Potamotrygon *sp. (freshwater sting
ray), from Castelnau, 1855-57 (9).*

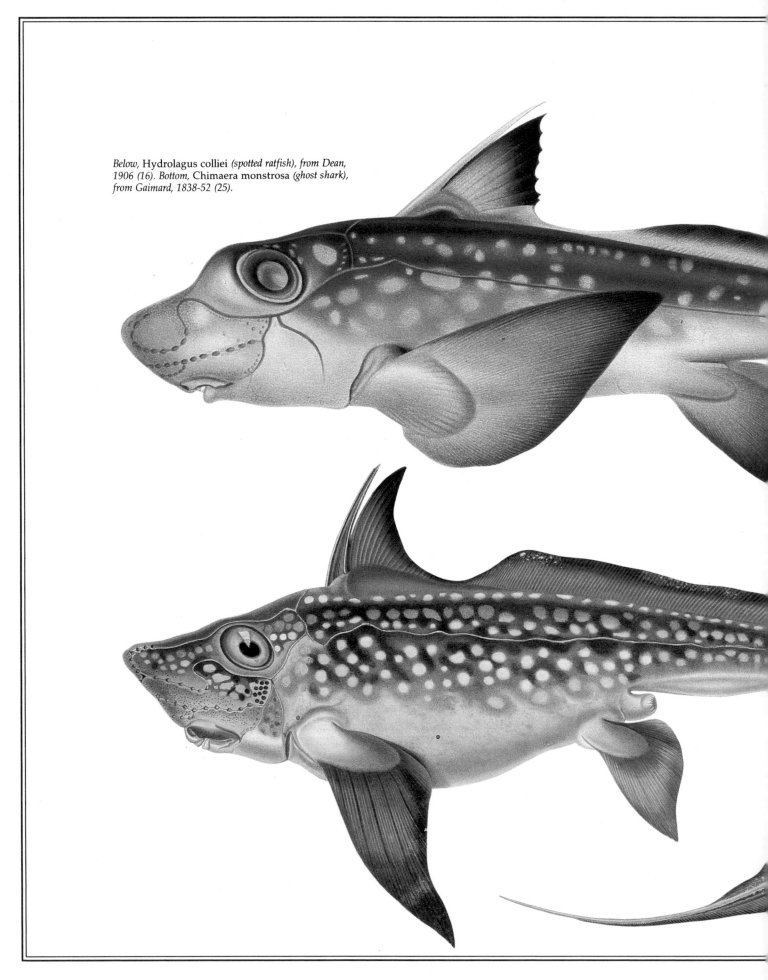

Below, Hydrolagus colliei *(spotted ratfish), from Dean, 1906 (16). Bottom,* Chimaera monstrosa *(ghost shark), from Gaimard, 1838-52 (25).*

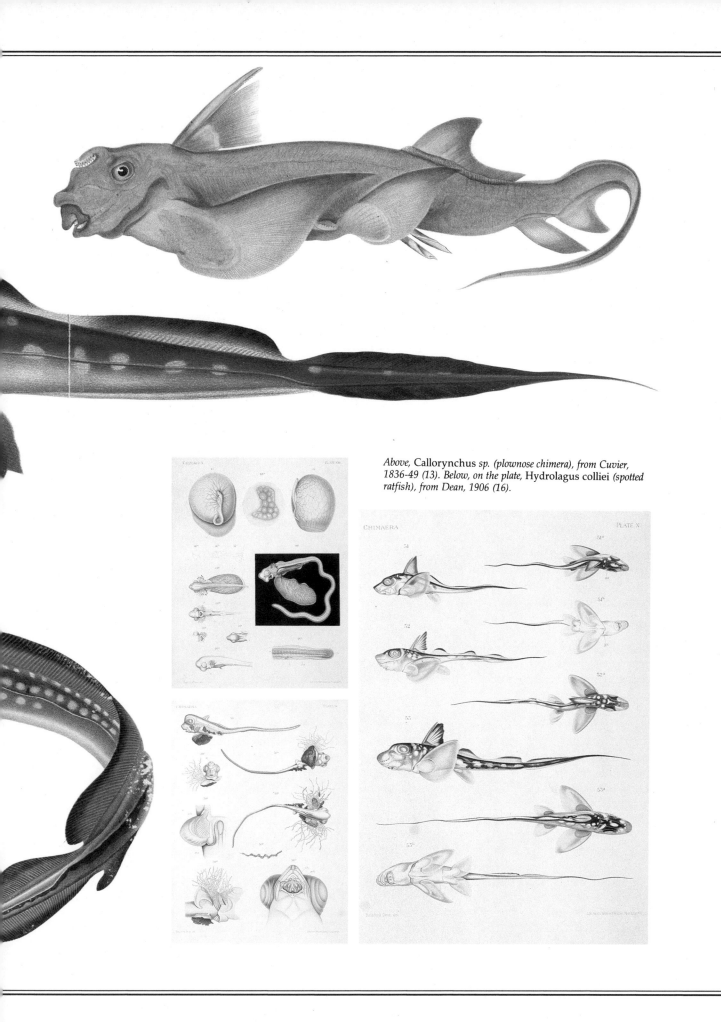

Above, Callorynchus *sp. (plownose chimera), from Cuvier, 1836-49 (13). Below, on the plate,* Hydrolagus colliei *(spotted ratfish), from Dean, 1906 (16).*

Not only teeth

Indiscriminate fear prevents us from viewing sharks not just as a threat to man, but also as a marvelous adjustment to the marine environment proven by a presence dating back hundreds of millions of years.

Fantasy, closely pressed by science and technology, is confined today within such a narrow space that its total disappearance can be considered imminent. Even so, it still keeps in the minds and hearts of men its unconquered strongholds in which dreams, poetry and fear exert their irrational control.

Decades of more and more widespread and perfected naturalistic information do not appear to have been of much use so far in establishing truer and more rational bases in the relationships among men and those animals that, since time immemorial, have always been condemned as dangerous threats to life. Therefore, even today, for most vacationers walking in the summer through mountain pastures and woods, the rustling noise of a snake can be nothing but the noise of a viper, ready to attack the unwary passerby. In the same way, more or less all over the world, any shark, whatever its species, is automatically associated by most people with mortal danger. As a consequence, many circuses put aside sometimes their usual equipment of lions, bears, and elephants and rely, to attract the audience, on images of pretty girls in bikinis face to face with dangerous sharks, images that bring together defenseless beauty and wild ferocity, the sure efficacy of which they are obviously well aware of; and in the "oceanic parks" not even the most gorgeous fish of the coral reef attract crowds as large as those drawn to the large pools ploughed by the fins of sharks, recalling — in the excited and frightened fantasy of the bystanders — exotic stories of shipwrecks ended in tragedies. But, as a matter of fact, the leading role in such performances is entrusted to nurse sharks, of the Orectolobidae family; and they show clearly — with the lazy ease of their movements, the small size of their teeth, the flattened shape of their body totally incompatible with sudden ferocious attacks — their unmistakable, mild character.

It is not easy to look with interest and objectivity at something we are afraid of. This is precisely what happens with sharks, all of which share the same bad reputation, a reputation that veils the many interesting aspects of these animals. First of these is their extraordinarily, unbelievably ancient origin. In fact, the fossil remains of Cladoselachii date back to three hundred million years ago, to the Devonian period: their general appearance already recalled present-day sharks. Originated — perhaps — in fresh water, Chondrichthyes (i.e., cartilaginous fishes) migrated early to the oceans, where their ensuing evolution took place. This was marked by the gradual progress — together with, then instead of, Cladoselachii, which became extinct over two hundred million years ago — of Squaliformes proper, which soon included genera (such as *Lamna, Carcharodon, Carcharias, Hemipristis*) still largely diffused in the oceans. But when years, like money, add up to much over a certain amount, we risk not being able to calculate their real value. In this case, a comparison like the following will be of some use to fully appreciate the extraordinary antiquity of sharks: dinosaurs, the big Mesozoic reptiles considered the preeminent example of "prehistoric" animals, appeared two hundred million years ago, only to disappear over a hundred million years ago!

By appearing on the stage for decades with uninterrupted success, an actor demonstrates his ability to play impeccably the roles entrusted to him, assisted among other things by his first-class *physique du rôle*. In a similar way, such animals as sharks, present on the stage of life for hundreds of millions of years, in the course of which they have seen numerous "fellow-travelers" appear and die out, must own an "existential uniqueness" of extraordinary efficiency. By examining the over two hundred species of sharks living today — from the large *Rhincodon typus* eighteen meters long to the very small *Squaliolus* hardly over a few inches long — we can observe that they all have substantially one structural scheme in common, with only a few slight variations, to which corresponds a substantially unique functional scheme. This anatomical, and consequently physiological, homogeneity, testifying to a reduced variability of the environmental conditions that have been the background for shark evolution, is first of all clearly visible in the unmistakable body profile of these animals. We can notice it, in its most typical and pure shape, in those powerful open-sea swimmers, the Isurides: the white shark (*Carcharodon carcharias*), the porbeagle shark (*Lamna nasus*), and makos (*Isurus oxyrhynchus, I. glaucus*). The shape of these fishes, often compared to the shape of an airship, can be schematically described, in geometric terms, as the junction of two cones, adhering to each other by two bases of the same size, the front one of which — less sharply pointed — is of shorter length. As a consequence, the body is of a gradually tapering, more elongated shape at the back than in front, thanks to which the turbulence that forms behind the fish and the friction are reduced to a minimum. This hydrodynamic trim, completed and improved by other anatomical elements, such as the big scythe-shaped caudal fin and the "stiffening ribs" running along the thin caudal peduncle, assigns the sharks of this family to the fastest roamers of the ocean wastes.

This structural homogeneity of sharks — and of cartilaginous fishes in general — appears even more remarkable when compared with the great anatomical differentiations characterizing osseous fishes, in comparison with which they present a rather simple structure that actually proves to be highly efficient. Side by side, the skulls of a big tunny fish and of a shark show that the first one appears to be a very complicated mosaic of bony *tesserae* of different shapes and sizes; the second one appears instead to be a massive single block of cartilage enclosing the encephalon, with which — in an essential as well as functional assemblage — the "seats" for smell and hearing organs and eye sockets form one single unit; in front, the rostral cartilages supporting the snout; underneath, the powerful jaws.

In comparison with an osseous fish, a shark shows structural handicaps, but these have been largely overcome. It can't be denied that a cartilagenous skeleton is less strong than an osseous one; however, in correspondence with the central portion of the vertebrae, which support the tensions and compressions exerted by the powerful muscular masses, it is permeated with calcium salts that make it much stronger; and this is proportional to the swimming habits of each species. On this subject, it must also be remembered that in correspondence with the back part of the body, which exerts the maximum effort for locomotion, each muscular segment is connected to two vertebrae instead of one, with obvious advantages as far as propulsion is concerned. The fact that sharks are not — as we usually say — lynx-eyed animals is widely known. But although their visual perception of their surroundings is somewhat blurred, the retina of their eyes — rich with rods — is very sensitive to any difference in light intensity, thus allowing them to detect easily any object that stands out against a contrasting background.

Thus prepared visually to search for food in conditions of dim light, sharks possess a powerful sense of smell. The enormous development of the front part of their central nervous system testifies to the sharpness of their sense of smell: in fact it is formed by a bulb and an olfactory lobe receiving the signals perceived by the sensory cells located inside the nasal cavities. And so, following the odorous "Ariadne's thread" left by the prey, sharks reach it swimming in a series of smaller and smaller circles, and this happens also in complete darkness and in the muddiest coastal waters. This hunting strategy has been effectively compared to a bloodhound's, but there is something more: their power to detect the presence of prey also by perceiving — through the sensory ends of the "lateral line" running along the sides and on the head — the movement of the water the prey makes by swimming.

The wanderer condemned by God to roam unceasingly the roads of the world until death is a character often mentioned in medieval legends. We are led to believe that a similar doom impends over sharks, condemned to wander unceasingly through ocean wastes not as an atonement for some horrible guilt, but as a compensation for an anatomic handicap, in this case a truly essential one: the absence of a swim bladder. Present in most osseous fishes, this unmistakable organ — similar to a small elongated bag whose skin tears easily — thanks to the gases inside it, adjusts the specific weight of the fish's body to the weight of the surrounding water, permitting it to hang motionless, or almost. Deprived of a swim bladder, sharks must fight actively — relentlessly — the effects of gravitation, which would cause their otherwise unavoidable, ruinous descent to the bottom. Two anatomic elements are mainly responsible for this vital function: the caudal fin and the pectoral fins. The lower lobe of the first one, besides contributing to the forward propulsion of the animal, tends to push toward the surface the tail part, with consequent inclination toward the bottom of the front part. But the large pectoral fins — slightly inclined toward the back like the wings of an aircraft — exert a pressure that works the opposite way, pushing upward the front part of the body and balancing perfectly the vertical push of the caudal fin. Hence, a perfectly horizontal trim of the body, ideal for a "navigation" with no time limits.

The ability to remain at the required level within the mass of water is vital for open-sea sharks, whereas it is of smaller consequence for sharks that, living in coastal waters or near the bottom, can find some solid surface on which to rest when required. Furthermore, for open-sea sharks, the relentless swimming contributes considerably to the breathing flow: in fact, water, flowing in through the mouth, which is constantly open, floods gills continuously, flowing out through the slits by means of which each of them opens separately to the outside. There are five of them on each side, with the exception of only a few species, with very primitive characteristics, that belong to the Hexanchidae family (seven and six respectively, genera *Heptranchias* and *Hexanchus*) and to the Chlamydoselachidae family (one single species, *Chlamidoselache anguineus*, equipped with six slits).

When admiring the refined hydrodynamic shape of a shark, it is natural to compare it to a race boat, the result of the most advanced marine engineering. However, we may be puzzled by the fact that the surface of this superb living "hull" is not perfectly smooth, as we would think it should be, to reduce the friction against water to minimum; on the contrary, it turns out to be very rough, so much as to cause dangerous wounds in cases of violent contacts.

In fact, the skin of this fish is densely strewn with tiny sharp placoid scales whose structure — an external shell of dentin enclosing a cavity full of blood vessels — resembles the structure of a tooth. However, the resulting coating of the skin — the shagreen — is still flexible enough so as not to impair the contraction of the mighty muscular masses that propel the animal, though, as a matter of fact, the bigger shark species give the impression of moving in a sort of stiff — though elegant — way.

If nothing has been said so far about the relationship between man and shark, this is not because of a prejudicial, antiscientific acquitting attitude against these animals. The correct attitude is to discriminate between the sharks (only a few) that man must really fear, and all other sharks, a much larger number, so as to get rid of an irrational fear that prevents us from really learning more about these extraordinary animals.

The most systematic, ample, detailed investigation of this controversial subject is perhaps still the one carried out many years ago by the Office of Naval Research of the United States by examining through a computerized analysis at the Mote Marine Laboratory of Sarasota the roughly 1,600 assumed shark attacks against man registered by the Smithsonian Institution. For 270 of these cases it was possible to ascertain, with sufficient certainty, the species of concerned sharks. The first place in the not very long list turned out to be firmly held by the already mentioned "white shark" (Carcharodon carcharias): a cosmopolitan giant with a frightening set of triangular teeth — up to 10 m long, and a weight of 3 tons — whose aggressiveness, together with its inexhaustible appetite, is undeniable. After this "public enemy number one," fortunately rather rare in all waters, comes the tiger shark (Galeocerdo cuvieri), a very common Carcharinidae of both coastal and open waters of warm seas. Its family is one of the shark families with the largest number of species, characterized by that remarkable asymmetry of the caudal fin — due to a much greater development of the upper lobe — that we usually associate with the image of a shark. Most of them belong to the genus Carcharinus, which includes three of them (Carcharinus zambesensis, C. gangeticus and C. nicaraguensis), with steady residence in river and lake areas, where their aggressiveness toward man is well known and much feared.

Something really striking, as far as shark dangerousness is concerned, is the varieties of opinions expressed on the subject by the many "experts" and observers. See for instance the case of the blue shark (Prionace glauca), the most elegant of all sharks thanks to its fusiform, elongated line and its greenish blue bright dress: considered as not dangerous for man by some, it is regarded instead as an animal to be feared and respected by the long-experienced scuba divers of Captain Cousteau's crew. Presumably, with this one as well as with other species, each personal experience may have had a different course and therefore a different outcome, depending on various factors, such as environment, climate, physiological conditions of the animal, attitude and reactions of the man; moreover, most times the "confrontation" takes place with a suddenness and unexpectedness that prevent a calm and objective evaluation of the facts.

Even sharks positively dangerous to man should not be labeled "ferocious." This word, which man has always applied to animals capable of injuring him, really fits perfectly only the being that has created it, as only man appears to be capable of inflicting totally unnecessary suffering. Instead, in the case of sharks, it is often a matter of perpetual necessity, as they must cope with food requirements made particularly pressing by the fact that they are doomed to move unceasingly through an environment such as the oceans, which except along the coast, are characterized by a very scarce biological productivity. In this liquid near-desert the search for food may become chronically distressing for a large ocean shark, for which the meeting with a possible "meal" is a vital opportunity that cannot be missed. And at that moment, any difference between a large fish, a seal, a young cetacean, or even — unfortunately — a man fallen into the water may become immaterial. A different explanation must be found for tropical sharks that attack man near the seashore, that is to say, in waters rich in food. On this subject, we must mention that such species — mostly Carcharinidae — are often characterized by a sort of laziness of behavior and appear to be a little less inclined to perform "maneuvers" when swimming than the open-sea species. Hence, they prefer — whenever possible — prey that is not very swift and agile; as a consequence, the clearly visible limb of an unsuspecting swimmer can be mistaken for a large fish in difficulty owing to some previous injury. And, having discovered how easily this kind of aggression can be carried out, the shark may be led to try it again, exactly like some Indian tigers that find it much easier to attack a poor peasant at the well than to pursue a deer in the woods.

One fact is undeniable: most existing sharks are totally harmless for man, as they feed on fish, squids, and bottom invertebrates such as crustaceans and mollusks. The relative size of a shark is no indication of its dangerousness: the largest extant sharks, which are also the largest living fish (the already mentioned whale shark and the basking shark, *Cetorhinus maximus*, which also reaches a length of 15 m), feed only on tiny planktonic crustaceans that they swallow in enormous quantities by filtering water through their gill-rakers, very thin horny filaments placed on the gill arches.

As surrealistic as paintings by Dali, the shapes of some sharks seem to have been created to set imagination free. This explains why Greeks and Romans, with their natural inclination to see wonders and myths in every natural phenomenon, made these fishes the leading characters of stories that, though retaining sometimes a small core of truth, enlarged and deformed it monstrously.

The thresher (*Alopias vulpinus*), for instance, is not an animal that does not strike the eye: the upper lobe of its caudal fin, in effect, has grown to such an extent that it is almost as long as the rest of the body. Hence it bears the name *alopex* ("fox"), created by the famous Aristotle, because of a certain similarity between that huge fish tail and the soft plume-shaped tail of the tawny ravager of hen-houses. About the thresher, the ancients used to write that by threshing the sea surface with its tail, it would frighten whales, forcing them to group into large shoals; and after doing that — often with the cooperation of the swordfish, goodness knows why — it would stuff itself with those moving mountains of flesh. Now, it is possible to trace in this legend the echo of a true fact, the real use the shark makes of its large tail, swinging it vigorously from side to side and stunning the fish it feeds on. But no connection with truth can exist when, arbitrarily developing the purely visual analogy between fox and shark, it has been maintained that the latter is provided with a diabolical cunning that enables it to untie knots in fishermen's fishing lines!

The feelings of tender parental care attributed by Oppian to the blue shark appear to have been a pure flight of fancy. According to this second-century Greek poet, the adults of this shark "control all movements of their young, moderate their speed, watch every breaker and in case of doubt show them the way," going to the extent, in case of serious danger, of sheltering them inside their enormous mouth, where the little ones feel safe "like a little bird inside its mossy nest." What may possibly be the origin of such an unlikely tale? One assumption, the first one that occurs to our minds on the subject, can be connected to the way blue sharks (and most sharks) reproduce: the female, after being fecundated internally by the male, ejects in the water live young, instead of laying eggs like the rest of fish. Well, the ascertainment of a "pregnancy" apparently similar to the pregnancy of mammals and even of humans may have led to the idea of motherhood, which is the equivalent of love and motherly care for their offspring. From there on, it was probably only a matter of imagination and also of some... self-assurance!

Saltwater fishes

To us, living within the lowest layer of the atmospheric strata in close contact with the ground, oceans and seas look like a sort of reversed world. In effect, life is concentrated in the upper water layer and decreases gradually as we descend into the depths locked in the grip of a cold, timeless obscurity.

However, if we consider the number of the species, we may conclude that marine fishes prefer the euphotic layer (that is, lighted up by solar light, which at a depth of 150 m is reduced to 1 percent in perfectly clear waters) only near the coasts, where about 10,200 species can be found, but not off the coasts. In fact, beyond the 200 m of depth of the continental shelf, bathyphylous or benthonic species prevail, and they are about 2,700, whereas only 250 lead an epipelagic life, keeping near the surface.

The distribution of the ichthyological species in the immense volume of the oceans (1,370 million cu. km with an average depth of 2,700 m) is irregular not only as regards bathymetry but also latitude and longitude. The maximum variety of forms populate tropical waters and the minimum populate circumpolar waters, though a few species of the boreal hemisphere that like icy waters form large populations with remarkable biomasses. The area that extends across the Indian Ocean and the southwestern Pacific (from the southeastern coasts of Africa to Australia and Polynesia) includes a very rich ichthyofauna, as does the Caribbean area, whereas the ichthyofauna of western Africa is very scarce.

At the moment the preeminent fishes of the sea environment are the teleosts, which succeeded in colonizing even its smallest recesses by developing an unbelievable variety of physiologic and behavioristic adaptations.

At a taxonomic level, the main difference between sea-water and fresh-water teleosts consists in the fact that the former belong mostly to Ostariophyses, a not much evolved group with primitive features, whereas the latter belong mostly to the Percidae order, which is composed of highly specialized and developed species. The difference in the two levels of evolutionary progress depends on different characteristics.

Ostariophyses lack hard spines in the structure of the fins and have only one dorsal fin, pelvic fins rather behind in the abdominal position, and pectoral fins positioned on the belly with a horizontal insertion; they have osteocytes in the bone of adult individuals and miospines, and the swim bladder is connected to the digestive apparatus through a pneumatic duct (physostomes). Percidae have fins strengthened by spines, two dorsal fins, pectoral fins, if present, in advanced positions at a thoracic level and pectoral fins positioned on the sides with a vertical insertion; they lack osteocytes, miospines, and pneumatic ducts (physoclysts). This last feature is particularly interesting, as the filling and emptying of the swim bladder cannot be effected through the introduction or emission of air through the mouth, as with physostomes, but only through gaseous exchanges with the blood. Therefore in a physoclystic bladder there are both a vascularized zone for gas reabsorption from the lumen in the blood (oval chamber) and a gas-concentrating apparatus from the blood in the lumen consisting of the gas gland and the rete mirabile. By means of a counter-current movement along the capillaries of the rete mirabile, the gland can pump gas into the swim bladder at enormous pressures (up to 700 atm. for the abyssal species).

The order of Percidae is the largest order of Teleosts, as it numbers as many as 150 families with 7,791 species, three quarters of which live in coastal sea waters, 10 percent in the ocean, and the rest in fresh water. Two suborders, Percoids and Gobioidea, include about two thirds of the Percidae.

Of the Percoids, the largest families are Cichlids (680 species), such as the Tilapia sparrmani and Cichlasoma labiatum (page 254) and other species distinguished by their peculiar parental care: in fact, the parents use their oral cavities to incubate the fecundated eggs or to hide their young; Serranidae (370 species), such as groupers of the genus Epinephelus (pages 83, 84, 86, 87), and sea perches of the genus Serranus (page 88); Demoiselles (235 species), such as clown-fishes of the genus Amphiprio (page 129) that live in symbiosis with large sea-anemones, swim in the middle of tentacles, and are not urticated.

Of the Gobioidea, the most important family is Gobiidae (150 species), the largest family of marine fishes and a typical component of the benthonic ichthyofauna of coastal waters. To this family belong also some species that can live a few days out of the water, such as Periophthalmodon schlosseri (page 125), which can move swiftly on the beach breathing air and looking around with lively pedunculate retractile eyes.

Among the other 20 suborders of Percidae we may mention the Blenniidae families (349 species), such as blennies of the genus Blennius (pages 120, 121) so called because of their bare viscid skin, which share several habitats with Gobiidae; Labridae (500 species), such as rainbow wrasses, Coris julis (page 133) or green wrasses of the genus Labrus, extremely different as to shapes, colors, and sizes, often of very different hues within one single species; Scombroidea (48 species), of great economic importance as they represent 9 percent of the fishing produce in the whole world, which include the tunny fish, Thunnus thynnus (page 115), a truly marvelous swimmer, and the mackerel, Scomber scombrus (page 116).

Besided Percidae, Pluronectiforms represent another rather developed order of exclusively marine and benthonic teleosts, composed of 538 species of flat fishes, such as the turbot, Scophthalmus rhombus (page 171), the flounder, Pleuronectes platessa (page 171), and the wart sole, Solea impar (page 169). The most surprising feature is the fact that the flat shape does not originate from a dorsal-ventral compression as in Chondroichthyes Batoids, but from their normal posture on one side, whereas the initial form of young individuals is upright, high, and thin. Another curious feature is the fact that some species lie on the left side, some others on the right side, and others include both dextrorse and sinistrose individuals.

Two more orders, Clupeids and Gadoids, are of enormous interest to the fishing industry, as together they supply about one third of the fishing of the whole world. The order of Clupeids consists of 331 species with a low evolutionary level, mostly marine and feeding on plankton, that constitute the prevailing element of the pelagic ichthyofauna, such as herrings, Clupea harengus (page 49), sardines, Sardina pilchardus (page 40), and anchovies of the genus Engraulis.

Gadoids number 414 carnivorous species, which often eat fish, such as the cod, Gadus morhua (page 56) and the hake, Merluccius merluccius (page 57). Unlike Clupeids, whose muscles are rich in miospines and lipidic deposits, the flesh of Gadoids has no miospines and very few lipids, which gather instead in the liver. Some species, such as the hake, migrate every year over a distance of up to 2,000 km with a trophic and reproductive purpose, but the maximum migratory distances are attained by some members of the Anguilliforms, such as the European eel, Anguilla anguilla (page 51) and Salmonidae, such as the salmon of the genus Oncorhynchus (pages 219, 220). These species swim for thousands of kilometers (even 4,000 km) not only in the oceans but also in internal waters, undergoing two morphological and functional processes in order to change from one environment to the other.

Eels are born in the Sargasso Sea and cross the Atlantic and the Mediterraneann to swim up the European fresh waters, from which, after completing the adult stage, they swim back to the sea for reproduction. Salmon Ochorhyncus instead follow a reverse course, swimming down the fresh waters in which they are born toward the Pacific Ocean, and swimming back to them as adult individuals for reproduction.

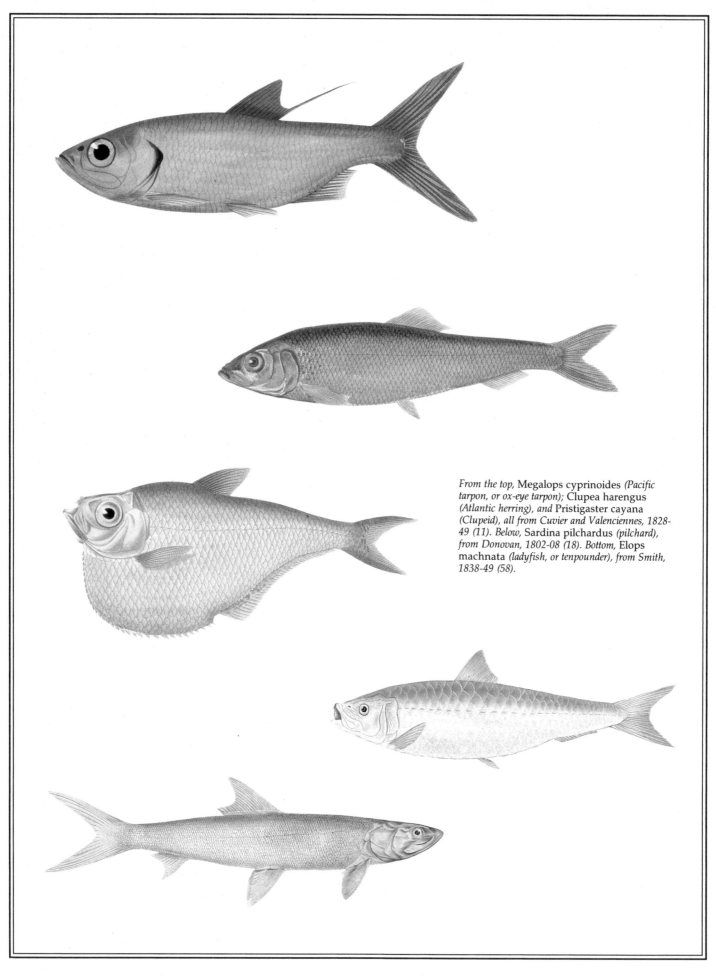

From the top, Megalops cyprinoides *(Pacific tarpon, or ox-eye tarpon);* Clupea harengus *(Atlantic herring), and* Pristigaster cayana *(Clupeid), all from Cuvier and Valenciennes, 1828-49 (11). Below,* Sardina pilchardus *(pilchard), from Donovan, 1802-08 (18). Bottom,* Elops machnata *(ladyfish, or tenpounder), from Smith, 1838-49 (58).*

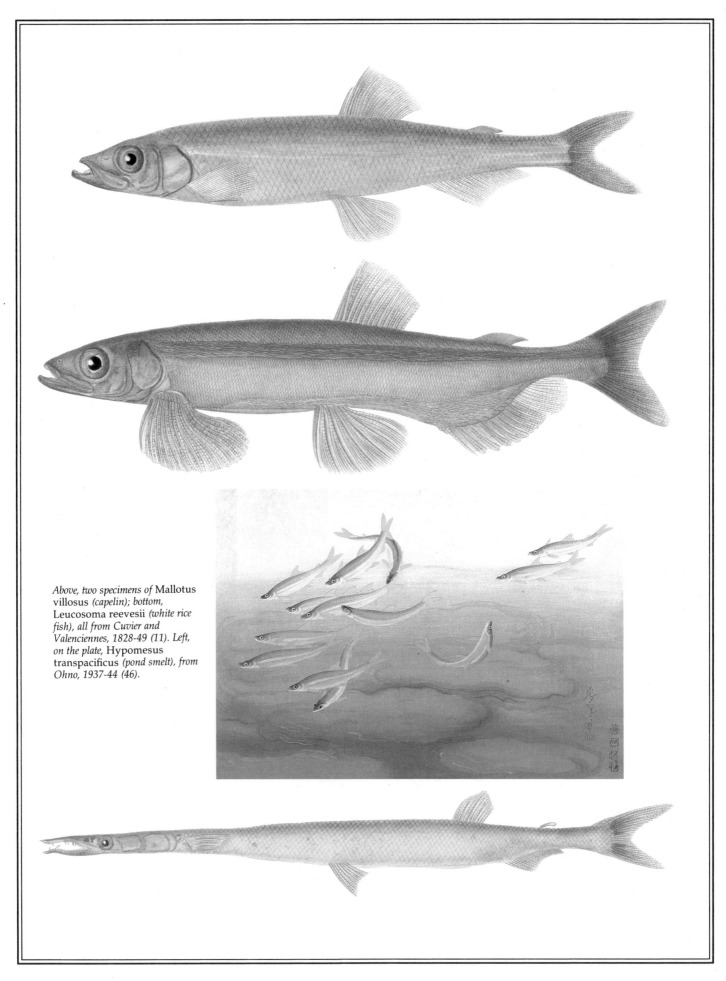

Above, two specimens of Mallotus villosus *(capelin); bottom,* Leucosoma reevesii *(white rice fish), all from Cuvier and Valenciennes, 1828-49 (11). Left, on the plate,* Hypomesus transpacificus *(pond smelt), from Ohno, 1937-44 (46).*

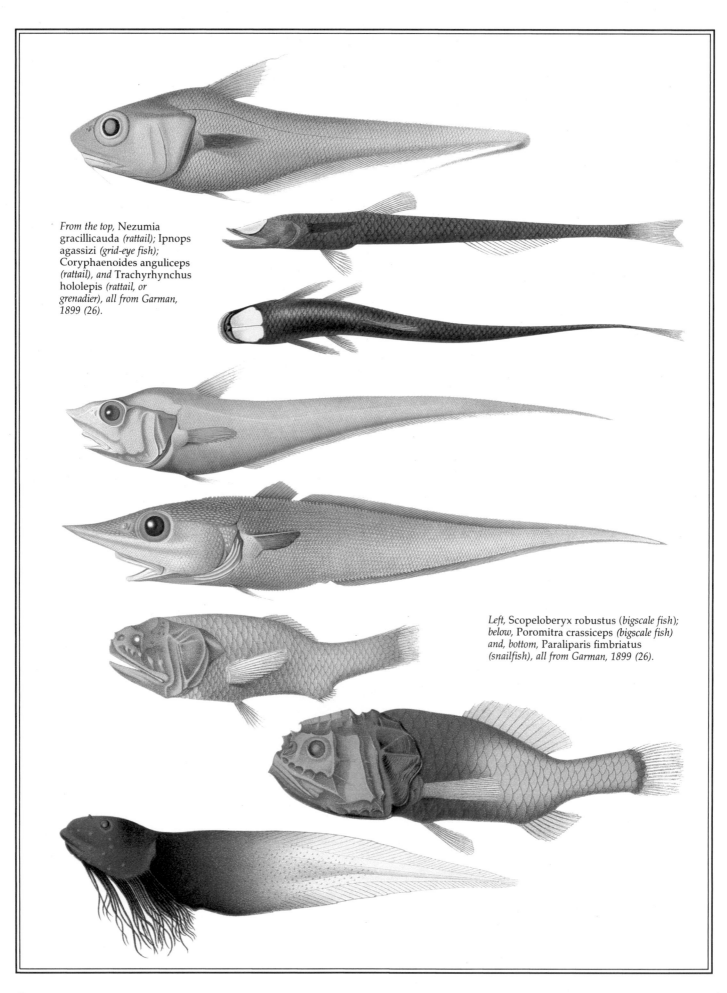

From the top, Nezumia gracillicauda *(rattail)*; Ipnops agassizi *(grid-eye fish)*; Coryphaenoides anguliceps *(rattail), and* Trachyrhynchus hololepis *(rattail, or grenadier), all from Garman, 1899 (26).*

Left, Scopeloberyx robustus (bigscale fish); *below,* Poromitra crassiceps *(bigscale fish) and, bottom,* Paraliparis fimbriatus *(snailfish), all from Garman, 1899 (26).*

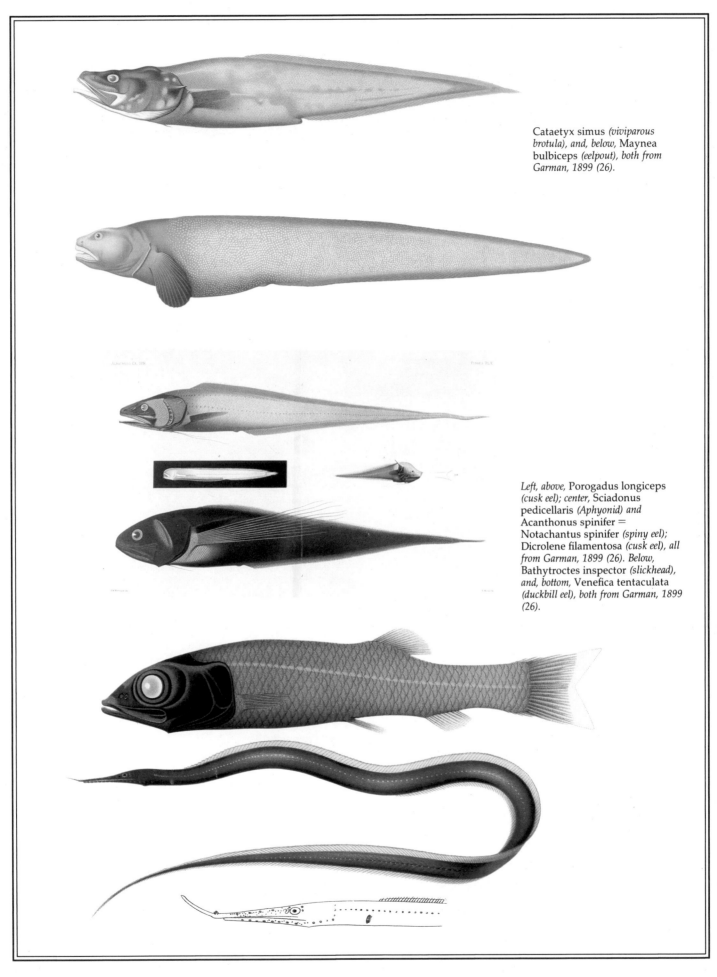

Cataetyx simus *(viviparous brotula), and, below,* Maynea bulbiceps *(eelpout), both from Garman, 1899 (26).*

Left, above, Porogadus longiceps *(cusk eel); center,* Sciadonus pedicellaris *(Aphyonid) and* Acanthonus spinifer = Notachantus spinifer *(spiny eel);* Dicrolene filamentosa *(cusk eel), all from Garman, 1899 (26). Below,* Bathytroctes inspector *(slickhead), and, bottom,* Venefica tentaculata *(duckbill eel), both from Garman, 1899 (26).*

43

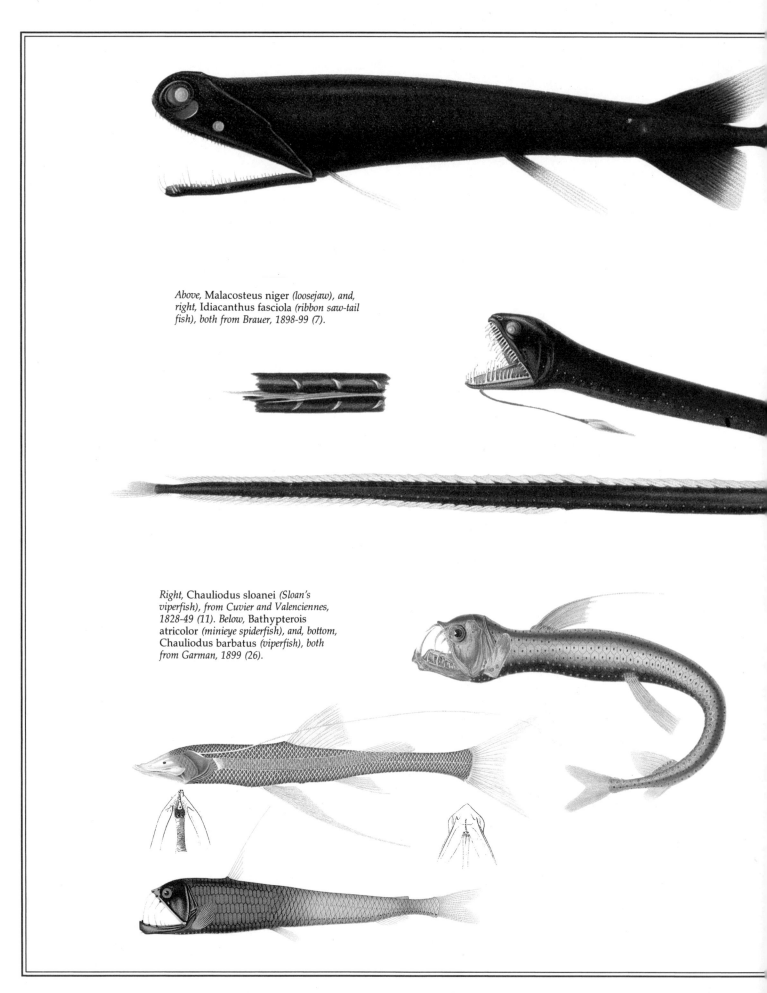

Above, Malacosteus niger *(loosejaw), and,* right, Idiacanthus fasciola *(ribbon saw-tail fish), both from Brauer, 1898-99 (7).*

Right, Chauliodus sloanei *(Sloan's viperfish), from Cuvier and Valenciennes, 1828-49 (11). Below,* Bathypterois atricolor *(minieye spiderfish), and, bottom,* Chauliodus barbatus *(viperfish), both from Garman, 1899 (26).*

Top, Neoscopelus macrolepidotus *(snouty lanternfish); above,* Bathypterois atricolor *(minieye spiderfish); below, from the top,* Stomias affinis *and* Macrostomias longibarbatus *(both scaly dragonfishes);* Bathophilus ater *(scaleless black dragonfish);* Melanostomias melanops *and* Melanostomias valdiviae *(both scaleless black dragonfishes), all from Brauer, 1898-99 (7).*

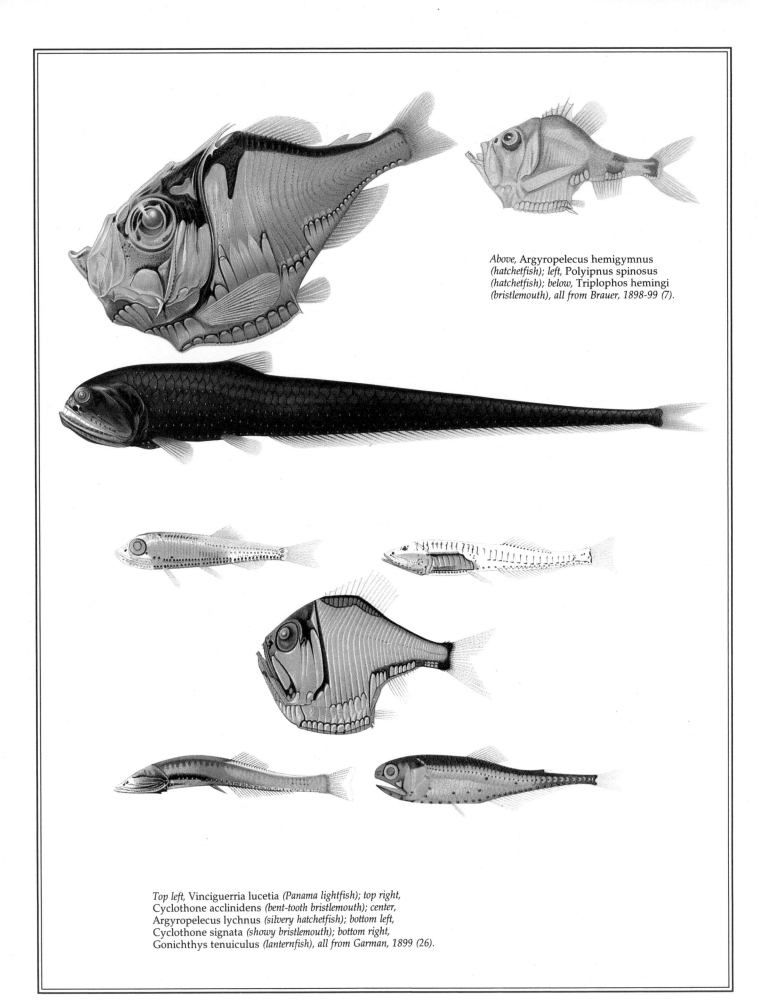

Above, Argyropelecus hemigymnus *(hatchetfish); left,* Polyipnus spinosus *(hatchetfish); below,* Triplophos hemingi *(bristlemouth), all from Brauer, 1898-99 (7).*

Top left, Vinciguerria lucetia *(Panama lightfish); top right,* Cyclothone acclinidens *(bent-tooth bristlemouth); center,* Argyropelecus lychnus *(silvery hatchetfish); bottom left,* Cyclothone signata *(showy bristlemouth); bottom right,* Gonichthys tenuiculus *(lanternfish), all from Garman, 1899 (26).*

Top, Anoplogaster cornuta
(fangtooth or ogrefish); center left,
Xenomystax rictus *(conger eel);*
center right, Notacanthus
spinosus *(spiny eel), all from*
Garman, 1899 (26). Center right
below, Alepocephalus rostratus
(slickhead), from Cuvier and
Valenciennes, 1828-49 (11). On the
plate, Idiacanthus fasciola
(ribbon saw-tail fish), from Brauer,
1898-99 (7).

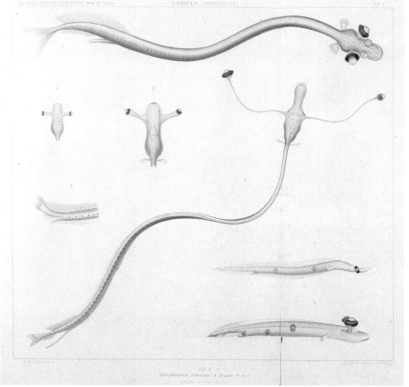

Top left, Cryptopsaras couesi *(deep-sea angler); top right,*
Caulophryne pelagica *(angler); center right,* Dolopichthys
niger *(Oneirodid); bottom,* Melanocetus murrayi *(Murray's
black devil), all from Brauer, 1898-99 (7).*

Top, Gigantactis vanhoeffeni *(Gigantactinid);*
bottom, Melanocetus johnsoni *(common black devil),*
both from Brauer, 1898-99 (7).

From the top, Coelophrys brevicaudata *(batfish);* Linophryne macrorhinus; Linophryne indica; Haplophryne mollis *(all Linophrynids), all from Brauer, 1898-99 (7). Bottom,* Chaunax coloratus *(sea toad), from Garrett and Günther, 1873-1910 (27).*

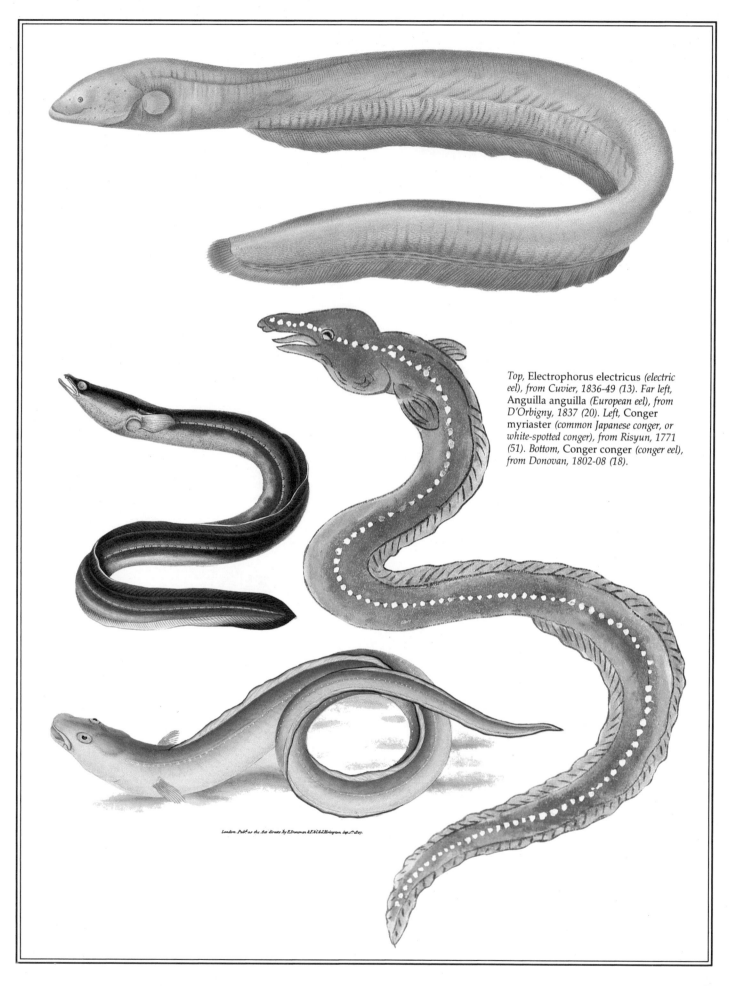

Top, Electrophorus electricus *(electric eel), from Cuvier, 1836-49 (13). Far left,* Anguilla anguilla *(European eel), from D'Orbigny, 1837 (20). Left, Conger myriaster *(common Japanese conger, or white-spotted conger), from Risyun, 1771 (51). Bottom,* Conger conger *(conger eel), from Donovan, 1802-08 (18).*

London. Pub.^d as the Act directs by E.Donovan &E.&J.Birington. Sep.1.st 1807.

Top left, Muraena porphyrea *(moray); top right,* Ophichthys remiger *(snake eel), both from Gay, 1844-71 (28). Center,* Muraena marmorea *(moray), from Du Petit-Thouars, 1846 (22). On the plate, top,* Echidna xanthospilus *(moray) and, bottom,* Ophichthys garretti *(snake eel), from Museum Godeffroy, 1873-1910 (44).*

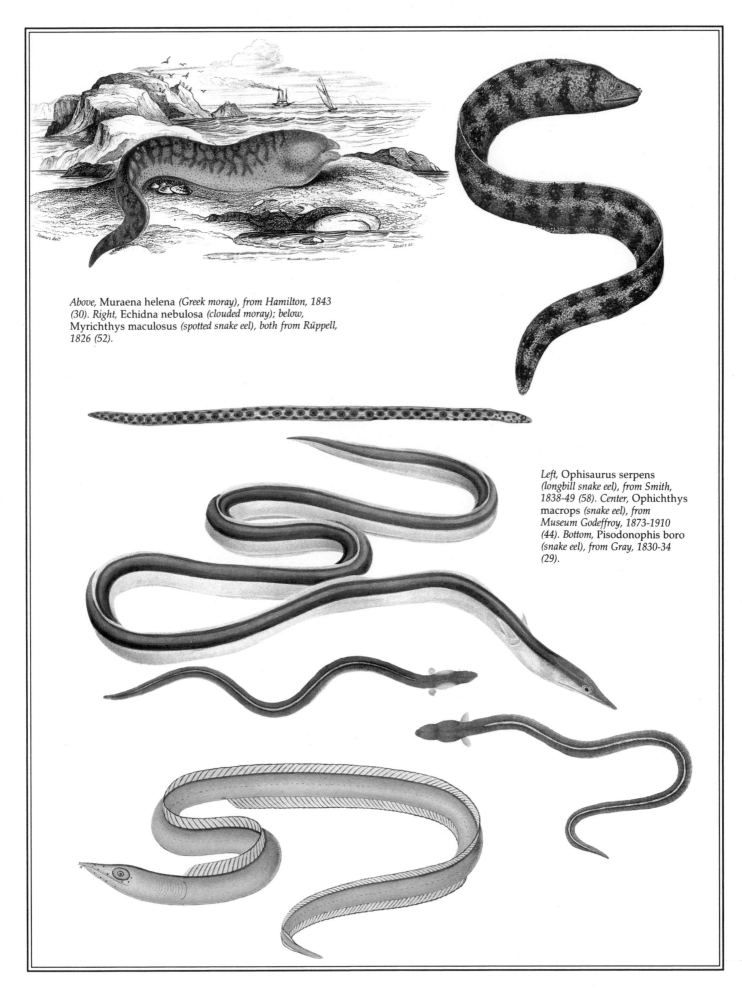

Above, Muraena helena *(Greek moray), from Hamilton, 1843 (30). Right,* Echidna nebulosa *(clouded moray); below,* Myrichthys maculosus *(spotted snake eel), both from Rüppell, 1826 (52).*

Left, Ophisaurus serpens *(longbill snake eel), from Smith, 1838-49 (58). Center,* Ophichthys macrops *(snake eel), from Museum Godeffroy, 1873-1910 (44). Bottom,* Pisodonophis boro *(snake eel), from Gray, 1830-34 (29).*

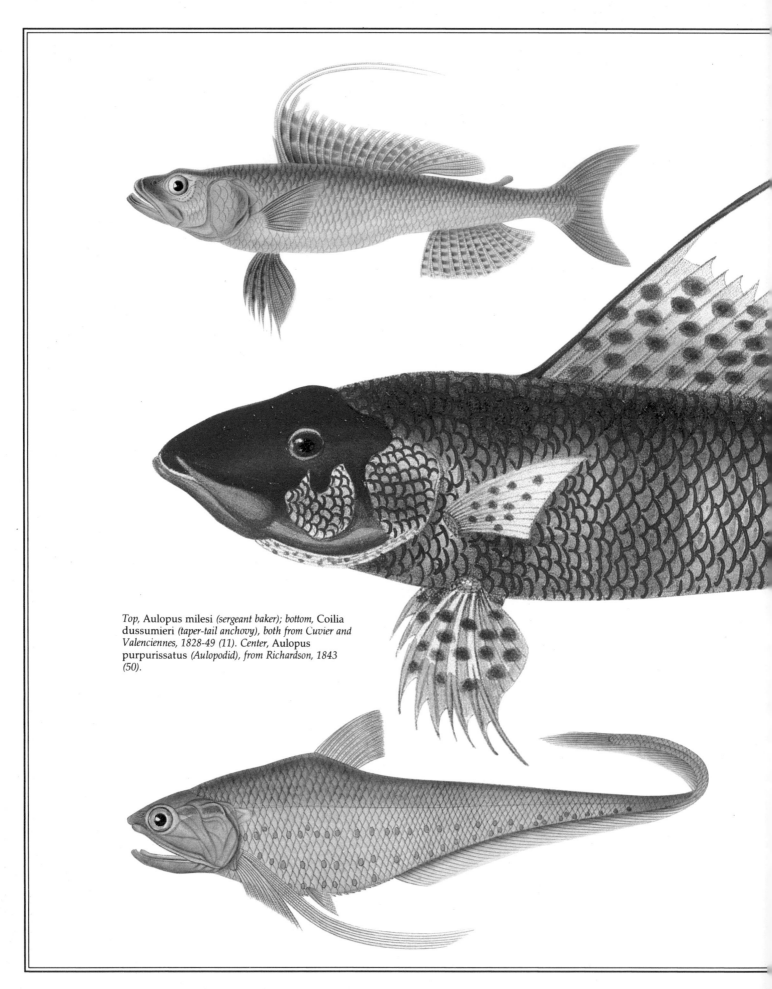

Top, Aulopus milesi *(sergeant baker); bottom,* Coilia dussumieri *(taper-tail anchovy), both from Cuvier and Valenciennes, 1828-49 (11). Center,* Aulopus purpurissatus *(Aulopodid), from Richardson, 1843 (50).*

Top, Paralepis coregonoides *(barracudina), from Cuvier, 1836-49 (13).* Bottom, Trachinocephalus myops *(offshore lizard fish, or painted saury), from* Illustrations of Fishes, *1868-1912 (33).*

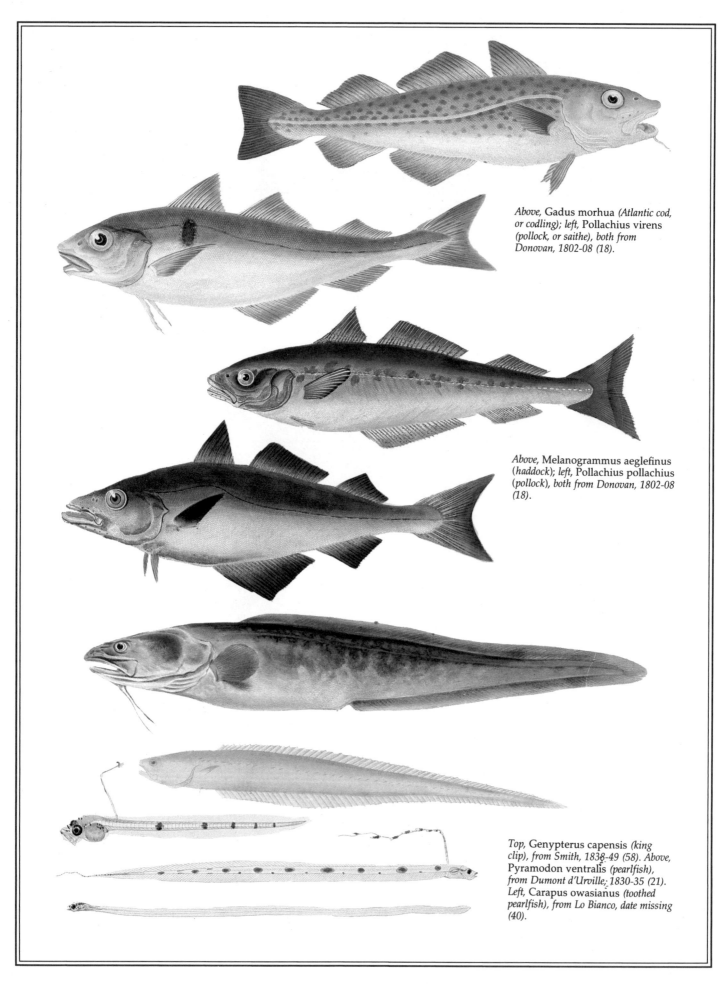

Above, Gadus morhua *(Atlantic cod, or codling); left,* Pollachius virens *(pollock, or saithe), both from Donovan, 1802-08 (18).*

Above, Melanogrammus aeglefinus *(haddock); left,* Pollachius pollachius *(pollock), both from Donovan, 1802-08 (18).*

Top, Genypterus capensis *(king clip), from Smith, 1838-49 (58). Above,* Pyramodon ventralis *(pearlfish), from Dumont d'Urville, 1830-35 (21). Left,* Carapus owasianus *(toothed pearlfish), from Lo Bianco, date missing (40).*

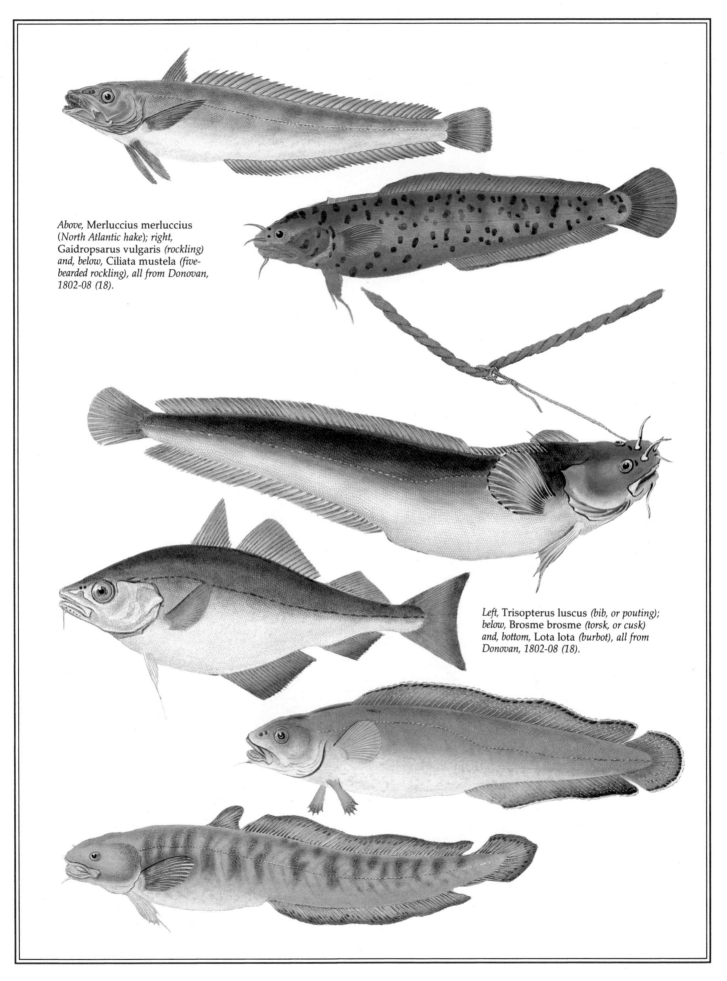

Above, Merluccius merluccius (*North Atlantic hake*); *right*, Gaidropsarus vulgaris *(rockling) and, below,* Ciliata mustela *(five-bearded rockling), all from Donovan, 1802-08 (18).*

Left, Trisopterus luscus *(bib, or pouting); below,* Brosme brosme *(torsk, or cusk) and, bottom,* Lota lota *(burbot), all from Donovan, 1802-08 (18).*

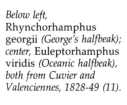

Below left,
Rhynchorhamphus
georgii *(George's halfbeak);*
center, Euleptorhamphus
viridis *(Oceanic halfbeak),*
both from Cuvier and
Valenciennes, 1828-49 (11).

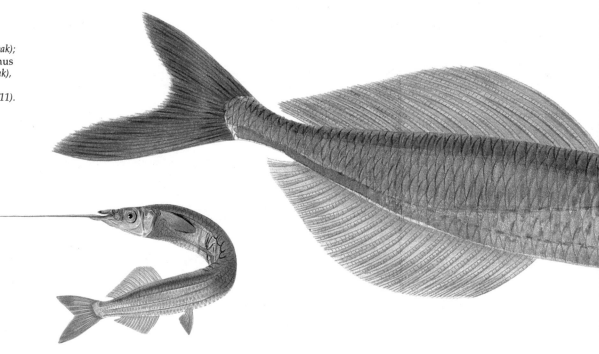

Left, Hemiramphus sajori
(halfbeak), from Ohno, 1937-44
(46). Bottom, Tylosurus acus
melanotus *(blackfin longtom),*
from Baien Mouri, date
missing, (3).

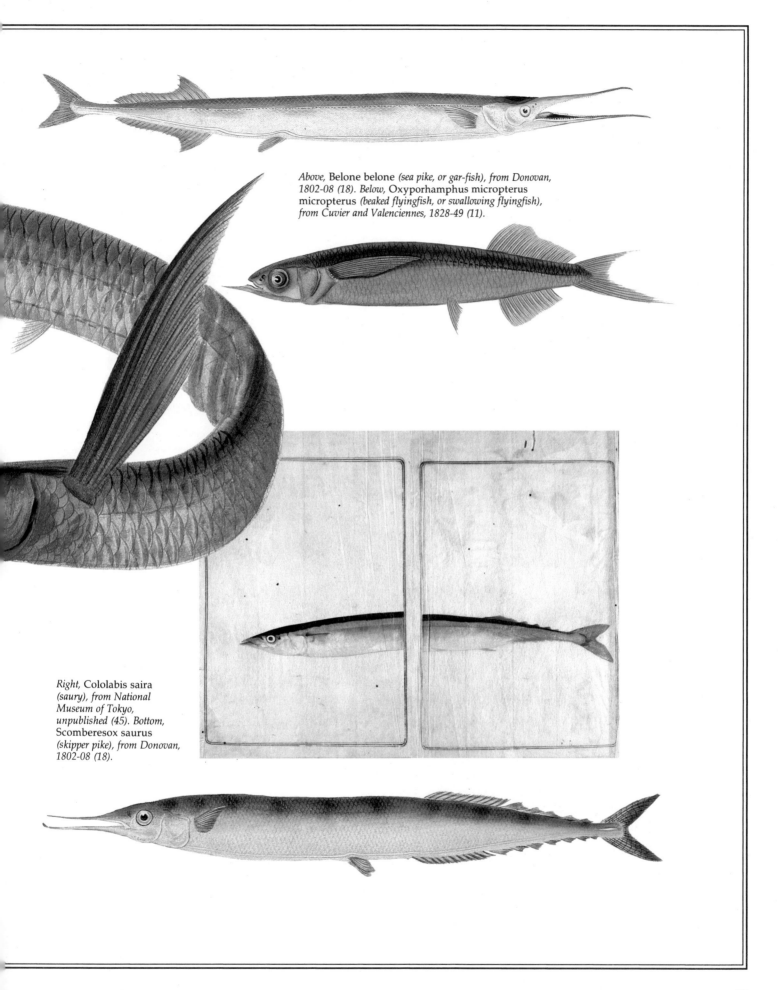

Above, Belone belone *(sea pike, or gar-fish), from Donovan, 1802-08 (18). Below,* Oxyporhamphus micropterus micropterus *(beaked flyingfish, or swallowing flyingfish), from Cuvier and Valenciennes, 1828-49 (11).*

Right, Cololabis saira *(saury), from National Museum of Tokyo, unpublished (45). Bottom,* Scomberesox saurus *(skipper pike), from Donovan, 1802-08 (18).*

Top, Exocoetus volitans (*common flyingfish*), *from Donovan, 1802-08 (18). Center and bottom*, Danichtys rondeletii *(okitobi), from Cuvier and Valenciennes, 1828-49 (11) and D'Orbigny, 1837 (29).*

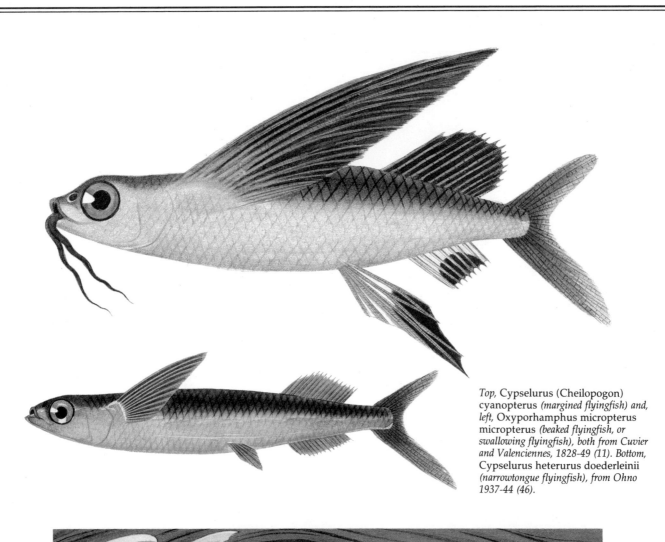

Top, Cypselurus (Cheilopogon) cyanopterus *(margined flyingfish) and, left,* Oxyporhamphus micropterus micropterus *(beaked flyingfish, or swallowing flyingfish), both from Cuvier and Valenciennes, 1828-49 (11). Bottom,* Cypselurus heterurus doederleinii *(narrowtongue flyingfish), from Ohno 1937-44 (46).*

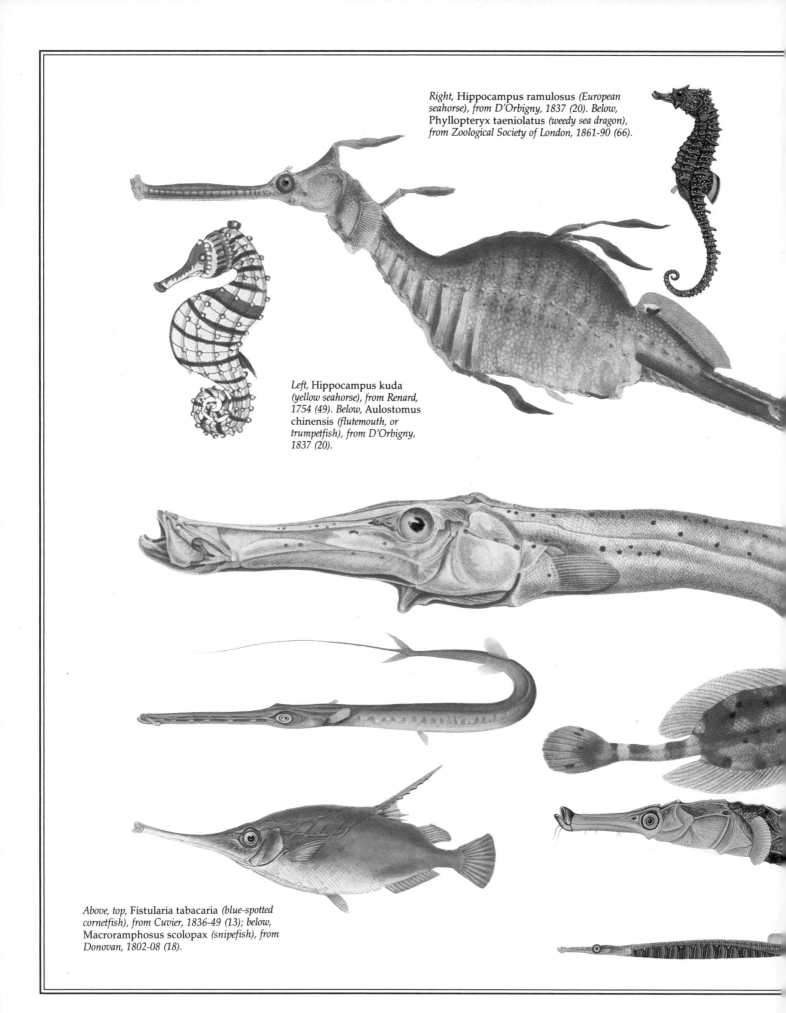

Right, Hippocampus ramulosus *(European seahorse), from D'Orbigny, 1837 (20). Below, Phyllopteryx taeniolatus *(weedy sea dragon), *from Zoological Society of London, 1861-90 (66).*

Left, Hippocampus kuda *(yellow seahorse), from Renard, 1754 (49). Below, Aulostomus chinensis *(flutemouth, or trumpetfish), from D'Orbigny, 1837 (20).*

Above, top, Fistularia tabacaria *(blue-spotted cornetfish), from Cuvier, 1836-49 (13); below,* Macroramphosus scolopax *(snipefish), from Donovan, 1802-08 (18).*

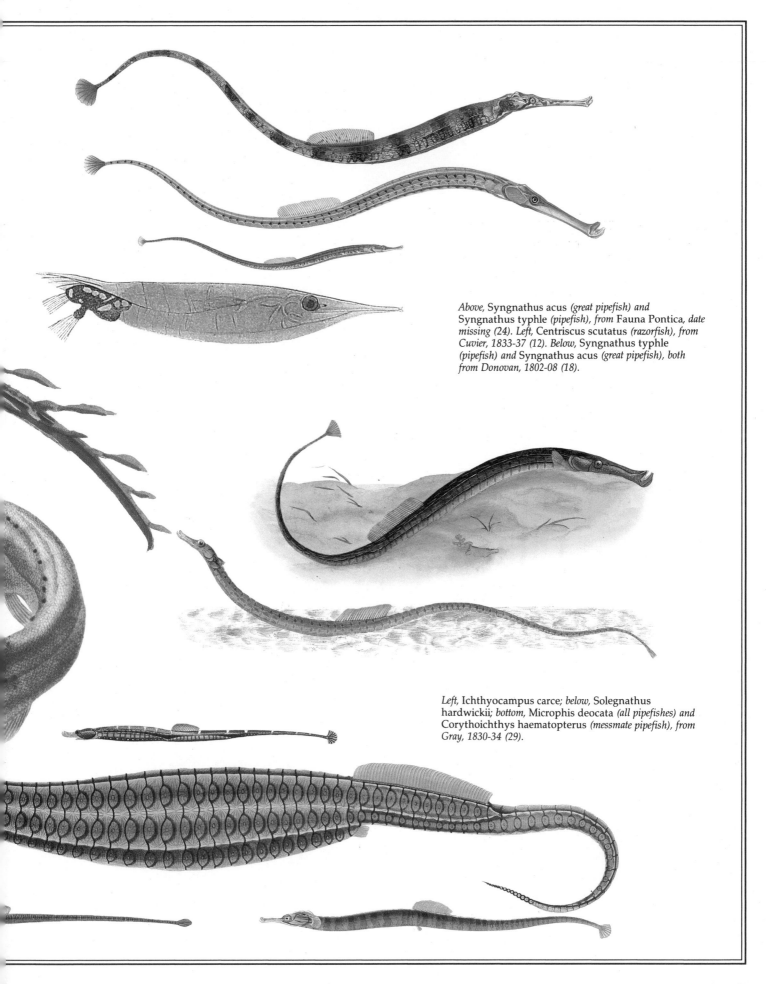

Above, Syngnathus acus *(great pipefish) and* Syngnathus typhle *(pipefish), from* Fauna Pontica, *date missing (24). Left*, Centriscus scutatus *(razorfish), from Cuvier, 1833-37 (12). Below*, Syngnathus typhle *(pipefish) and* Syngnathus acus *(great pipefish), both from Donovan, 1802-08 (18).

Left, Ichthyocampus carce; *below*, Solegnathus hardwickii; *bottom*, Microphis deocata *(all pipefishes) and* Corythoichthys haematopterus *(messmate pipefish), from Gray, 1830-34 (29).*

Top, Hoplostethus pacificus *(slimy head),* *from Garman, 1899 (26). Left,* Sargocentron caudimaculatum *(silverspot soldier), from Bennett, 1830 (4). Bottom left,* Sargocentron spiniferum *(scarlet squirrelfish) and, bottom right,* Sargocentron hastatum *(squirrelfish), both from Cuvier and Valenciennes, 1828-49 (11).*

Top left, Myripristis murdjan *(crimson squirrelfish, or blotcheye), and, top right,* Sargocentron diadema *(crowned soldierfish), both from Rüppell, 1826 (52). Center, above,* Beryx decadactylus *(broad alfonsino) and, below,* Plectrypops lima *(Ryukyu squirrelfish), both from Cuvier, 1836-49 (13). Left,* Osthichtys japonicus *(hardscale soldierfish, or ebisu perch), from Tansyu, date missing (64).*

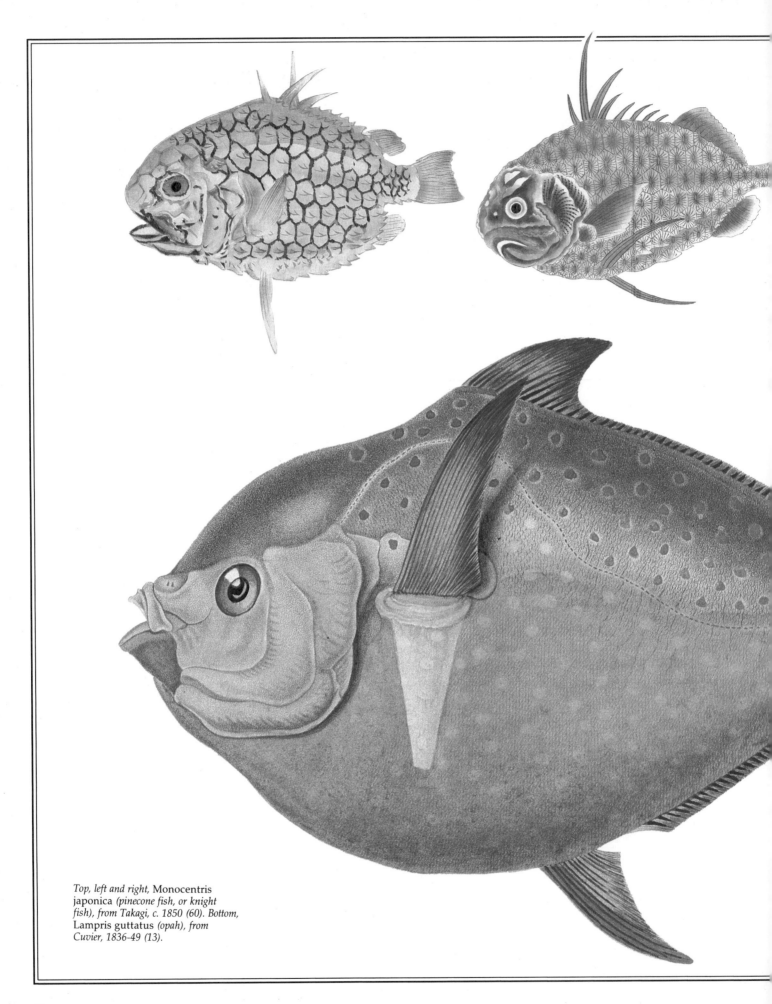

Top, left and right, Monocentris
japonica *(pinecone fish, or knight
fish), from Takagi, c. 1850 (60). Bottom,*
Lampris guttatus *(opah), from
Cuvier, 1836-49 (13).*

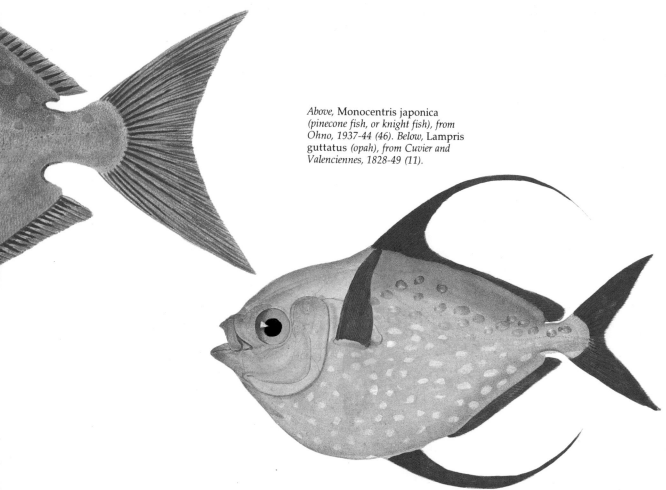

Above, Monocentris japonica
*(pinecone fish, or knight fish), from
Ohno, 1937-44 (46). Below,* Lampris
guttatus *(opah), from Cuvier and
Valenciennes, 1828-49 (11).*

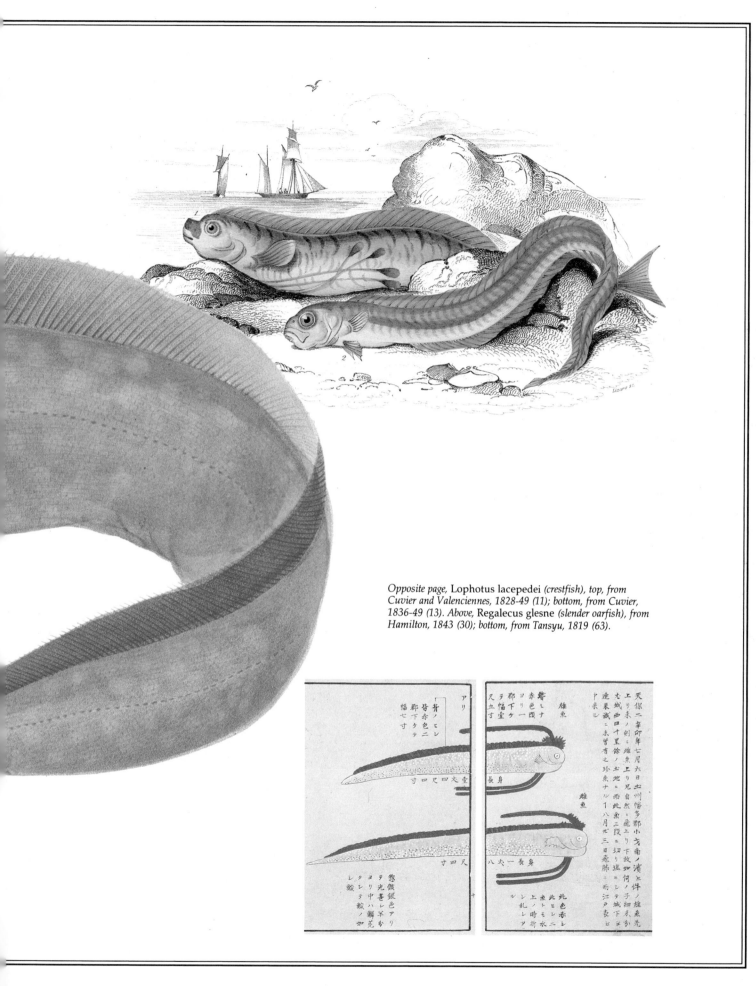

Opposite page, Lophotus lacepedei *(crestfish), top, from Cuvier and Valenciennes, 1828-49 (11); bottom, from Cuvier, 1836-49 (13). Above,* Regalecus glesne *(slender oarfish), from Hamilton, 1843 (30); bottom, from Tansyu, 1819 (63).*

Top, Trachipterus arcticus *(lowsail ribbonfish), from Gaimard, 1838-52 (25). Bottom,* Trachipterus trachypterus *(deal fish), from D'Orbigny, 1837 (20).*

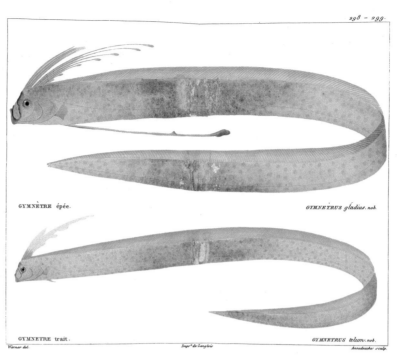

GYMNETRE épée.

GYMNETRUS gladius. nob.

GYMNETRE trait.

GYMNETRUS telum. nob.

Werner del.

Impr.ᵉ de Langlois

Annedouche sculp.

Above, Regalecus glesne *(slender oarfish), from Cuvier and* *Valenciennes, 1828-49 (11); below, from National Museum of Tokyo,* *unpublished (45); bottom, from Tansyu, 1819 (63).*

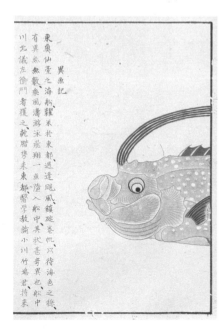

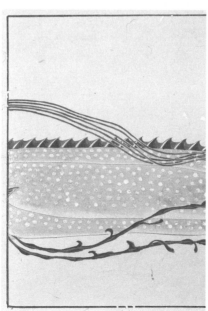

異魚記

東奧仙臺之海船米太郎東都遞逢颶風釀碰卷帆以待海色之穩有異無數乗風濤游泳飛翔一魚陷入船中其状甚奇異也船中川北儀左衛門者獲之乾腊賫來東都醫学教諭小川竹堵君持來

同小異ナリ蓋九州四國ノ邊二三十年ヲ經テ如此奇状ノ魚ヲ獲ルヿアリト云辛甲仲冬飢望七十五翁雲瑞仙院法印手摹

Antigonia capros *(boarfish), from*
Illustrations of Fishes, *1868-1912 (33).*

Top, left and right, Capros aper (boarfish), from Cuvier and Valenciennes, 1828-49 (11); center and left, Zeus faber (John Dory), respectively from Cuvier and Valenciennes, 1828-49 (11) and from Donovan, 1802-08 (18). Bottom, Zenopsis nebulosa (mirror Dory), from National Museum of Tokyo, unpublished (45).

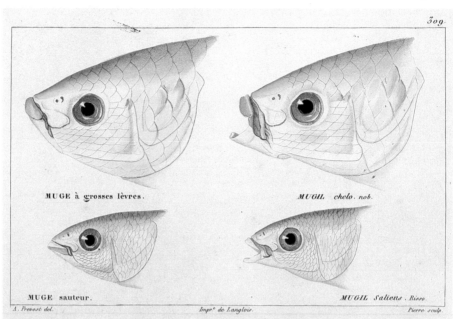

On the plate, top, Chelon labrosus *(thick-lipped gray mullet)* and, bottom, Liza saliens *(leaping gray mullet)*, both from Cuvier and Valenciennes, 1828-49 (11). Below, top, Austromenidia laticlavia *(pejerrey, or silverside)*, from Gay, 1844-71 (28); center, Liza macrolepis *(largescale mullet)*, from Day, 1865 (15); bottom, Atherina presbyter *(sand smelt)*, from Donovan, 1802-08 (18).

MUGE à grosses lèvres.

MUGIL chelo. nob.

MUGE sauteur.

MUGIL Saliens. Risso.

A. Prevost del.

Impr.e de Langlois.

Pierre sculp.

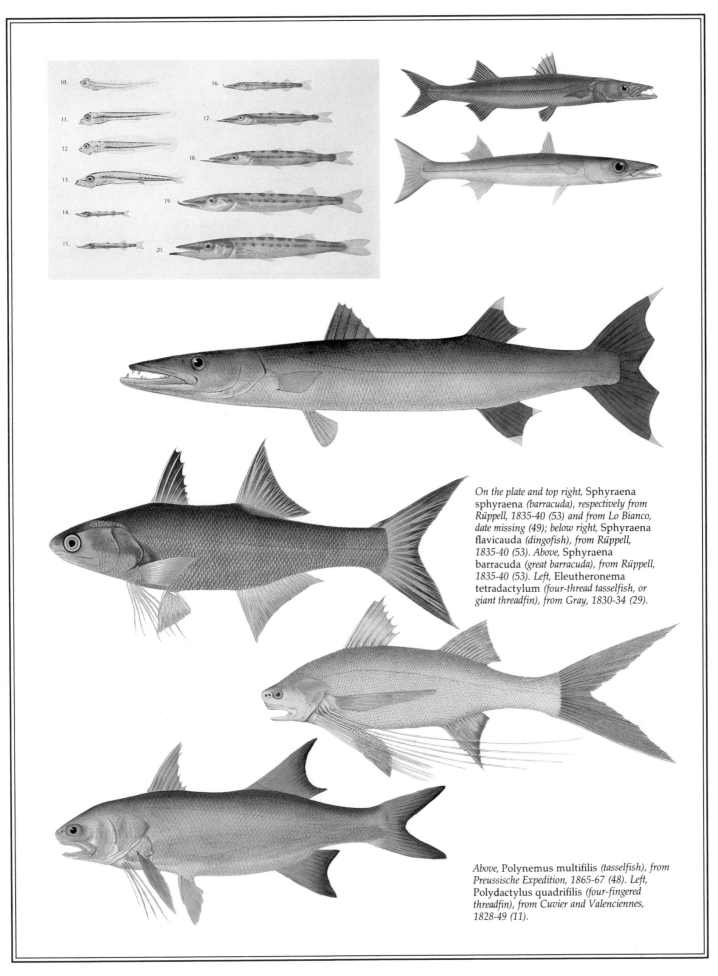

On the plate and top right, Sphyraena sphyraena *(barracuda), respectively from Rüppell, 1835-40 (53) and from Lo Bianco, date missing (49); below right,* Sphyraena flavicauda *(dingofish), from Rüppell, 1835-40 (53). Above,* Sphyraena barracuda *(great barracuda), from Rüppell, 1835-40 (53). Left,* Eleutheronema tetradactylum *(four-thread tasselfish, or giant threadfin), from Gray, 1830-34 (29).*

Above, Polynemus multifilis *(tasselfish), from Preussische Expedition, 1865-67 (48). Left,* Polydactylus quadrifilis *(four-fingered threadfin), from Cuvier and Valenciennes, 1828-49 (11).*

Right, Oplegnathus fasciatus *(Japanese parrotfish, or striped beak-perch), from Kruzenshtern, 1809-10 (37). Center left,* Ditrema viridis *(surf perch), from Ohno, 1937-44 (46); center right,* Pempheris otaitensis *(sweeper), from Cuvier and Valenciennes, 1828-49 (11). Bottom,* Mullus surmuletus *(red mullet), from Donovan, 1802-08 (18).*

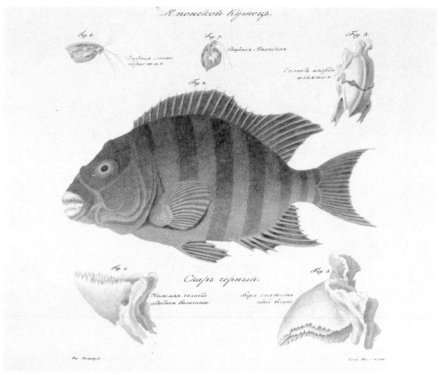

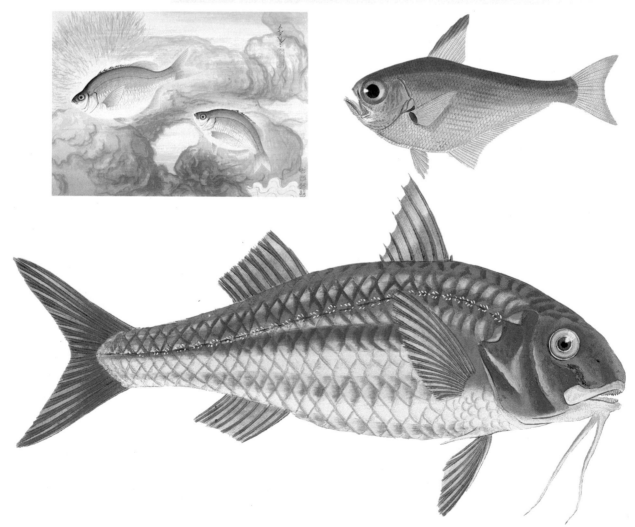

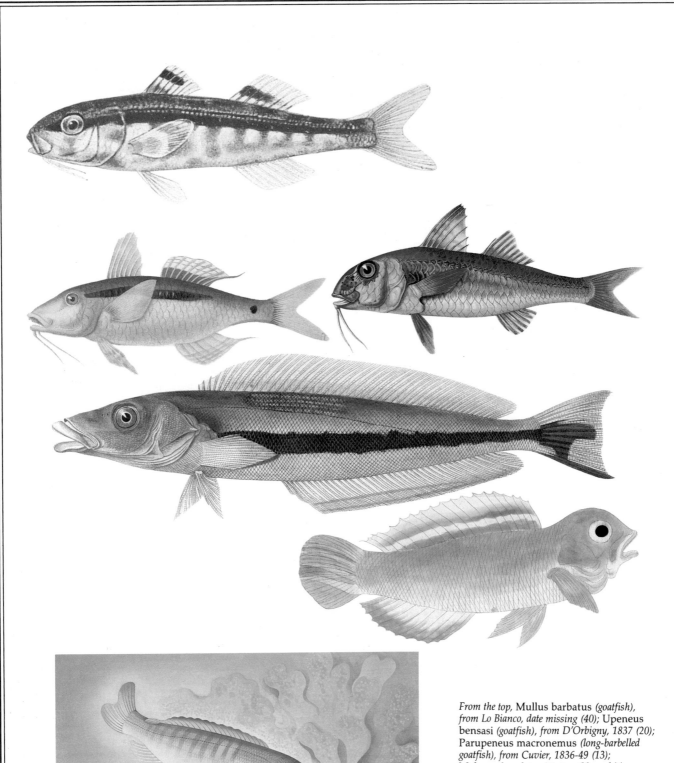

From the top, Mullus barbatus *(goatfish),
from Lo Bianco, date missing (40);* Upeneus
bensasi *(goatfish), from D'Orbigny, 1837 (20);*
Parupeneus macronemus *(long-barbelled
goatfish), from Cuvier, 1836-49 (13);*
Malacanthus latovittatus *(blue whiting, or
eye of the sea), from Dumont d'Urville, 1830-35
(21);* Branchiostegus argentatus *(yellow
horsehead), from National Museum of Tokyo,
unpublished (45). Left,* Branchiostegus
japonicus *(red horsehead, or Japanese tile fish),
from Ohno, 1937-44 (46).*

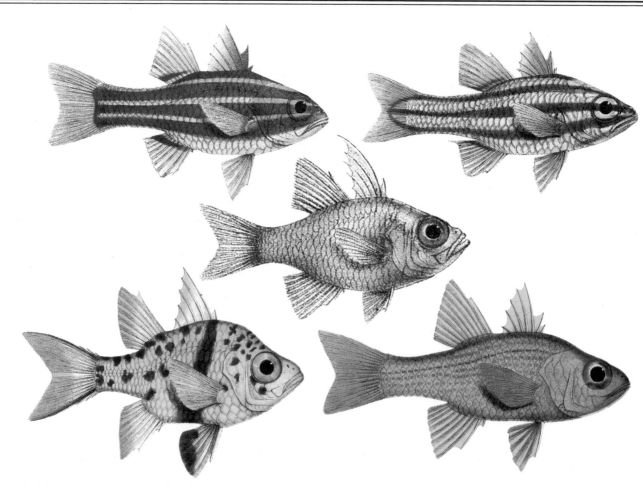

Top left, Apogon nigrofasciatus *(broadband cardinalfish); center,* Apogon leptacanthus *(threadfin cardinalfish); above, left,* Sphaeramia orbicularis *(polka dot cardinalfish, or pajama cardinalfish) and, above right,* Apogon maculiferus *(cardinalfish), all from Garrett and Günther, 1873-1910 (27).*

Top right, Apogon novemfasciatus *(nine-band cardinalfish); bottom,* Apogon endekataenia *(eleven-band cardinalfish), both from Siebold, 1833-50 (57).*

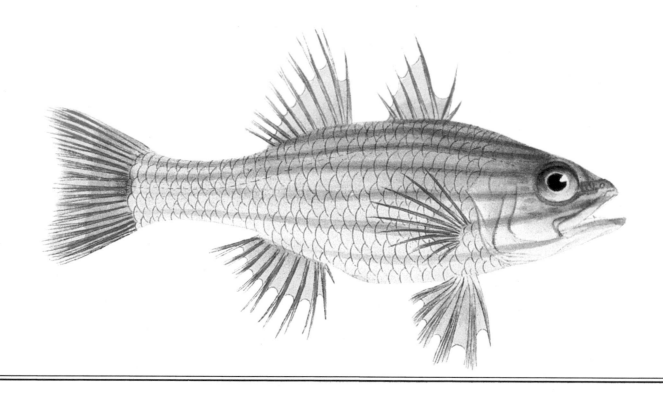

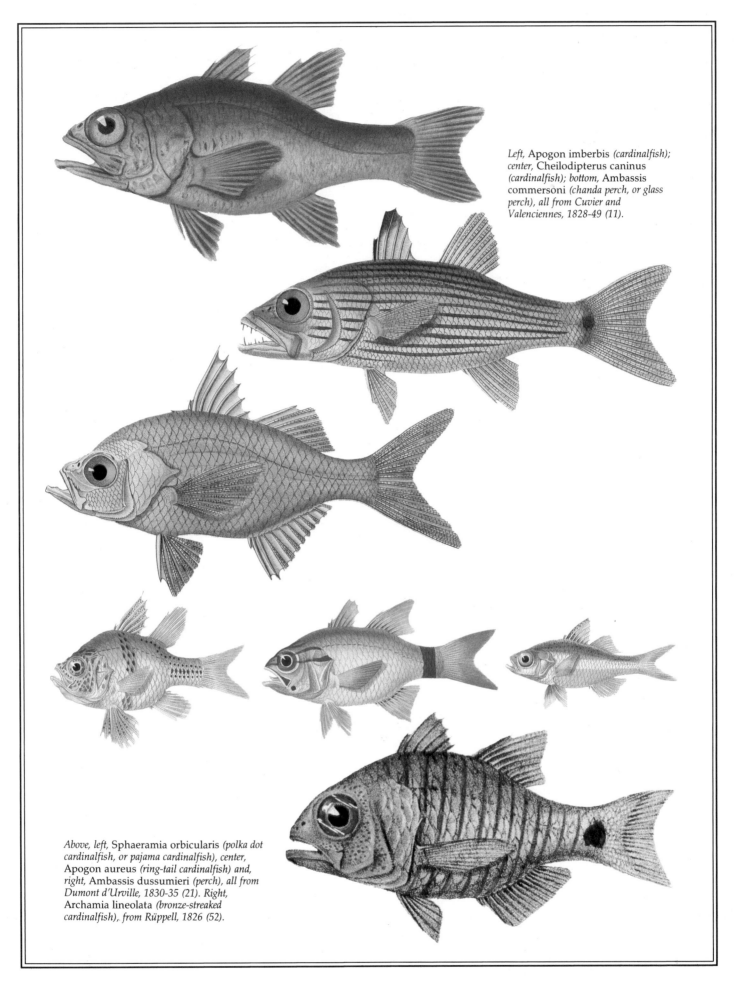

Left, Apogon imberbis *(cardinalfish);* center, Cheilodipterus caninus *(cardinalfish); bottom,* Ambassis commersoni *(chanda perch, or glass perch), all from Cuvier and Valenciennes, 1828-49 (11).*

Above, left, Sphaeramia orbicularis *(polka dot cardinalfish, or pajama cardinalfish), center,* Apogon aureus *(ring-tail cardinalfish) and, right,* Ambassis dussumieri *(perch), all from Dumont d'Urville, 1830-35 (21). Right,* Archamia lineolata *(bronze-streaked cardinalfish), from Rüppell, 1826 (52).*

79

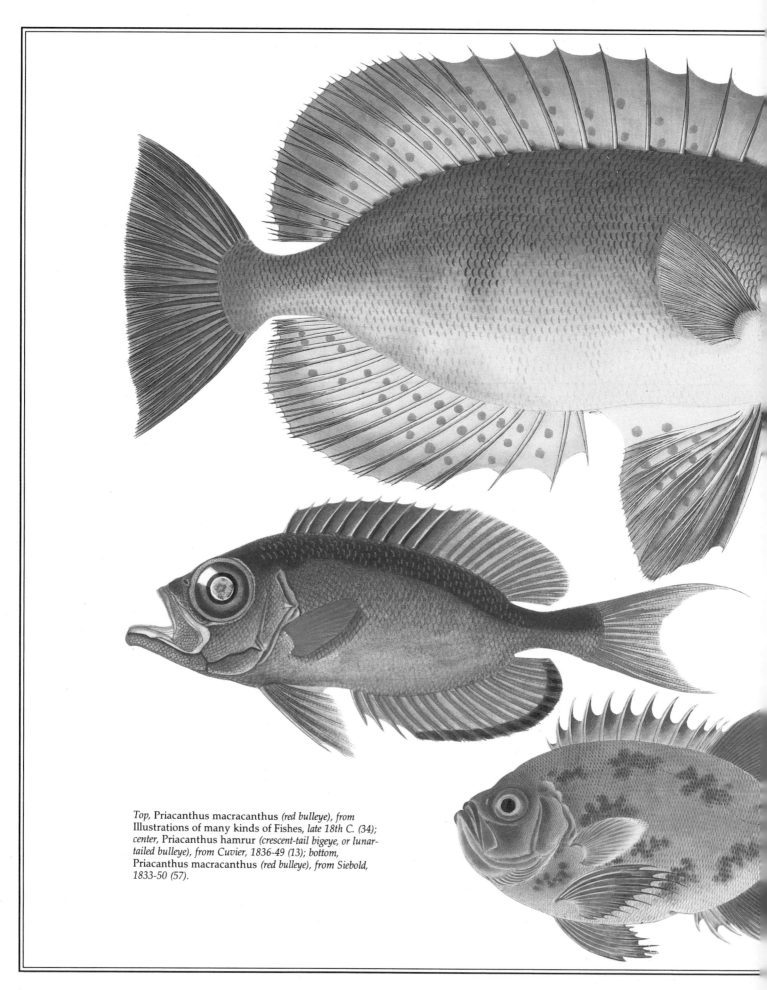

Top, Priacanthus macracanthus *(red bulleye), from* Illustrations of many kinds of Fishes, *late 18th C. (34); center,* Priacanthus hamrur *(crescent-tail bigeye, or lunar-tailed bulleye), from Cuvier, 1836-49 (13); bottom,* Priacanthus macracanthus *(red bulleye), from Siebold, 1833-50 (57).*

Top, Kuhlia caudivittata *(flagtail), from Cuvier, 1836-49 (13); center*, Kuhlia mugil *(barred flagtail), from Bennett, 1830 (4); bottom,* Cookeolus boops *(black-finned bigeye), from Dumont d'Urville, 1830-35 (21).*

Top left, Enoplosus armatus *(old wife), from Jardine, 1843 (35); top right,* Evistius acutirostris *(banded boarhead), from Syuntei, 1868-1912 (59). Left,* Pentaceros capensis *(pelagic armorhead), from Cuvier and Valenciennes, 1828-49 (11).*

Above, Banjos banjos *(banjofish), from Siebold, 1833-50 (57). Left,* Pentaceros richardsoni *(pelagic armorhead), from Smith, 1838-49 (58).*

From the top, Epinephelus akaara *(red grouper, or garrupa);* Epinephelus awoara *(green hata), both from Siebold, 1833-50 (57);* Epinephelus septemfasciatus *(sevenband grouper);* Epinephelus fario *(black-saddled grouper, or trout rockcod), from Kruzenshtern, 1809-10 (37);* Epinephelus moara *(kelp bass), from Siebold, 1833-50 (57);* Cephalopholis miniata *(blue spot rockcod), from Cuvier, 1836-49 (13).*

Top, Hypoplectrodes nigrorubrum; *right,* Othos dentex *(both Serranids). On the plate, from top,* Cephalopholis argus *(blue-spotted grouper);* Variola albimarginata *(rockcod);* Epinephelus miliaris *(grouper);* Cephalopholis boenak *(brown-banded rockcod), all from Dumont d'Urville, 1830-35 (21).*

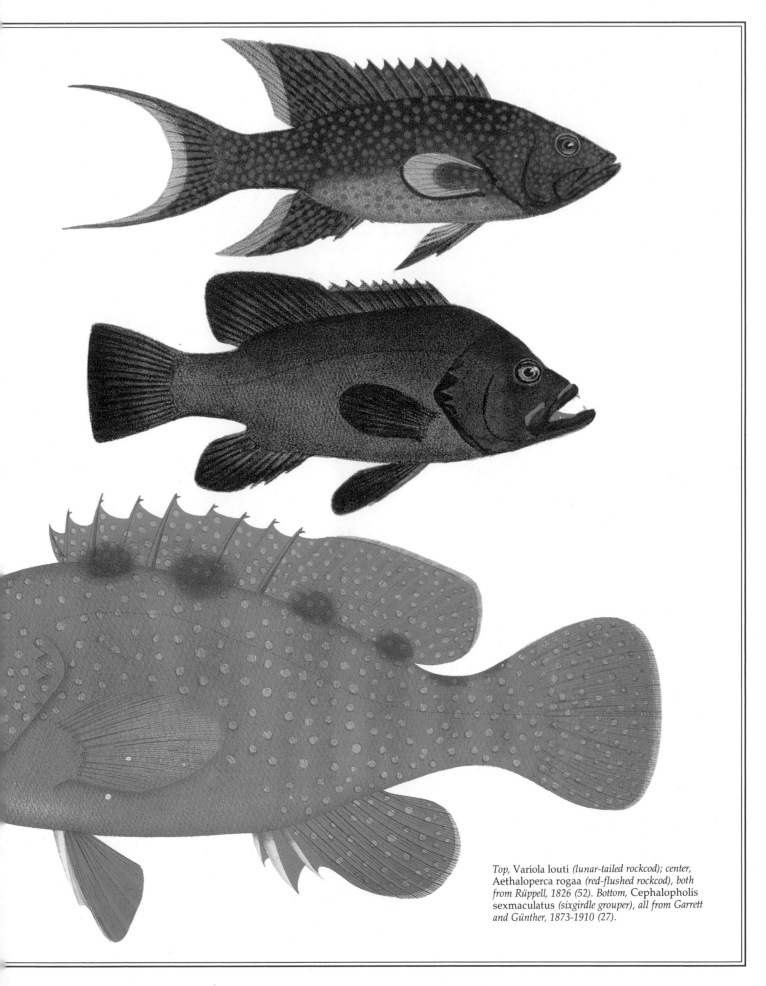

Top, Variola louti *(lunar-tailed rockcod); center,* Aethaloperca rogaa *(red-flushed rockcod), both from Rüppell, 1826 (52). Bottom,* Cephalopholis sexmaculatus *(sixgirdle grouper), all from Garrett and Günther, 1873-1910 (27).*

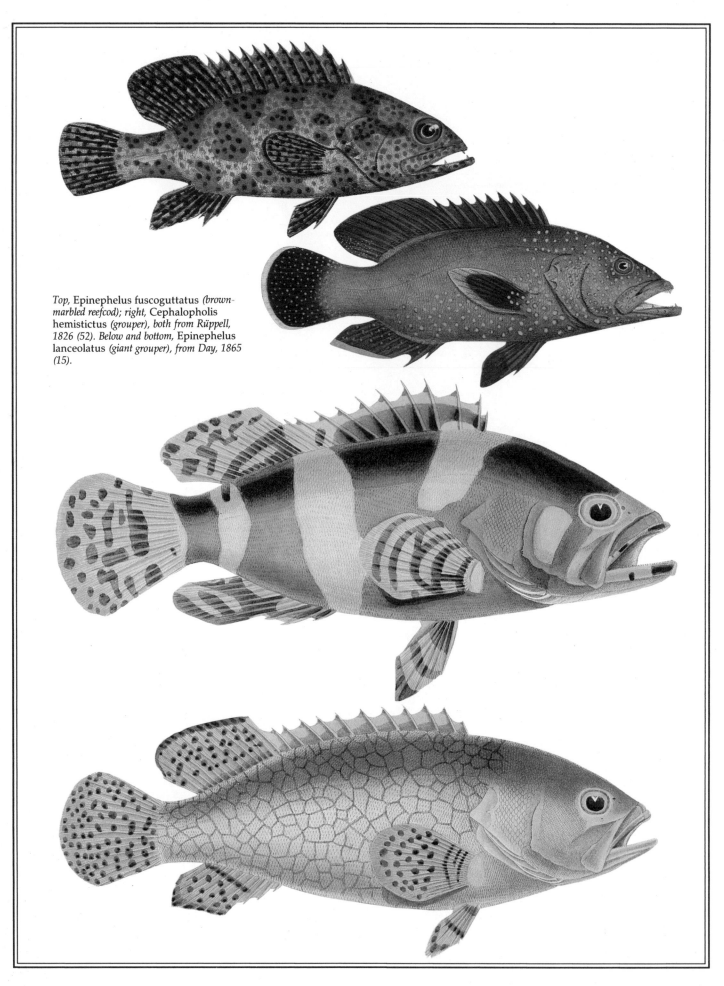

Top, Epinephelus fuscoguttatus *(brown-marbled reefcod); right,* Cephalopholis hemistictus *(grouper), both from Rüppell, 1826 (52). Below and bottom,* Epinephelus lanceolatus *(giant grouper), from Day, 1865 (15).*

Top, Epinephelus falvocaeruleus *(blue-and-yellow grouper), from Bennett, 1830 (4). Center,* Cephalopholis leopardus *(red-spotted rockcod); bottom,* Cephalopholis urodelus *(banded-tail coralcod), both from Garrett and Günther, 1873-1910 (27).*

Left, Grammistes sexlineatus *(six-lined perch, or gold-striped rockcod), from Jardine, 1843 (35). Below*, Rypticus bicolor *(soapfish), from Du Petit-Thouars, 1846 (22). Center left*, Serranus tigrinus *(tiger seaperch), from Bloch, 1785-89 (6); center right*, Serranus psittacinus *(sea perch), from Du Petit-Thouras, 1846 (22).*

Above, Aulacocephalus temmincki *(gold ribbon grouper), from Siebold, 1833-50 (57). Right*, Diploprion bifasciatus *(yellow emperor), from Cuvier, 1833-37 (12).*

Top, Polyprion americanus *(stone bass, or wreckfish), from* Cuvier, 1836-49 *(13). Center left,* Siniperca chuatsi *(Chinese perch), from* Ohno, 1937-44 *(46); center right,* Gilbertia semicincta *(Serranid), from* Gay, 1844-71 *(28).* Below, Hypoplectrus puella *(butter hamlet), from* Jardine, 1843 *(35).*

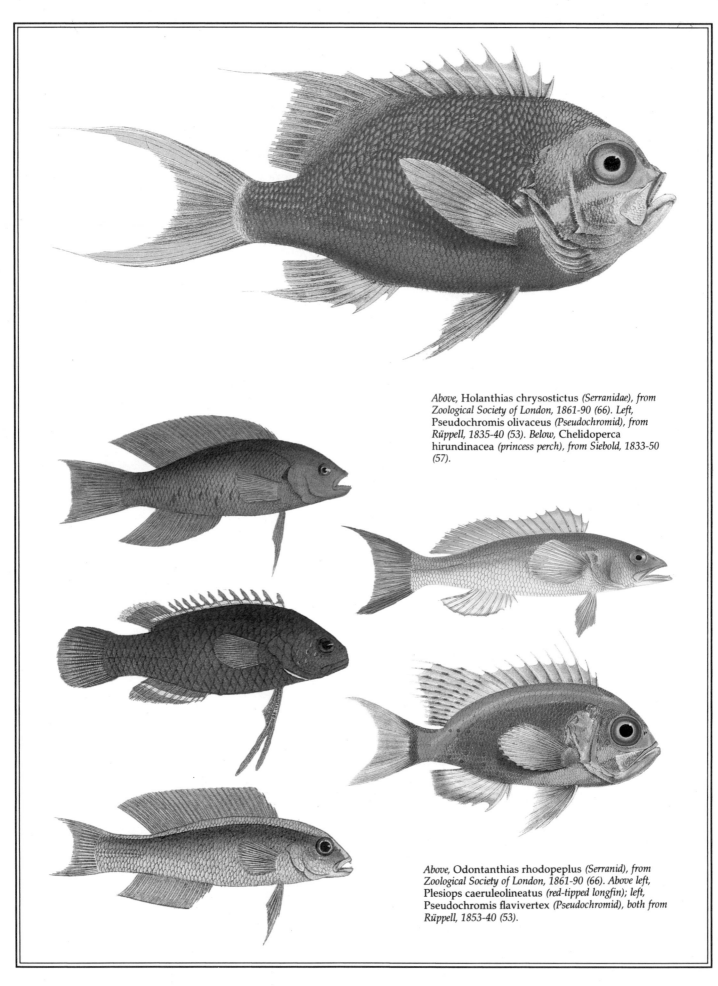

Above, Holanthias chrysostictus *(Serranidae), from Zoological Society of London, 1861-90 (66). Left,* Pseudochromis olivaceus *(Pseudochromid), from Rüppell, 1835-40 (53). Below,* Chelidoperca hirundinacea *(princess perch), from Siebold, 1833-50 (57).*

Above, Odontanthias rhodopeplus *(Serranid), from Zoological Society of London, 1861-90 (66). Above left,* Plesiops caeruleolineatus *(red-tipped longfin); left,* Pseudochromis flavivertex *(Pseudochromid), both from Rüppell, 1853-40 (53).*

From the top, Anthias anthias *(Serranid), from Cuvier and Valenciennes, 1828-49 (11);* Paranthias furcifer *(Creole fish), from Du Petit-Thouars, 1846 (22);* Plesiops corallicola *(ocellated longfin) and* Paraplesiops bleekeri *(longfin), both from Garrett and Günther, 1873-1910 (27).*

Left, Pogonias chromis *(black drum); below right,* Sciaena umbra *(corb, or brown mearge), both from Cuvier, 1836-49 (13). On the plate,* Argyrosomus argentatus *(white croaker) and* Nibea mitsukurii *(nibe croaker, or blue drum), from* Illustrations of Fishes, *1868-1912 (33).*

Left, Equetus lanceolatus *(jackknife fish), from Cuvier, 1836-49 (13). Above,* Sciaena umbra *(corb, or brown mearge), from Lo Bianco, date missing (40).*

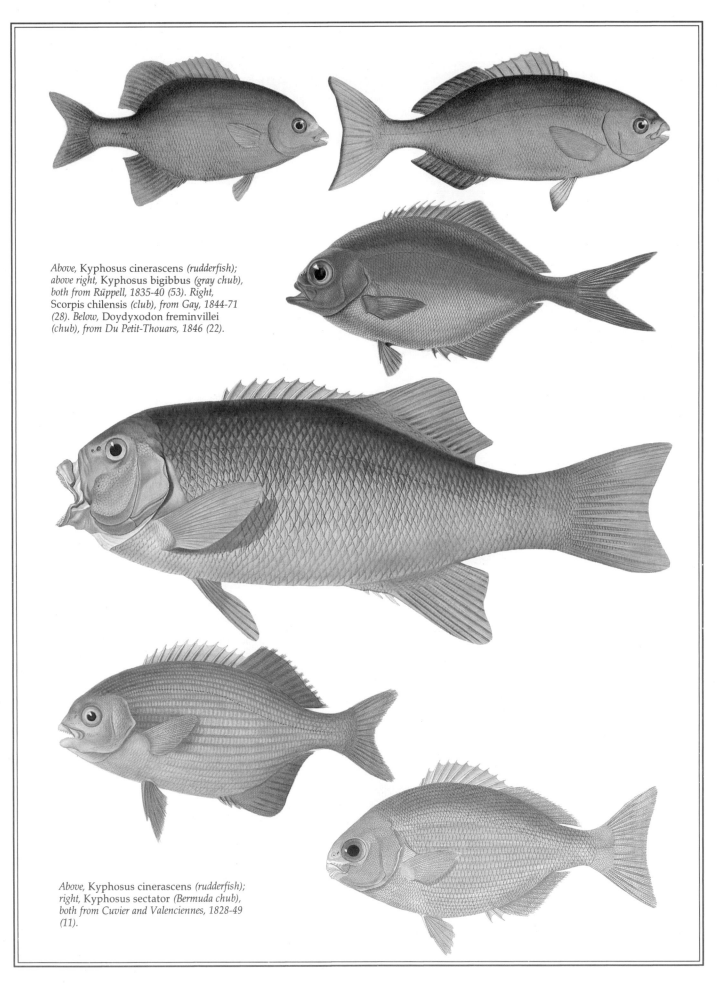

Above, Kyphosus cinerascens *(rudderfish); above right,* Kyphosus bigibbus *(gray chub), both from Rüppell, 1835-40 (53). Right,* Scorpis chilensis *(club), from Gay, 1844-71 (28). Below,* Doydyxodon freminvillei *(chub), from Du Petit-Thouars, 1846 (22).*

Above, Kyphosus cinerascens *(rudderfish); right,* Kyphosus sectator *(Bermuda chub), both from Cuvier and Valenciennes, 1828-49 (11).*

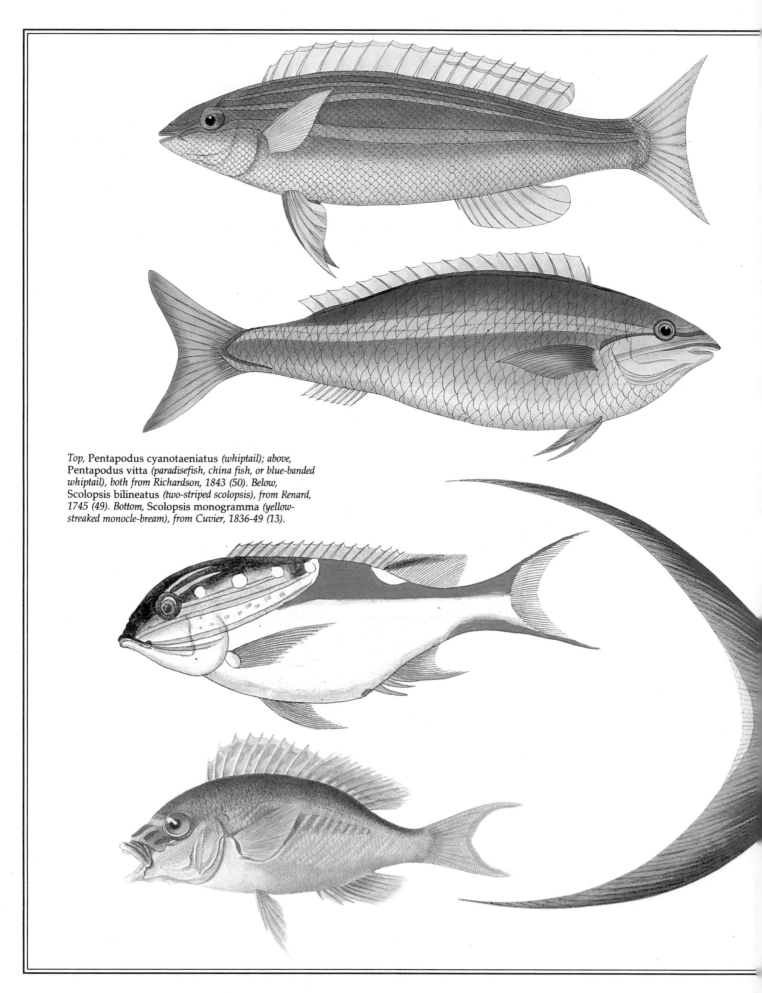

Top, Pentapodus cyanotaeniatus *(whiptail); above,*
Pentapodus vitta *(paradisefish, china fish, or blue-banded
whiptail), both from Richardson, 1843 (50). Below,*
Scolopsis bilineatus *(two-striped scolopsis), from Renard,
1745 (49). Bottom,* Scolopsis monogramma *(yellow-
streaked monocle-bream), from Cuvier, 1836-49 (13).*

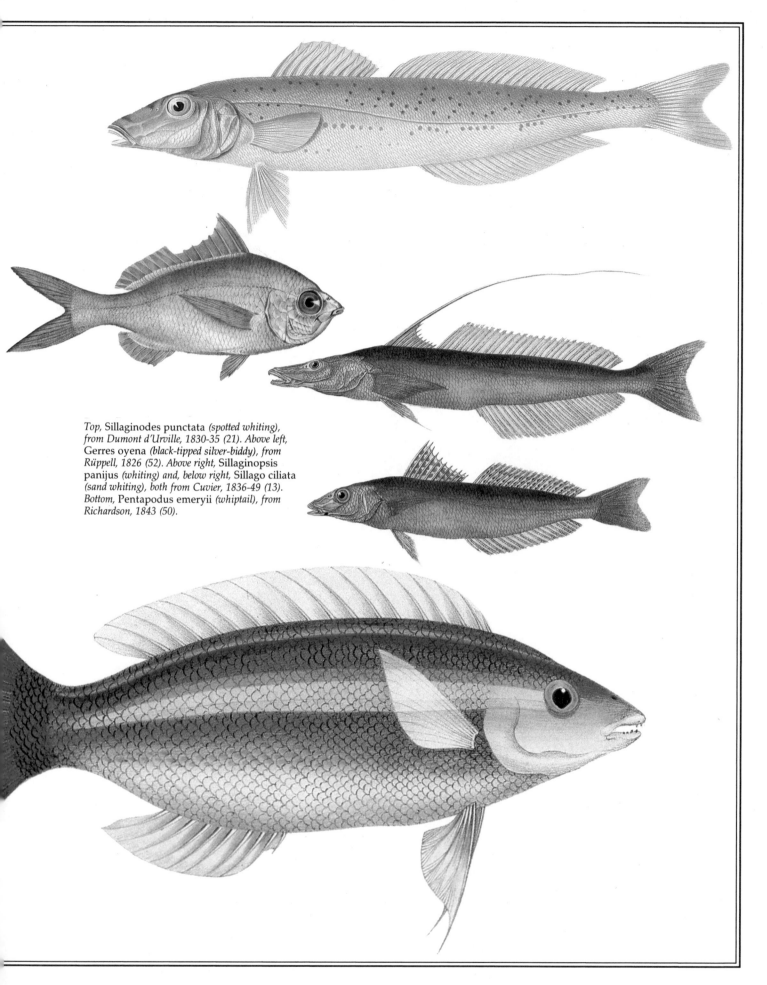

Top, Sillaginodes punctata *(spotted whiting),
from Dumont d'Urville, 1830-35 (21). Above left,*
Gerres oyena *(black-tipped silver-biddy), from
Rüppell, 1826 (52). Above right,* Sillaginopsis
panijus *(whiting) and, below right,* Sillago ciliata
*(sand whiting), both from Cuvier, 1836-49 (13).
Bottom,* Pentapodus emeryii *(whiptail), from
Richardson, 1843 (50).*

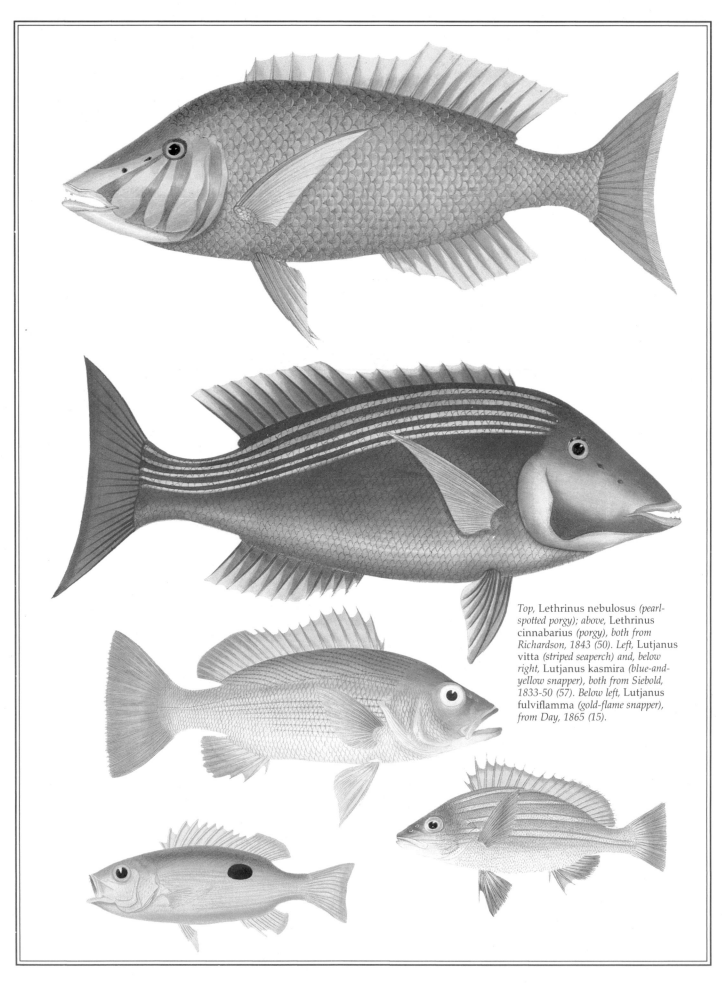

Top, Lethrinus nebulosus *(pearl-spotted porgy); above*, Lethrinus cinnabarius *(porgy), both from Richardson, 1843 (50). Left*, Lutjanus vitta *(striped seaperch) and, below right*, Lutjanus kasmira *(blue-and-yellow snapper), both from Siebold, 1833-50 (57). Below left*, Lutjanus fulviflamma *(gold-flame snapper), from Day, 1865 (15).*

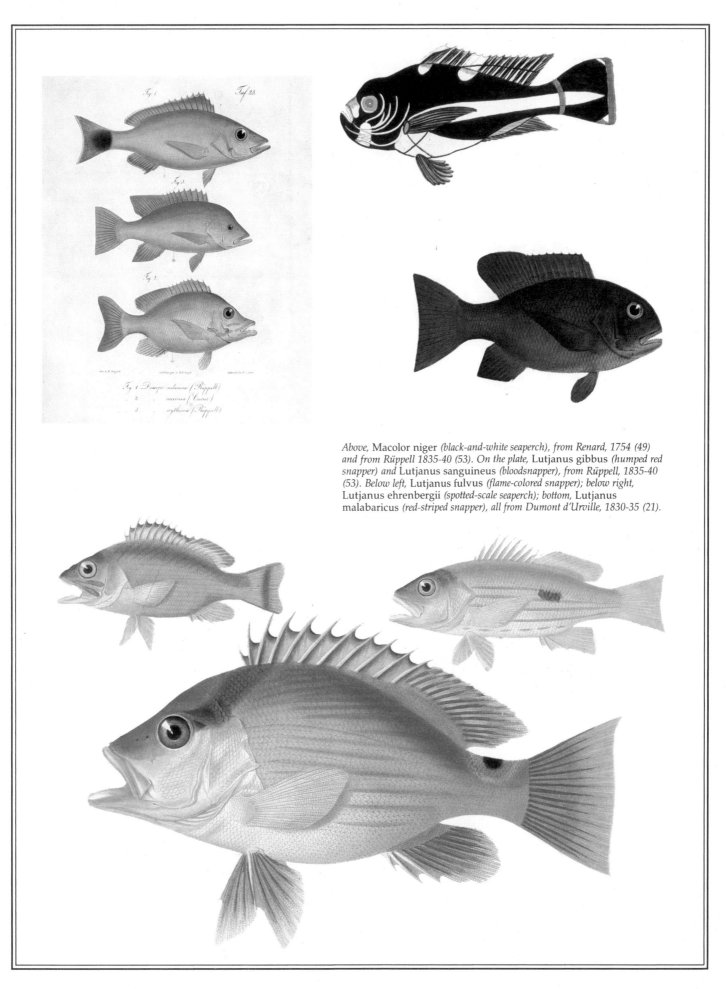

Above, Macolor niger *(black-and-white seaperch), from Renard, 1754 (49) and from Rüppell 1835-40 (53). On the plate,* Lutjanus gibbus *(humped red snapper) and* Lutjanus sanguineus *(bloodsnapper), from Rüppell, 1835-40 (53). Below left,* Lutjanus fulvus *(flame-colored snapper); below right,* Lutjanus ehrenbergii *(spotted-scale seaperch); bottom,* Lutjanus malabaricus *(red-striped snapper), all from Dumont d'Urville, 1830-35 (21).*

Above, Plectorhynchus punctatissimus *(grunt), from Garrett and Günther, 1873-1910 (27). Right,* Genyatremus luteus *(torroto) and, bottom right,* Plectorhynchus pictus *(oriental sweetlip), both from Cuvier and Valenciennes, 1828-49 (11). Below, on the plate,* Plectorhynchus gaterinus *(grunt) and* Diagramma pictum *(painted sweetlip), from Rüppell, 1826 (52).*

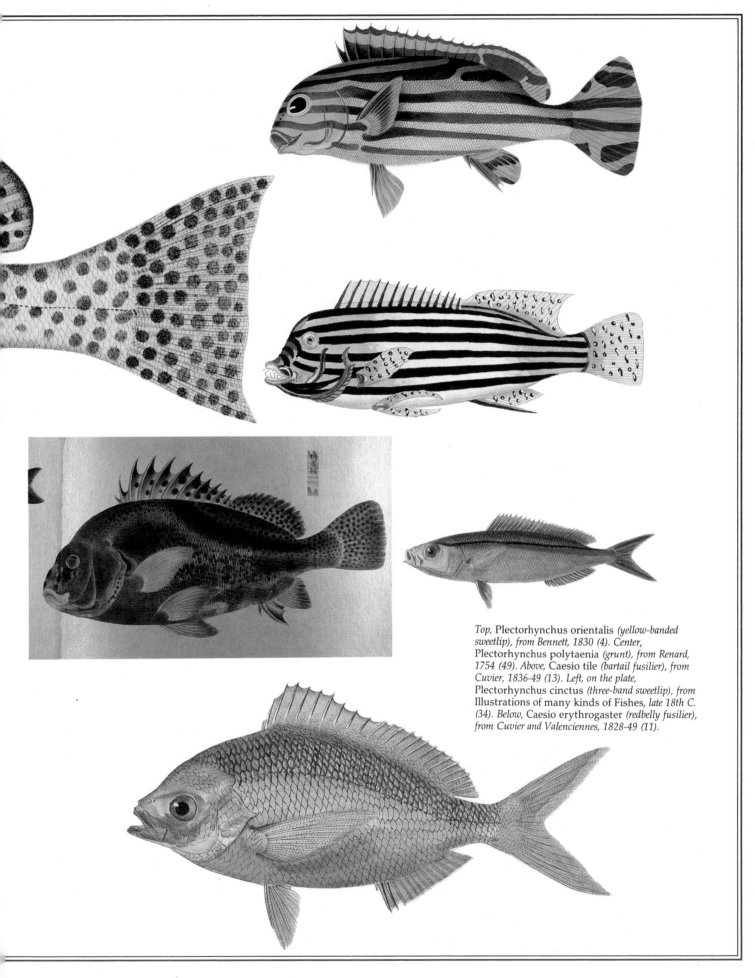

Top, Plectorhynchus orientalis *(yellow-banded sweetlip), from Bennett, 1830 (4). Center,* Plectorhynchus polytaenia *(grunt), from Renard, 1754 (49). Above,* Caesio tile *(bartail fusilier), from Cuvier, 1836-49 (13). Left, on the plate,* Plectorhynchus cinctus *(three-band sweetlip), from* Illustrations of many kinds of Fishes, *late 18th C. (34). Below,* Caesio erythrogaster *(redbelly fusilier), from Cuvier and Valenciennes, 1828-49 (11).*

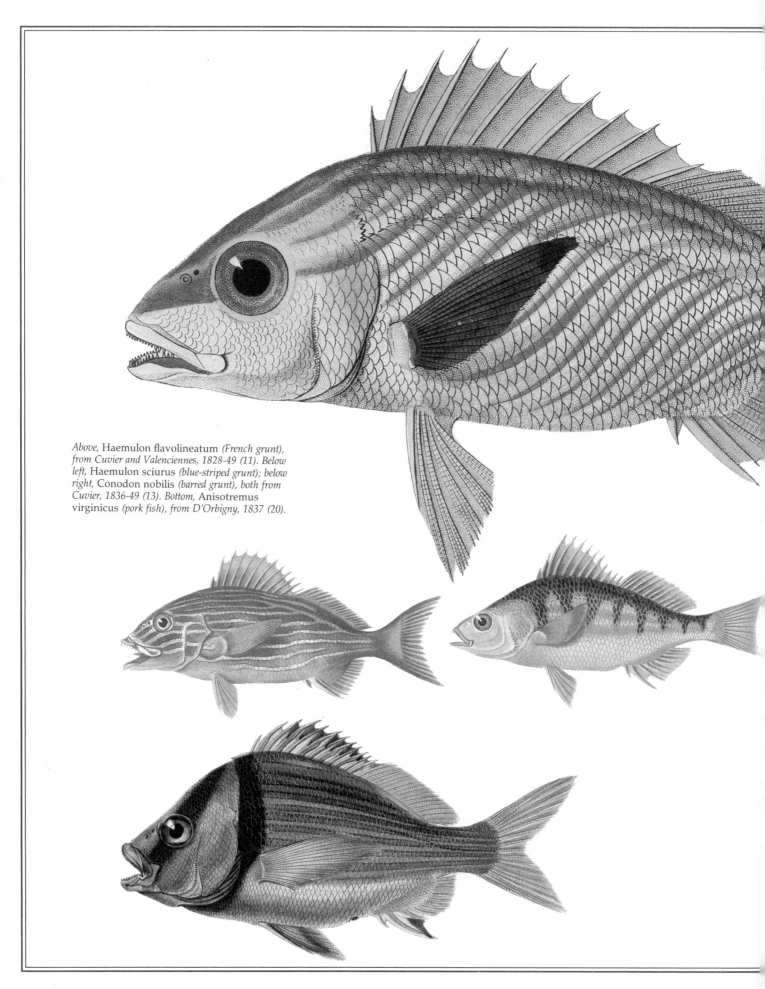

Above, Haemulon flavolineatum *(French grunt)*, *from Cuvier and Valenciennes, 1828-49 (11). Below left*, Haemulon sciurus *(blue-striped grunt); below right*, Conodon nobilis *(barred grunt), both from Cuvier, 1836-49 (13). Bottom*, Anisotremus virginicus *(pork fish), from D'Orbigny, 1837 (20).*

漢名鼠頭魚

シマイサキ

Above, Terapon oxyrhynchus *(sharp-nosed tigerfish), from* Illustrations of Fishes, *1868-1912 (33). Left,* Pelates quadrilineatus *(four-barred grunt), from Cuvier, 1836-49 (13). Below,* Parapristipoma trilineatum *(chicken grunt, or three-line grunt), from Ohno, 1937-44 (46).*

Above, Monotaxis grandoculis *(bigeye barenose), from Rüppell, 1835-40 (53). Below,* Pagellus bogaraveo *(lunulated gilt-head), from Donovan, 1802-08 (18).*

Left, Acanthopagrus schlegeli *(sea bream), from Ohno, 1937-44 (46). Below,* Petrus rupestris *(red steenbras, or yellow steenbras), from Smith, 1838-49 (58).*

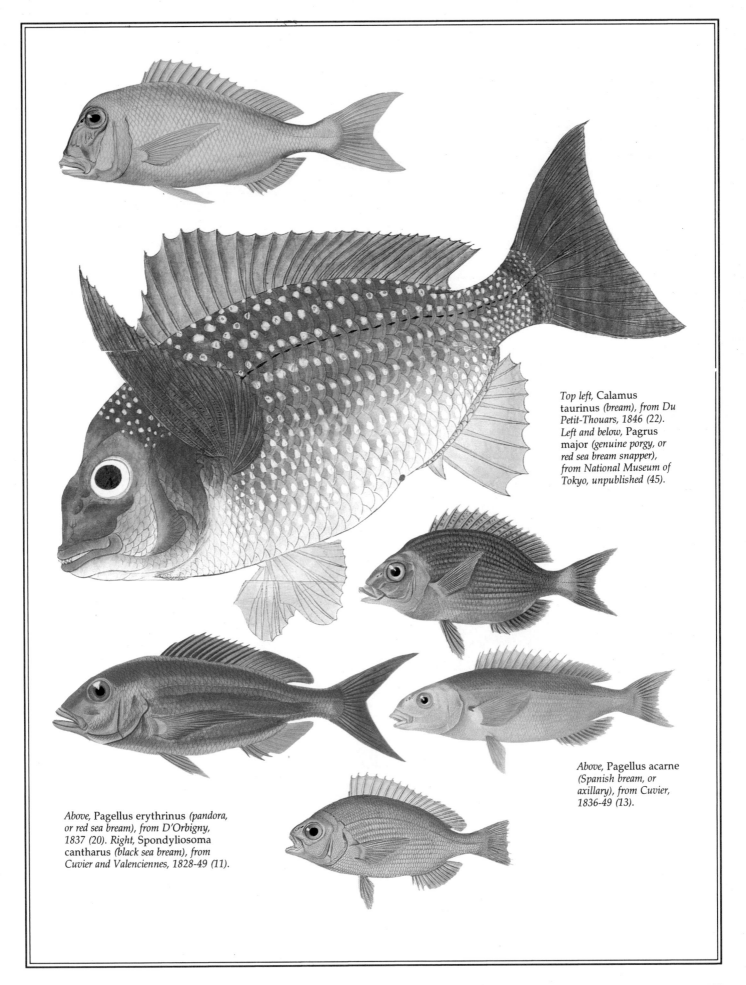

Top left, Calamus taurinus *(bream), from Du Petit-Thouars, 1846 (22). Left and below,* Pagrus major *(genuine porgy, or red sea bream snapper), from National Museum of Tokyo, unpublished (45).*

Above, Pagellus acarne *(Spanish bream, or axillary), from Cuvier, 1836-49 (13).*

Above, Pagellus erythrinus *(pandora, or red sea bream), from D'Orbigny, 1837 (20). Right,* Spondyliosoma cantharus *(black sea bream), from Cuvier and Valenciennes, 1828-49 (11).*

Top, Paracirrhites forsteri *(blacksides hawkfish), from Bennett, 1830 (4). Above left,* Cirrihitichthys aureus *(golden curlyfin), from Siebold, 1833-50 (57); above right,* Cirrhitops fasciatus *(hawkfish), from Cuvier and Valenciennes, 1828-49 (11).*

Above, Cirrhitus rivulatus *(hawkfish), from Du Petit-Thouars, 1846 (22). Right,* Paracirrhites arcatus *(ring-eyed hawkfish), from Cuvier, 1836-49 (13).*

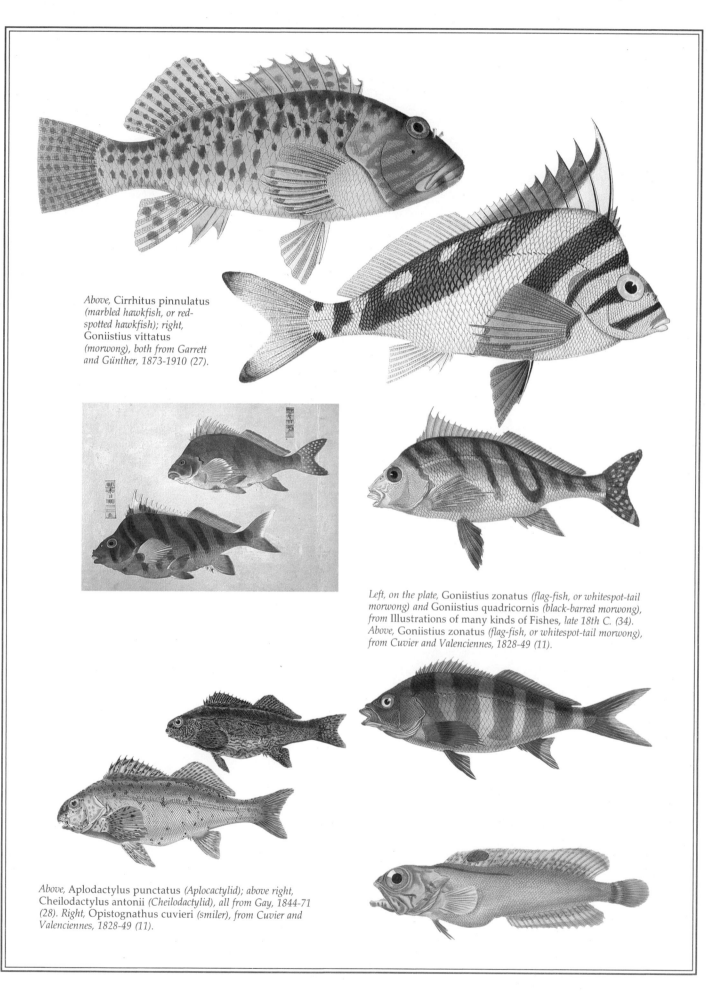

Above, Cirrhitus pinnulatus *(marbled hawkfish, or red-spotted hawkfish)*; *right*, Goniistius vittatus *(morwong), both from Garrett and Günther, 1873-1910 (27).*

Left, on the plate, Goniistius zonatus (flag-fish, or whitespot-tail morwong) and Goniistius quadricornis (black-barred morwong), from Illustrations of many kinds of Fishes, late 18th C. (34). Above, Goniistius zonatus (flag-fish, or whitespot-tail morwong), from Cuvier and Valenciennes, 1828-49 (11).

Above, Aplodactylus punctatus *(Aplocactylid)*; *above right*, Cheilodactylus antonii *(Cheilodactylid), all from Gay, 1844-71 (28)*. *Right*, Opistognathus cuvieri *(smiler), from Cuvier and Valenciennes, 1828-49 (11).*

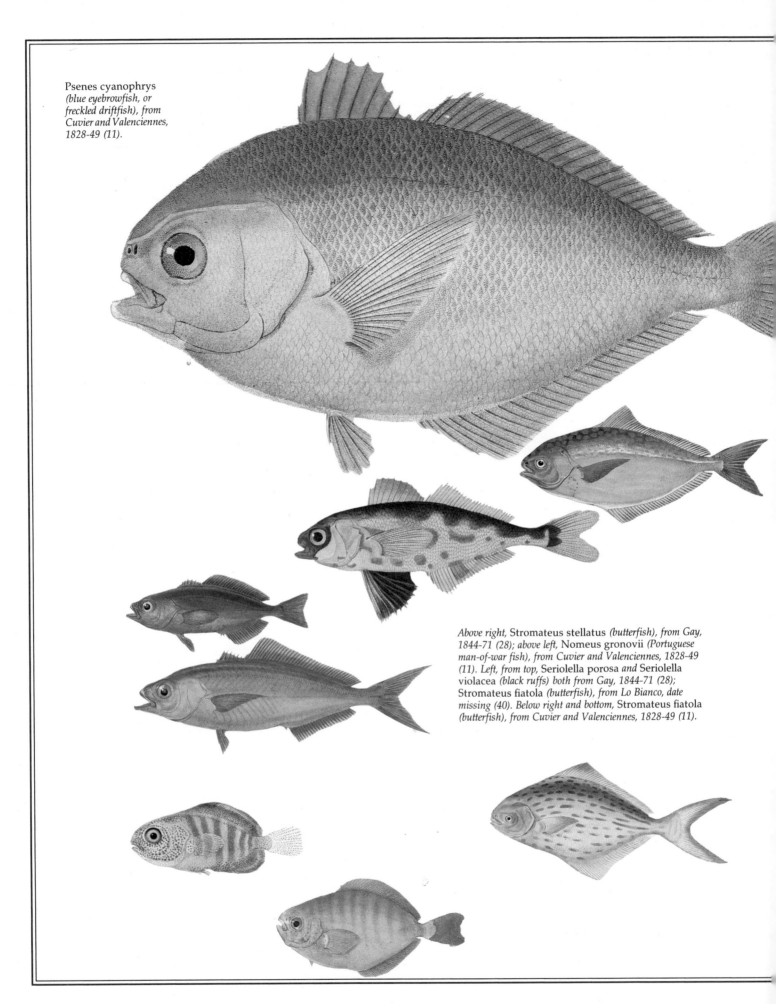

Psenes cyanophrys *(blue eyebrowfish, or freckled driftfish), from Cuvier and Valenciennes, 1828-49 (11).*

Above right, Stromateus stellatus (butterfish), from Gay, 1844-71 (28); above left, Nomeus gronovii (Portuguese man-of-war fish), from Cuvier and Valenciennes, 1828-49 (11). Left, from top, Seriolella porosa and Seriolella violacea (black ruffs) both from Gay, 1844-71 (28); Stromateus fiatola (butterfish), from Lo Bianco, date missing (40). Below right and bottom, Stromateus fiatola (butterfish), from Cuvier and Valenciennes, 1828-49 (11).

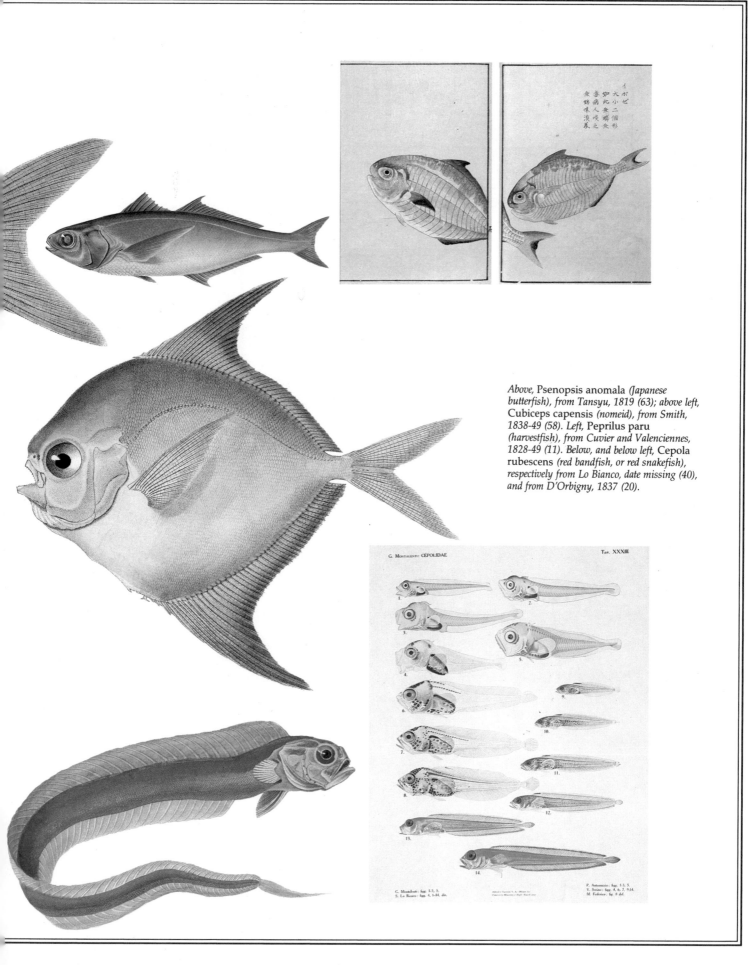

イバゼ
大小二個
如此魚蝶形
喜病人喷之
魚肪味浪
養

Above, Psenopsis anomala *(Japanese butterfish), from Tansyu, 1819 (63); above left,* Cubiceps capensis *(nomeid), from Smith, 1838-49 (58). Left,* Peprilus paru *(harvestfish), from Cuvier and Valenciennes, 1828-49 (11). Below, and below left,* Cepola rubescens *(red bandfish, or red snakefish), respectively from Lo Bianco, date missing (40), and from D'Orbigny, 1837 (20).*

G. MONTALENTI: CEPOLIDAE   Tav. XXXIII.

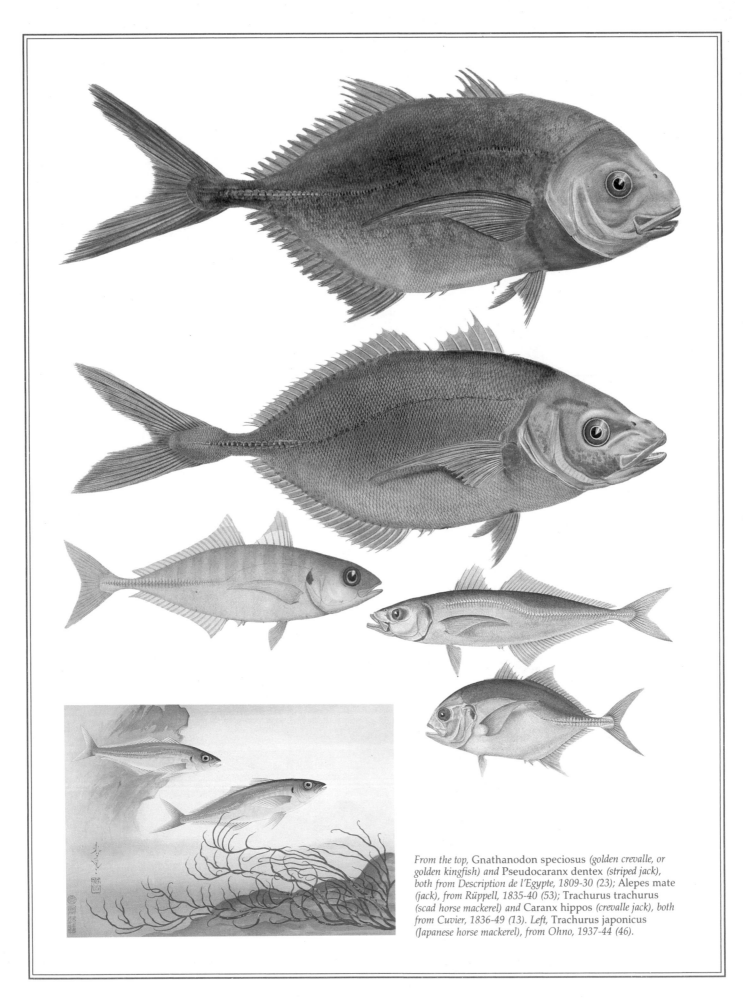

From the top, Gnathanodon speciosus *(golden crevalle, or golden kingfish) and* Pseudocaranx dentex *(striped jack), both from* Description de l'Egypte, *1809-30 (23); Alepes mate (jack), from Rüppell, 1835-40 (53); Trachurus trachurus (scad horse mackerel) and Caranx hippos (crevalle jack), both from Cuvier, 1836-49 (13). Left, Trachurus japonicus (Japanese horse mackerel), from Ohno, 1937-44 (46).*

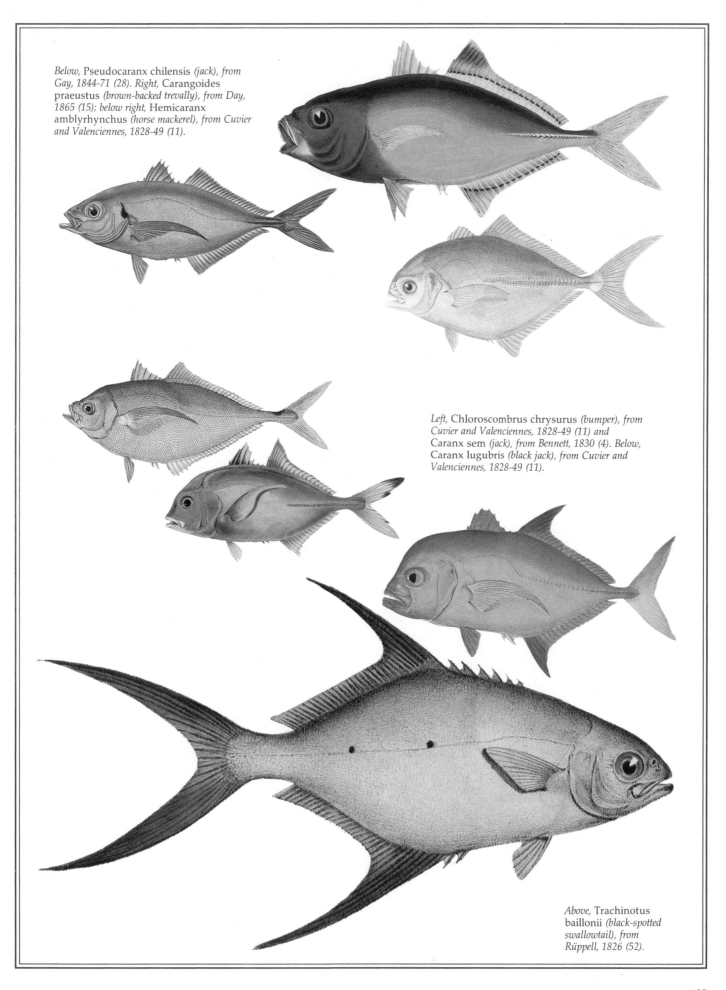

Below, Pseudocaranx chilensis *(jack), from Gay, 1844-71 (28).* Right, Carangoides praeustus *(brown-backed trevally), from Day, 1865 (15); below right,* Hemicaranx amblyrhynchus *(horse mackerel), from Cuvier and Valenciennes, 1828-49 (11).*

Left, Chloroscombrus chrysurus *(bumper), from Cuvier and Valenciennes, 1828-49 (11) and* Caranx sem *(jack), from Bennett, 1830 (4). Below,* Caranx lugubris *(black jack), from Cuvier and Valenciennes, 1828-49 (11).*

Above, Trachinotus baillonii *(black-spotted swallowtail), from Rüppell, 1826 (52).*

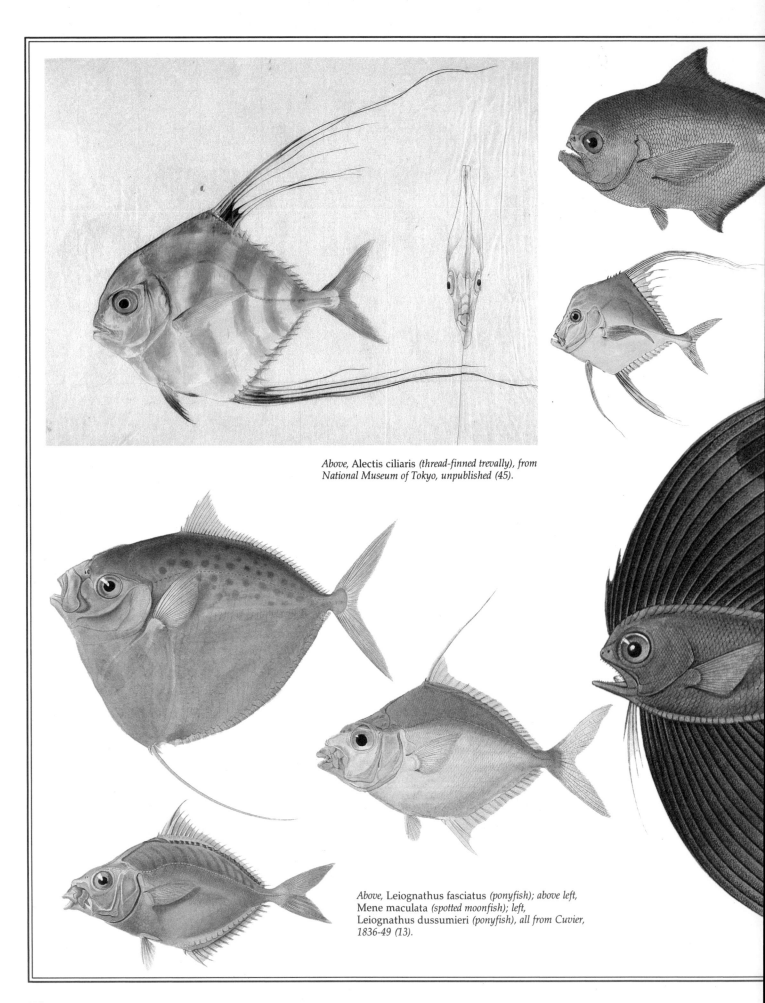

Above, Alectis ciliaris *(thread-finned trevally), from National Museum of Tokyo, unpublished (45).*

Above, Leiognathus fasciatus *(ponyfish); above left,* Mene maculata *(spotted moonfish); left,* Leiognathus dussumieri *(ponyfish), all from Cuvier, 1836-49 (13).*

Top left, on the double page, Brama brama *(Atlantic pomfret); below,* Alectis indicus *(Indian thread-fin) and* Carangoides hedlandensis *(armed trevally, or long-finned crevalle), all from Cuvier and Valenciennes, 1828-49 (11).*

On the plate, top, Selene vomer *(Atlantic lookdown); center,* Selene browni *(lookdown); bottom,* Alectis alexandrinus *(thread-fin), from Cuvier, 1836-49 (13). Below,* Carangoides armatus *(armed trevally, or kingfish), from Cuvier and Valenciennes, 1828-49 (11). Bottom,* Taractichthys steindachneri *(Steindachner's pomfret fish), from Takagi, c. 1850 (60). Below left, on the double page,* Pteraclis velifera *(fanfish), from Cuvier, 1836-49 (13).*

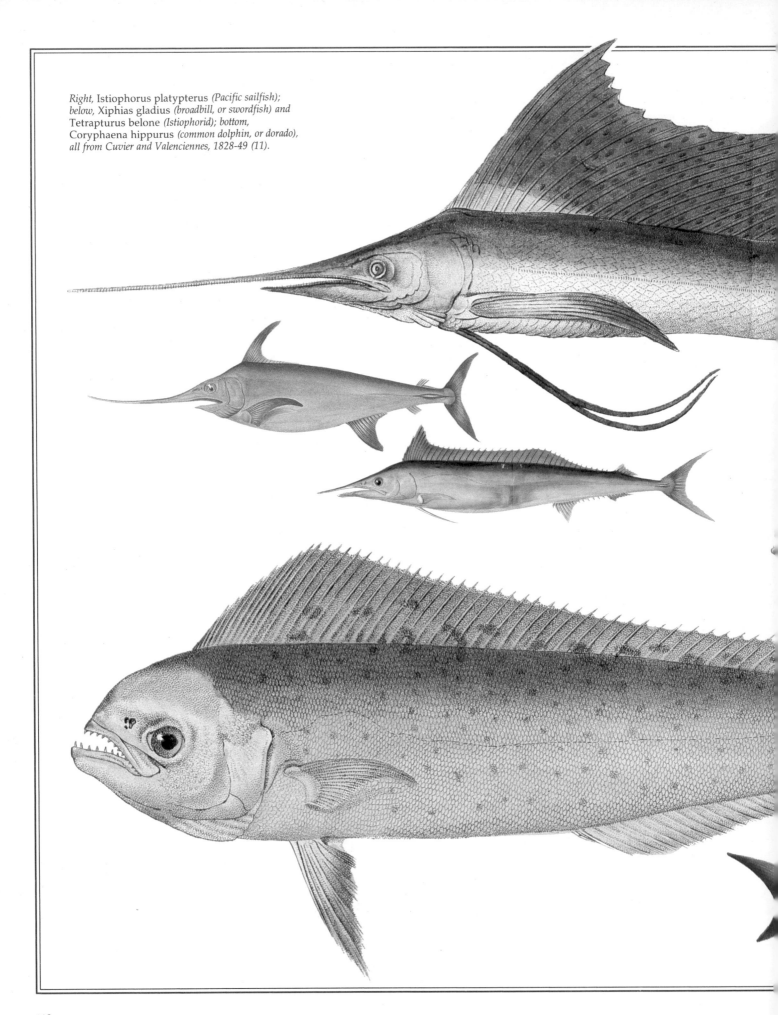

Right, Istiophorus platypterus *(Pacific sailfish)*;
below, Xiphias gladius *(broadbill, or swordfish) and*
Tetrapturus belone *(Istiophorid)*; *bottom*,
Coryphaena hippurus *(common dolphin, or dorado)*,
all from Cuvier and Valenciennes, 1828-49 (11).

Center, Luvarus imperialis *(luvar); above,* Naucrates ductor *(pilot fish), both from Cuvier, 1836-49 (13). Left,* Rachycentron canadum *(black bonito), from Rüppell, 1835-40 (53).*

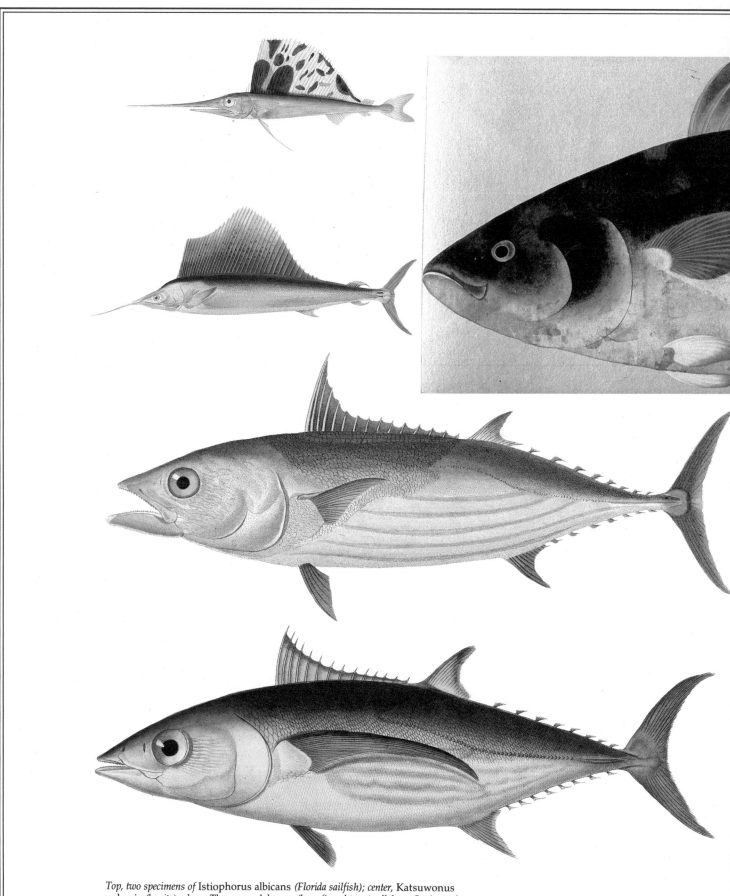

Top, two specimens of Istiophorus albicans *(Florida sailfish); center,* Katsuwonus pelamis *(bonito); above,* Thunnus alalunga *(long-finned tuna), all from Cuvier and Valenciennes, 1828-49 (11).*

此宗西海極多長崎方多有
名梅可得而聞矣

まぐろ

Top, on the double page, Thunnus albacares *(yellowfin albacore, or allison), from* Illustrations of many kinds of Fishes, *late 18th C. (34). Above,* Euthynnus alletteratus *(little tuna, or false albacore); below,* Thunnus thynnus *(tunny, or Atlantic bluefin tuna), both from Cuvier, 1836-49 (13).*

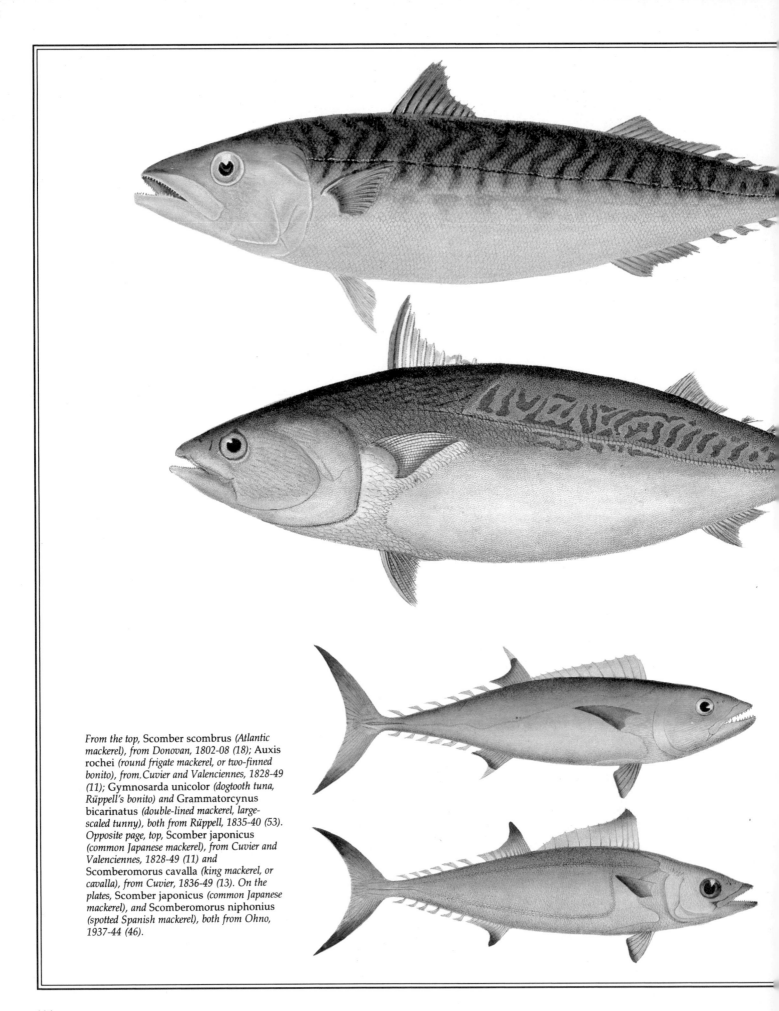

From the top, Scomber scombrus (Atlantic mackerel), from Donovan, 1802-08 (18); Auxis rochei (round frigate mackerel, or two-finned bonito), from Cuvier and Valenciennes, 1828-49 (11); Gymnosarda unicolor (dogtooth tuna, Rüppell's bonito) and Grammatorcynus bicarinatus (double-lined mackerel, large-scaled tunny), both from Rüppell, 1835-40 (53). Opposite page, top, Scomber japonicus (common Japanese mackerel), from Cuvier and Valenciennes, 1828-49 (11) and Scomberomorus cavalla (king mackerel, or cavalla), from Cuvier, 1836-49 (13). On the plates, Scomber japonicus (common Japanese mackerel), and Scomberomorus niphonius (spotted Spanish mackerel), both from Ohno, 1937-44 (46).

On the plate, Trichiurus lepturus *(ribbonfish, or scabbardfish), from Ohno, 1937-44 (46). Top, left,* Lepturacanthus savala *(small-headed ribbonfish) and, right,* Lepidopus caudatus *(scabbardfish, or frostfish), both from Cuvier, 1836-49 (13). Above left,* Trichiurus lepturus *(ribbonfish, or scabbardfish), from Day, 1865 (15); above right,* Eleginops macrovinus *(Antarctic cod), from Day, 1844-71 (28). Below, left,* Thyrsites atun *(barracouta), from Cuvier, 1836-49 (13); right,* Echiichthys vipera *(weever), from Donovan, 1802-08 (18).*

Above, Parapercis pulchella *(rosy grubfish), from Siebold, 1833-50 (57). Right,* Parapercis hexophthalma *(grubfish), from Rüppell, 1826 (52). Below,* Parapercis colias *(grubfish), from Cuvier, 1836-49 (13).*

Below left, Echiichthys vipera *(weever), from Lo Bianco, date missing (40); below right,* Trachinus draco *(greater draco), from Donovan, 1802-08 (18).*

Above, Uranoscopus japonicus *(Japanese stargazer, or mishima pufferfish)* and Gnathagnus elongatus *(stargazer), both from Siebold, 1833-50 (57). On the plate, top,* Uranoscopus scaber; *center,* Uranoscopus guttatus *and, bottom,* Ichthyoscopus tebeck tebeck *(all stargazers), from Cuvier, 1836-49 (13).*

119

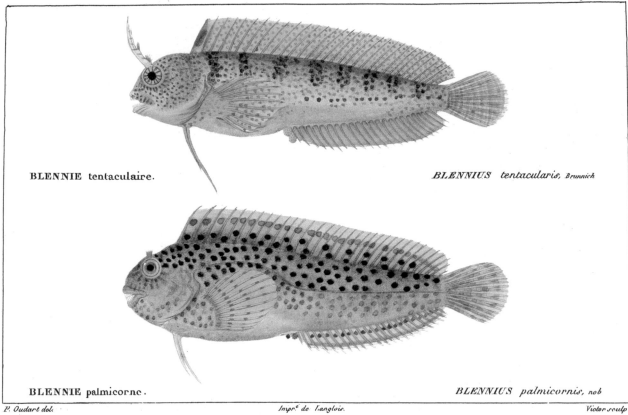

BLENNIUS tentacularis, Brunnich

BLENNIE palmicorne.

BLENNIUS palmicornis, nob

P. Oudart del.

Impr.e de Langlois.

Victor sculp.

On the plate, top, Parablennius tentacularis *(horned blenny); bottom,* Parablennius sanguinolentus *(red-speckled blenny), from Cuvier and Valenciennes, 1828-49 (11). Above,* Parablennius gattorugine *(rock blenny), from Donovan, 1802-08 (18).*

Above, Lipophrys pholis *(shanny blenny), from Donovan, 1802-08 (18). Below,* Blennius ocellaris *(butterfly blenny), from Cuvier, 1836-49 (13). Left,* Istiblennius flaviumbrinus *and* Atrosalarias fuscus fuscus *(blennies), both from Rüppell, 1835-40 (53).*

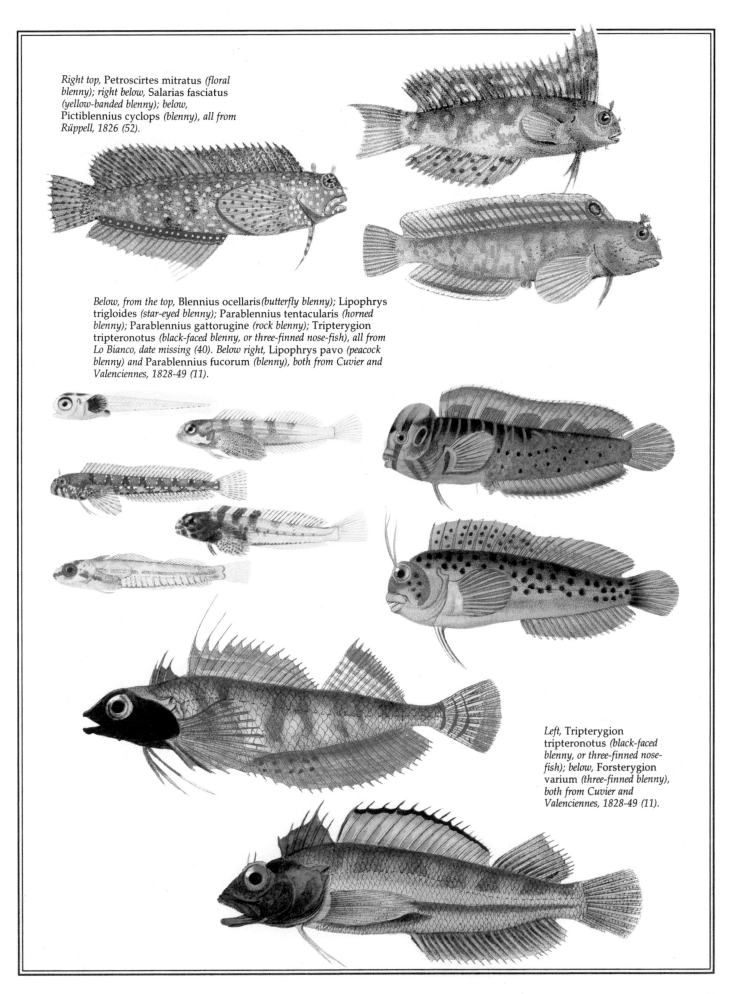

Right top, Petroscirtes mitratus *(floral blenny); right below,* Salarias fasciatus *(yellow-banded blenny); below,* Pictiblennius cyclops *(blenny), all from Rüppell, 1826 (52).*

Below, from the top, Blennius ocellaris *(butterfly blenny);* Lipophrys trigloides *(star-eyed blenny);* Parablennius tentacularis *(horned blenny);* Parablennius gattorugine *(rock blenny);* Tripterygion tripteronotus *(black-faced blenny, or three-finned nose-fish), all from Lo Bianco, date missing (40). Below right,* Lipophrys pavo *(peacock blenny) and* Parablennius fucorum *(blenny), both from Cuvier and Valenciennes, 1828-49 (11).*

Left, Tripterygion tripteronotus *(black-faced blenny, or three-finned nose-fish); below,* Forsterygion varium *(three-finned blenny), both from Cuvier and Valenciennes, 1828-49 (11).*

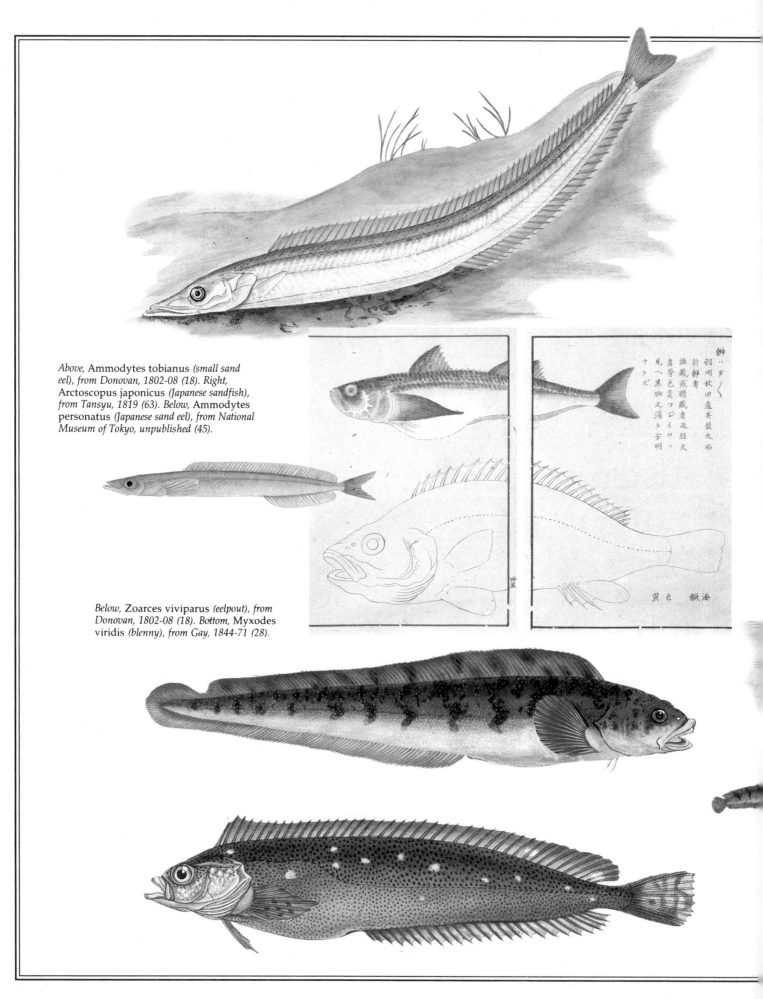

Above, Ammodytes tobianus *(small sand eel), from Donovan, 1802-08 (18). Right,* Arctoscopus japonicus *(Japanese sandfish), from Tansyu, 1819 (63). Below,* Ammodytes personatus *(Japanese sand eel), from National Museum of Tokyo, unpublished (45).*

鯱ハタハ
羽州秋田産其最大而
新鮮者
塩蔵或糟蔵者及短久
者骨色変ツジイ口ニ
見ハ黒斑文消ラ分明
ナラズ

黄色　鰰海

Below, Zoarces viviparus *(eelpout), from Donovan, 1802-08 (18). Bottom,* Myxodes viridis *(blenny), from Gay, 1844-71 (28).*

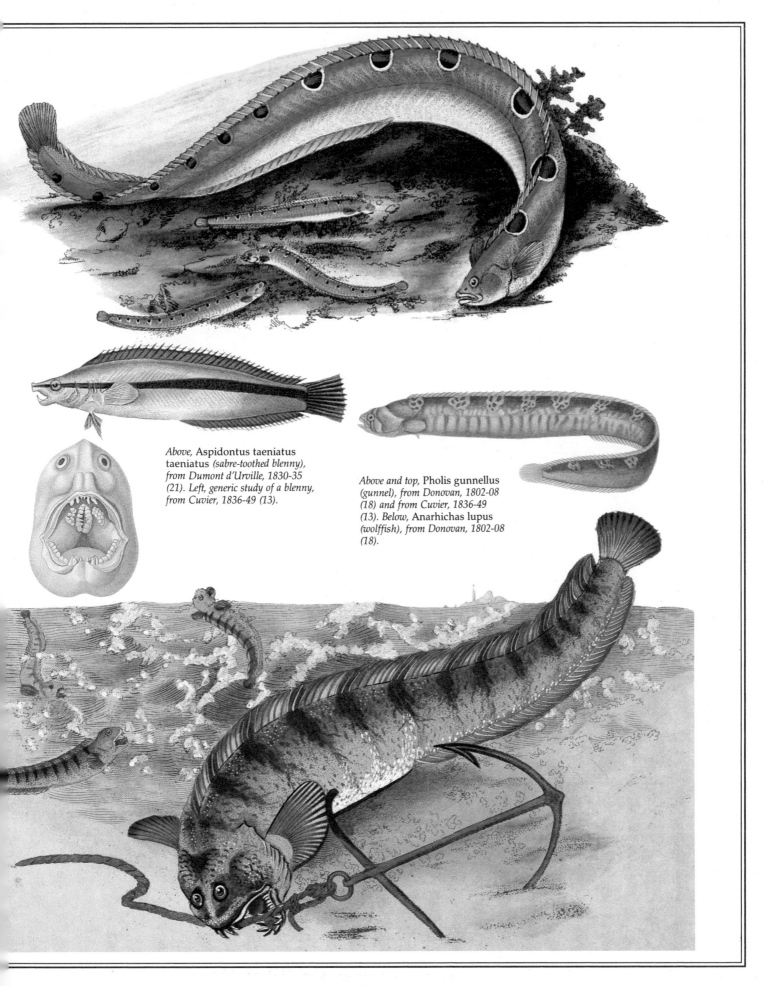

Above, Aspidontus taeniatus taeniatus *(sabre-toothed blenny), from Dumont d'Urville, 1830-35 (21). Left, generic study of a blenny, from Cuvier, 1836-49 (13).*

Above and top, Pholis gunnellus *(gunnel), from Donovan, 1802-08 (18) and from Cuvier, 1836-49 (13). Below*, Anarhichas lupus *(wolffish), from Donovan, 1802-08 (18).*

From the top, Periophthalmus papilio *(African mudskipper), from Cuvier and Valenciennes, 1828-49 (11);* Neogobius melanostomus *and* Neogobius ratan, *from Fauna Pontica, date missing (24);* Stenogobius malabaricus *(all gobies), from Day, 1865 (15).*

Above, Gymneleotris seminuda *(sleeper), from Zoological Society of London, 1861-90 (66). Below,* Leucopsarion petersi *(ice goby, or whitefish), from Tansyu, 1819 (63).*

From the top, Periophthalmodon schlosseri *(mudhopper) and* Eleotris gyrinus *(sleeper), both from Cuvier and Valenciennes, 1836-49 (13);* Cryptocentrus cryptocentrus *(goby);* Gobiodon histrio *(blue-spotted coralgoby), both from Cuvier and Valenciennes, 1828-49 (11). Below left,* Sicyopterus cynocephalus, *from Cuvier and Valenciennes, 1828-49 (11); below right,* Heterogobius chiloensis *(both gobies), from Gay, 1844-71 (28).*

Below, Pterogobius virgo *(maiden goby), from National Museum of Tokyo, unpublished (45). Center left,* Valenciennea muralis *(goby), from Richardson, 1843 (59). Center right, on the double page,* Aphia minuta *(transparent goby), from Donovan, 1802-08 (18). Bottom, on the plate,* Odontobutis obscura *(dark sleeper), from Ohno, 1937-44 (46).*

Top, Valenciennea muralis *(goby), from Cuvier and Valenciennes, 1828-49 (11). On the plate, from top,* Gobius cruentatus *(bloody-mouthed goby);* Padogobius martensi *(goby);* Gobioides broussoneti *(violet goby); bottom,* Taenioides broussoneti *(goby), from Cuvier, 1836-49 (13). Left,* Gobiusculus flavescens *(black goby), from Donovan, 1802-08 (18).*

Left, Abudefduf vaigiensis *(five-banded damselfish), from Bennett, 1830 (4). Below, left,* Chromis crusma *(demoiselle, or blacksmith), from Cuvier, 1836-49 (13); center,* Dascyllus trimaculatus *(three-spot humbug, or domino) and, right,* Dascyllus marginatus *(red sea humbug), both from Rüppell, 1826 (52).*

Left, Amblyglyphidodon aureus *(Pomacentrid), from Cuvier, 1836-49 (13). Below,* Dischistodus fasciatus *(Pomacentrid), from Cuvier and Valenciennes, 1828-49 (11). Right,* Chrysiptera biocellata *(damselfish), from Bennett, 1830 (4).*

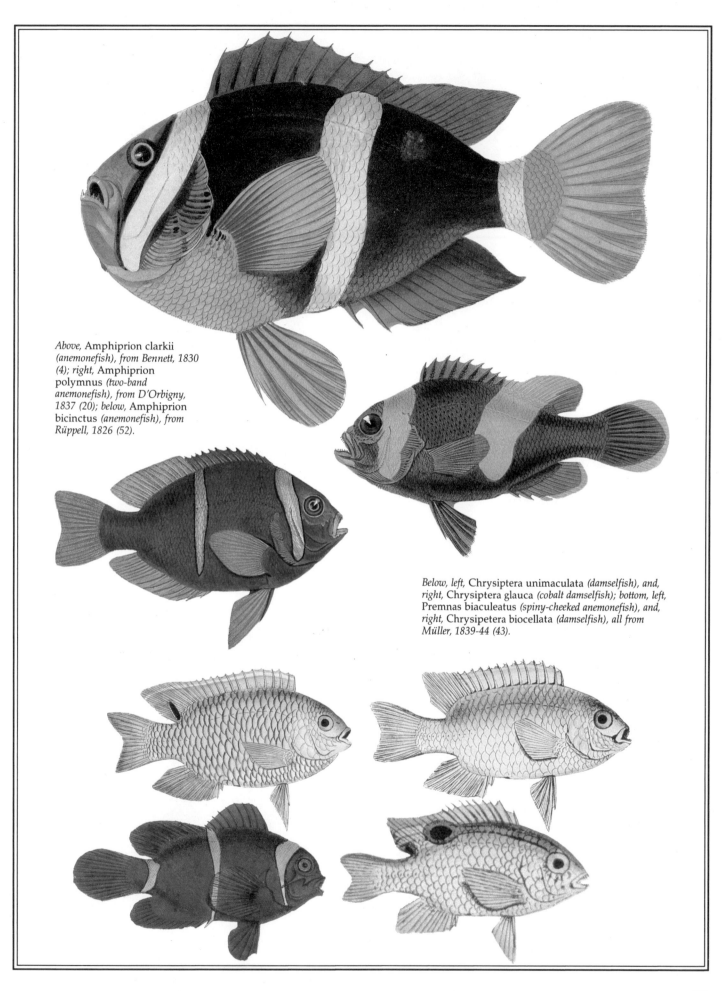

Above, Amphiprion clarkii *(anemonefish), from Bennett, 1830 (4); right,* Amphiprion polymnus *(two-band anemonefish), from D'Orbigny, 1837 (20); below,* Amphiprion bicinctus *(anemonefish), from Rüppell, 1826 (52).*

Below, left, Chrysiptera unimaculata *(damselfish), and, right,* Chrysiptera glauca *(cobalt damselfish); bottom, left,* Premnas biaculeatus *(spiny-cheeked anemonefish), and, right,* Chrysipetera biocellata *(damselfish), all from Müller, 1839-44 (43).*

Top left, Bodianus hirsutus *(blackfin hogfish); above left,* Bodianus bilunulatus *(crescent-band wrasse), both from Garrett and Günther, 1873-1910 (27). Top right,* Bodianus elancheri *(wrasse, or hogfish), and, above right,* Pimelometopon darwini *(sheep-head), both from Du Petit-Thouars, 1846 (22). Below,* Lachnolaimus maximus *(hogfish), from Cuvier and Valenciennes, 1828-49 (11).*

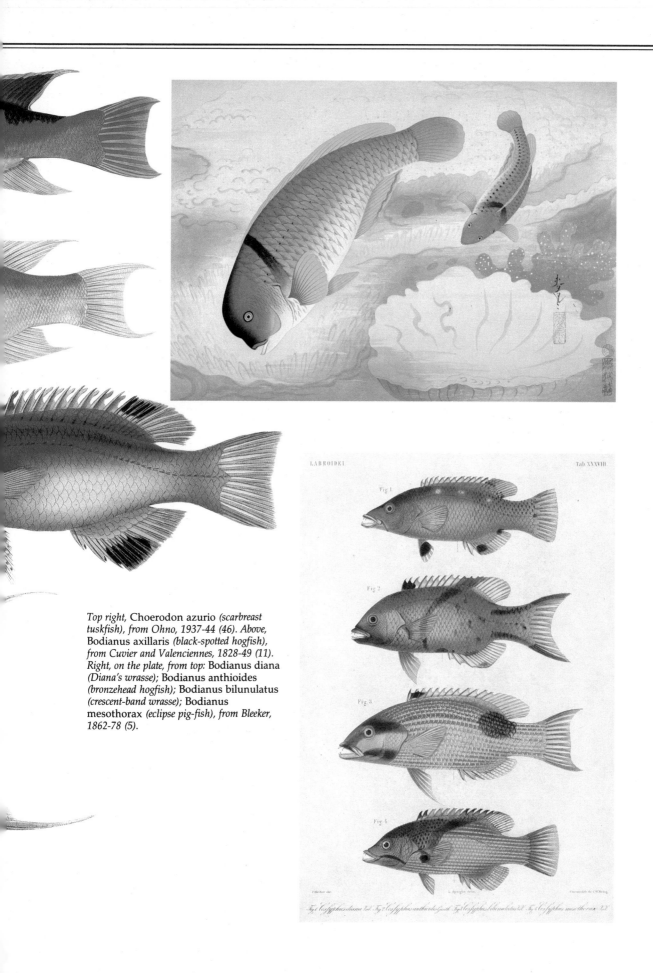

Top right, Choerodon azurio *(scarbreast tuskfish), from Ohno, 1937-44 (46). Above,* Bodianus axillaris *(black-spotted hogfish), from Cuvier and Valenciennes, 1828-49 (11). Right, on the plate, from top:* Bodianus diana *(Diana's wrasse);* Bodianus anthioides *(bronzehead hogfish);* Bodianus bilunulatus *(crescent-band wrasse);* Bodianus mesothorax *(eclipse pig-fish), from Bleeker, 1862-78 (5).*

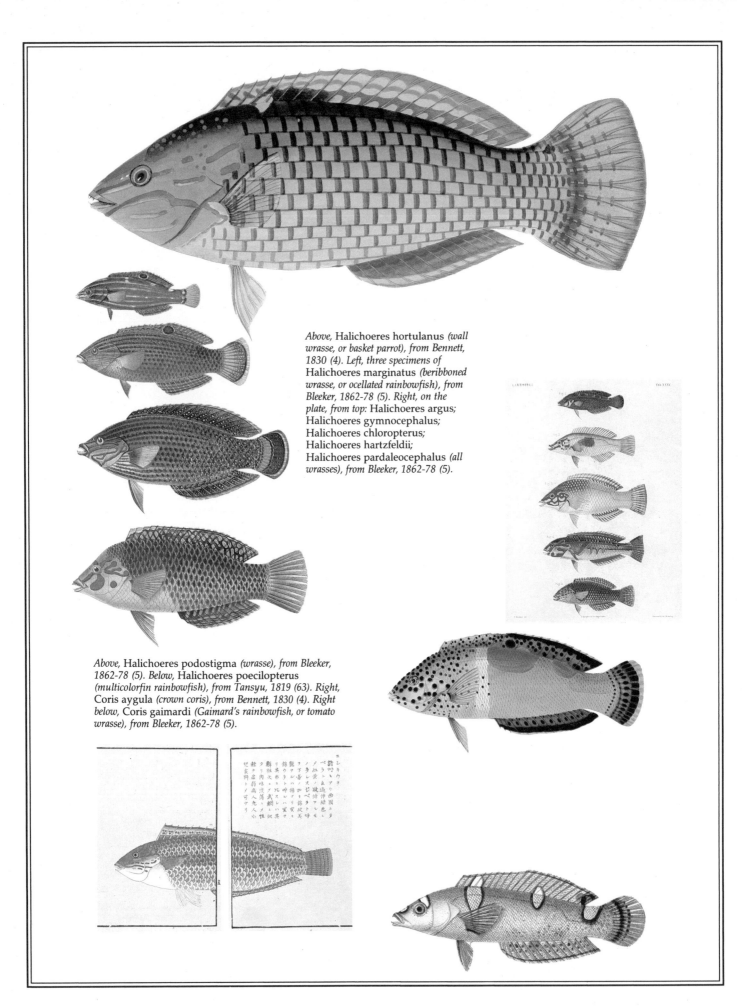

Above, Halichoeres hortulanus *(wall wrasse, or basket parrot), from Bennett, 1830 (4). Left, three specimens of* Halichoeres marginatus *(beribboned wrasse, or ocellated rainbowfish), from Bleeker, 1862-78 (5). Right, on the plate, from top:* Halichoeres argus; Halichoeres gymnocephalus; Halichoeres chloropterus; Halichoeres hartzfeldii; Halichoeres pardaleocephalus *(all wrasses), from Bleeker, 1862-78 (5).*

Above, Halichoeres podostigma *(wrasse), from Bleeker, 1862-78 (5). Below,* Halichoeres poecilopterus *(multicolorfin rainbowfish), from Tansyu, 1819 (63). Right,* Coris aygula *(crown coris), from Bennett, 1830 (4). Right below,* Coris gaimardi *(Gaimard's rainbowfish, or tomato wrasse), from Bleeker, 1862-78 (5).*

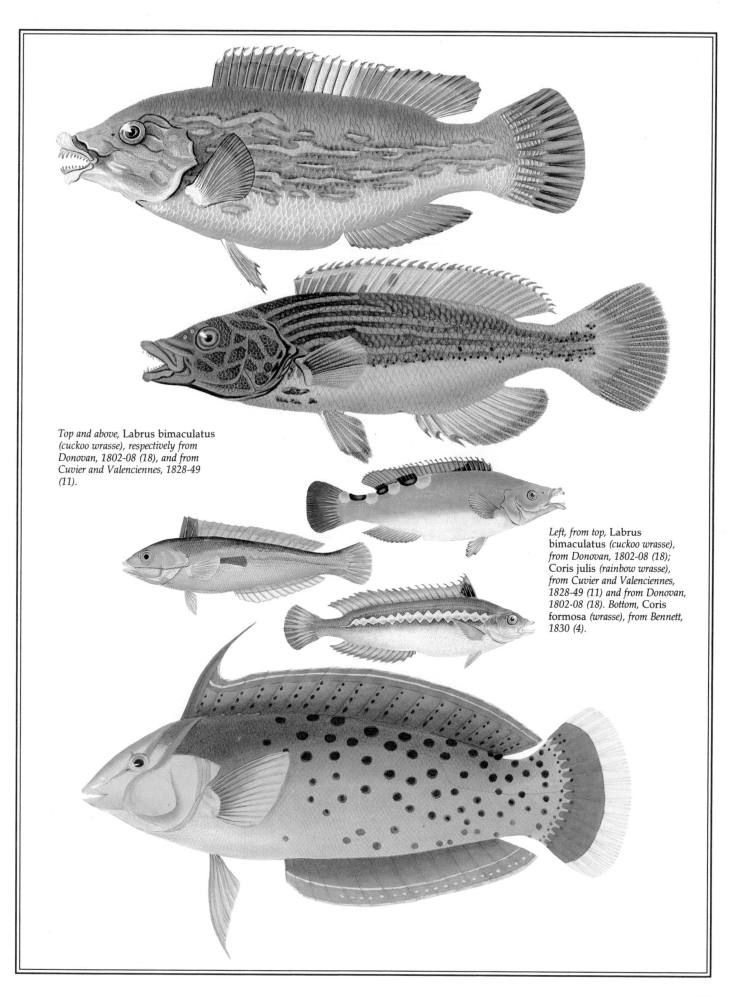

Top and above, Labrus bimaculatus *(cuckoo wrasse), respectively from Donovan, 1802-08 (18), and from Cuvier and Valenciennes, 1828-49 (11).*

Left, from top, Labrus bimaculatus *(cuckoo wrasse), from Donovan, 1802-08 (18);* Coris julis *(rainbow wrasse), from Cuvier and Valenciennes, 1828-49 (11) and from Donovan, 1802-08 (18). Bottom,* Coris formosa *(wrasse), from Bennett, 1830 (4).*

Below, Anampses caeruleopunctatus *(blue-spotted tamarin), from Rüppell, 1826 (52). Right,* Thalassoma lunare *(crescent-tail wrasse, or moon wrasse), from Gray 1830-34 (29). Center page,* Thalassoma purpureum *(purple wrasse), from Bennett, 1830 (4).*

Top left, Thalassoma whitmii; *center left,* Thalassoma duperreyi; *bottom left,* Thalassoma ballieui *(wrasses), all from Museum Godeffroy, 1873-1910 (44). Above,* Thalassoma hardwickii *(Hardwick's wrasse, or six-barred wrasse), from Bennett, 1830 (4).*

Top, Stethojulis trilineata *(three-line rainbowfish); above,* Stethojulis interrupta *(spotted-belly rainbowfish), both from Beeker, 1862-78 (5).*

Above, from top, Hologymnosus doliatus *(finescale wrasse);* Coris caudimaculata *(wrasse);* Thalassoma hebraicum *(wrasse);* Cymolutes lecluse *(Tateyama wrasse);* Thalassoma hardwickii *(Hardwick's wrasse, or six-barred wrasse), all from Dumont d'Urville, 1830-35 (21). Below,* Thalassoma pavo *(ornate wrasse); bottom,* Anampses geographicus *(cheek-lined wrasse), both from Cuvier and Valenciennes, 1828-49 (11).*

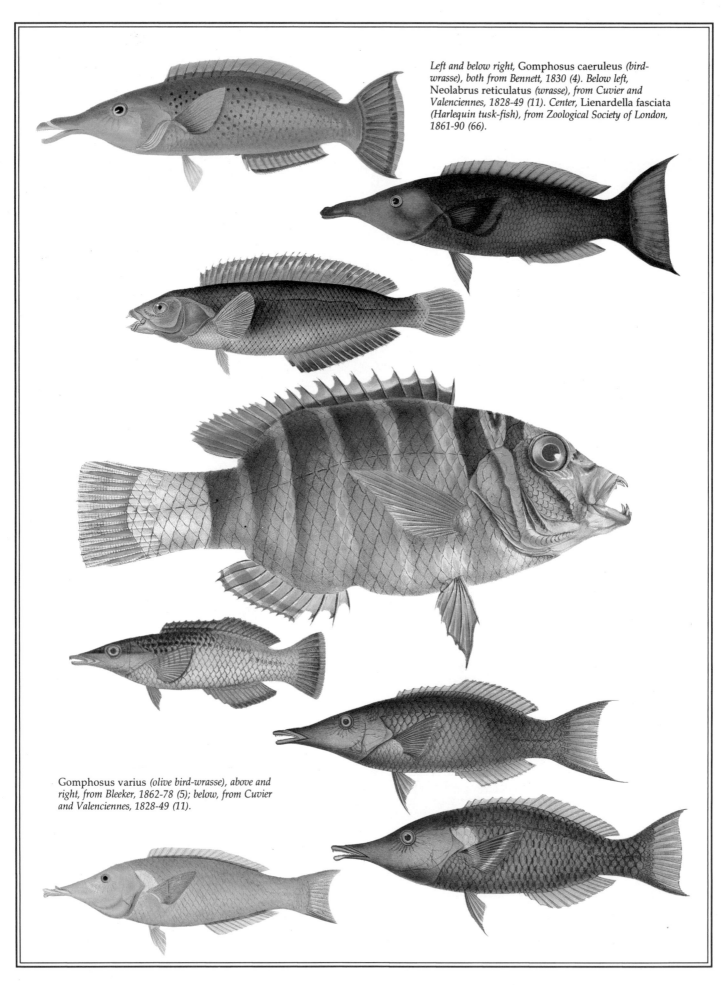

Left and below right, Gomphosus caeruleus (bird-wrasse), both from Bennett, 1830 (4). Below left, Neolabrus reticulatus (wrasse), from Cuvier and Valenciennes, 1828-49 (11). Center, Lienardella fasciata (Harlequin tusk-fish), from Zoological Society of London, 1861-90 (66).

Gomphosus varius *(olive bird-wrasse), above and right, from Bleeker, 1862-78 (5); below, from Cuvier and Valenciennes, 1828-49 (11).*

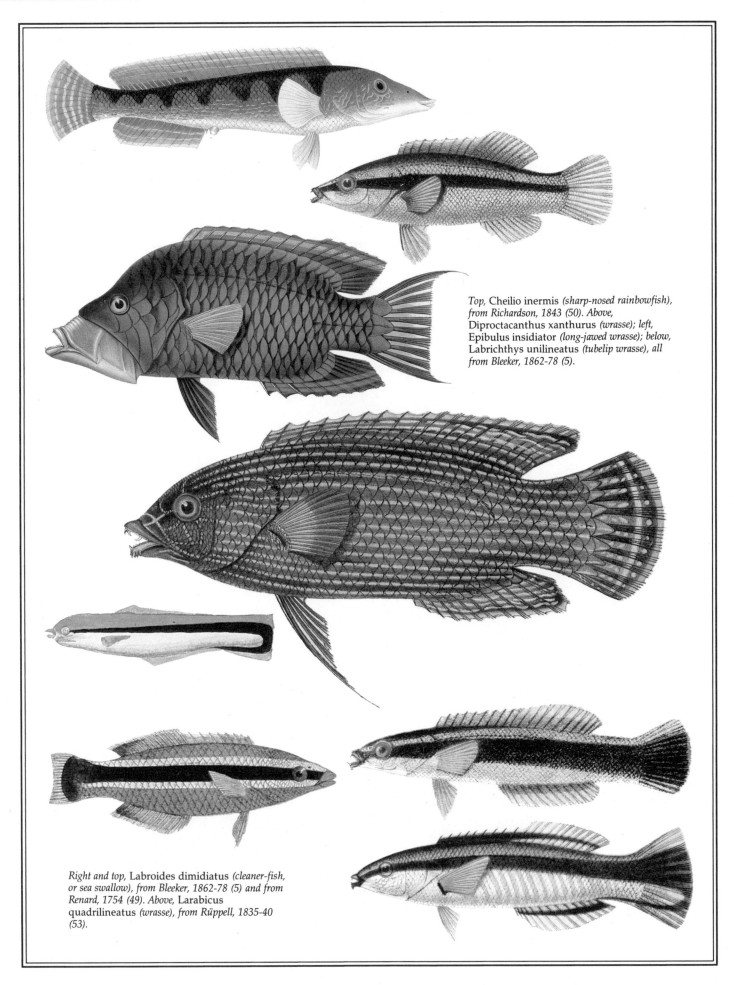

Top, Cheilio inermis *(sharp-nosed rainbowfish), from Richardson, 1843 (50). Above,* Diproctacanthus xanthurus *(wrasse); left,* Epibulus insidiator *(long-jawed wrasse); below,* Labrichthys unilineatus *(tubelip wrasse), all from Bleeker, 1862-78 (5).*

Right and top, Labroides dimidiatus *(cleaner-fish, or sea swallow), from Bleeker, 1862-78 (5) and from Renard, 1754 (49). Above,* Larabicus quadrilineatus *(wrasse), from Rüppell, 1835-40 (53).*

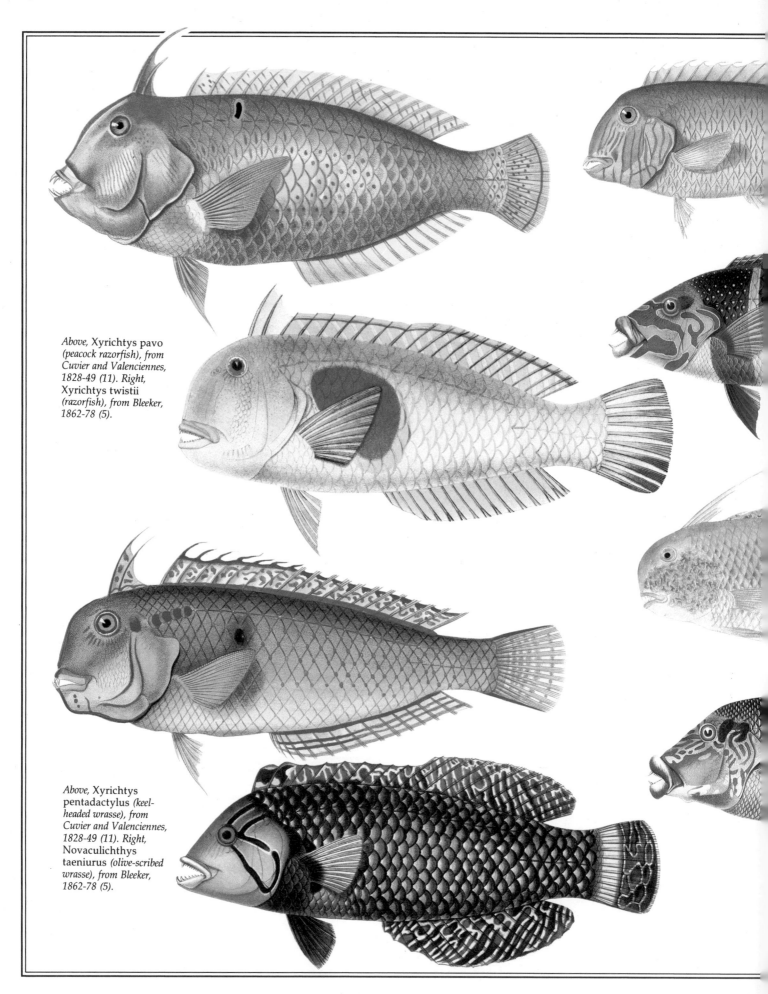

Above, Xyrichtys pavo *(peacock razorfish), from Cuvier and Valenciennes, 1828-49 (11). Right,* Xyrichtys twistii *(razorfish), from Bleeker, 1862-78 (5).*

Above, Xyrichtys pentadactylus *(keel-headed wrasse), from Cuvier and Valenciennes, 1828-49 (11). Right,* Novaculichthys taeniurus *(olive-scribed wrasse), from Bleeker, 1862-78 (5).*

Left, from top, Xyrichtys novacula *(razorfish), from Cuvier and Valenciennes, 1828-49 (11);* Hemigymnus fasciatus *(five-banded wrasse), from Bleeker, 1862-78 (5);* Xyrichtys dea *(goddess razorfish), from* Illustrations of Fishes, *1868-1912 (33);* Hemigymnus melapterus *(thick-lipped wrasse), from Bleeker, 1862-78 (5).*

Right, from top, Hologymnosus doliatus *(narrow-banded rainbowfish), from Cuvier, 1828-49 (11);* Hologymnosus annulatus *(wrasse) and* Choerodon anchorago *(orange-dotted tusk-fish), both from Bleeker, 1862-78 (5);* Cheilinus arenatus *(wrasse), from Cuvier and Valenciennes, 1828-49 (11).*

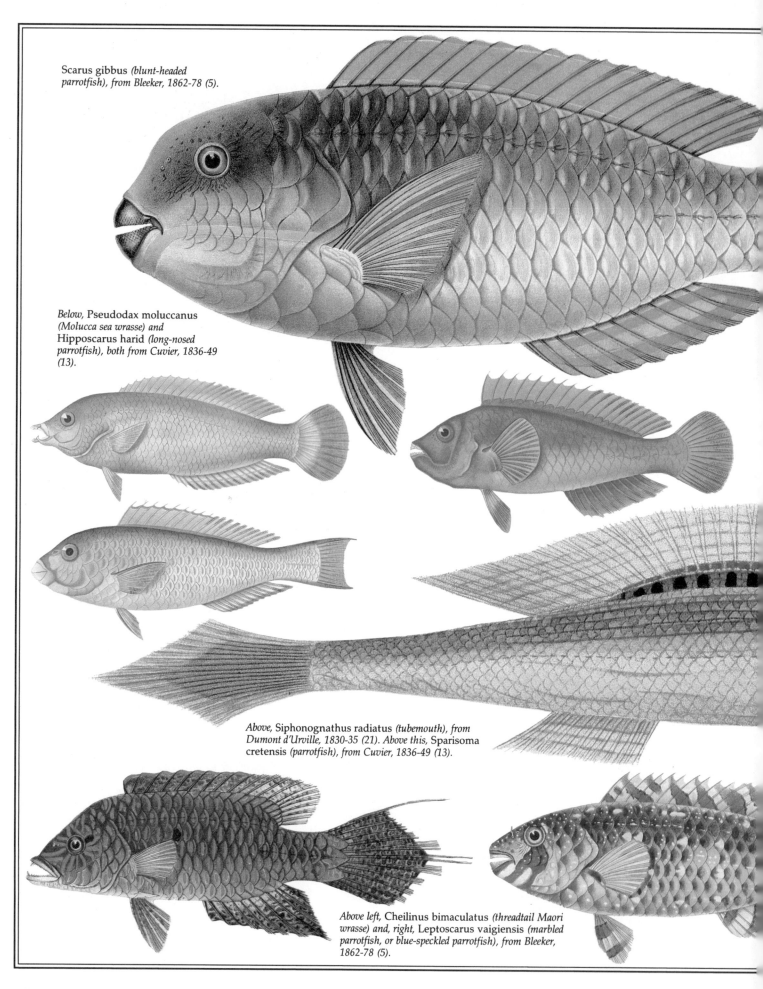

Scarus gibbus *(blunt-headed parrotfish), from Bleeker, 1862-78 (5).*

Below, Pseudodax moluccanus *(Molucca sea wrasse) and* Hipposcarus harid *(long-nosed parrotfish), both from Cuvier, 1836-49 (13).*

Above, Siphonognathus radiatus *(tubemouth), from Dumont d'Urville, 1830-35 (21). Above this,* Sparisoma cretensis *(parrotfish), from Cuvier, 1836-49 (13).*

Above left, Cheilinus bimaculatus *(threadtail Maori wrasse) and, right,* Leptoscarus vaigiensis *(marbled parrotfish, or blue-speckled parrotfish), from Bleeker, 1862-78 (5).*

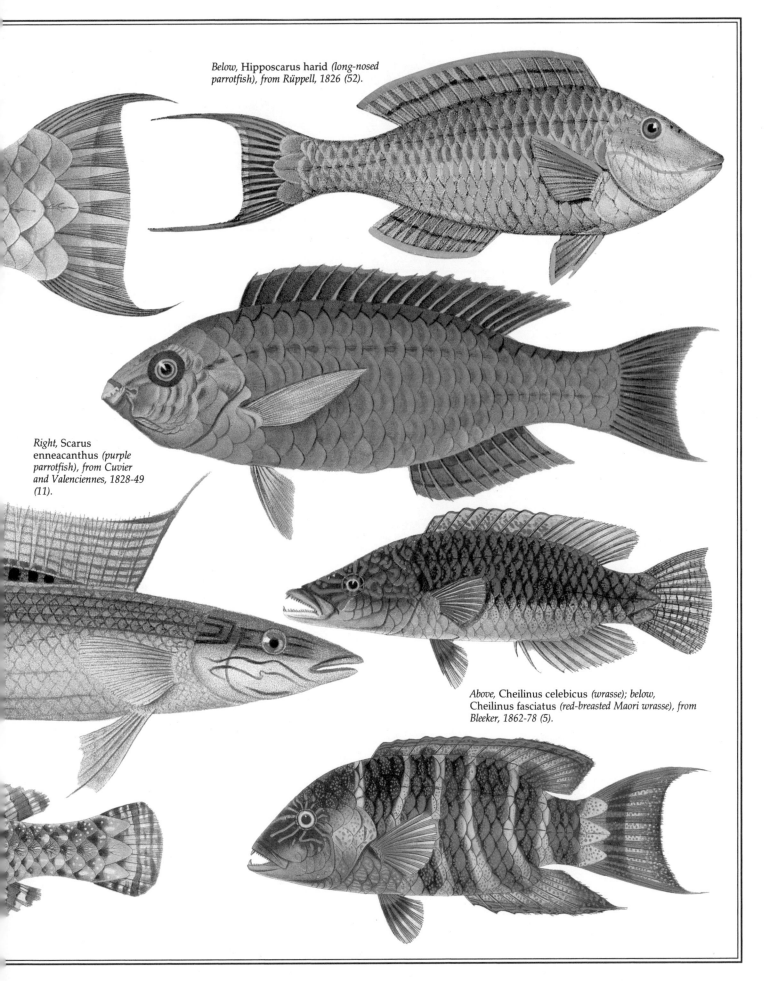

Below, Hipposcarus harid *(long-nosed parrotfish), from Rüppell, 1826 (52).*

Right, Scarus enneacanthus *(purple parrotfish), from Cuvier and Valenciennes, 1828-49 (11).*

Above, Cheilinus celebicus *(wrasse); below,* Cheilinus fasciatus *(red-breasted Maori wrasse), from Bleeker, 1862-78 (5).*

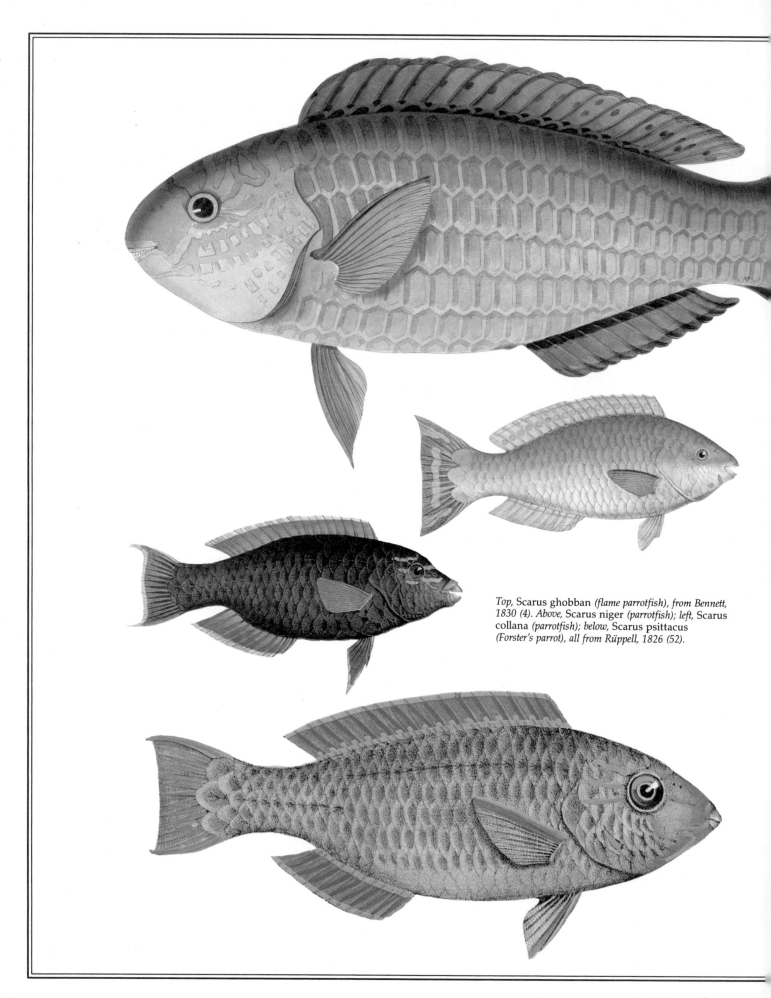

Top, Scarus ghobban *(flame parrotfish), from Bennett, 1830 (4). Above,* Scarus niger *(parrotfish); left,* Scarus collana *(parrotfish); below,* Scarus psittacus *(Forster's parrot), all from Rüppell, 1826 (52).*

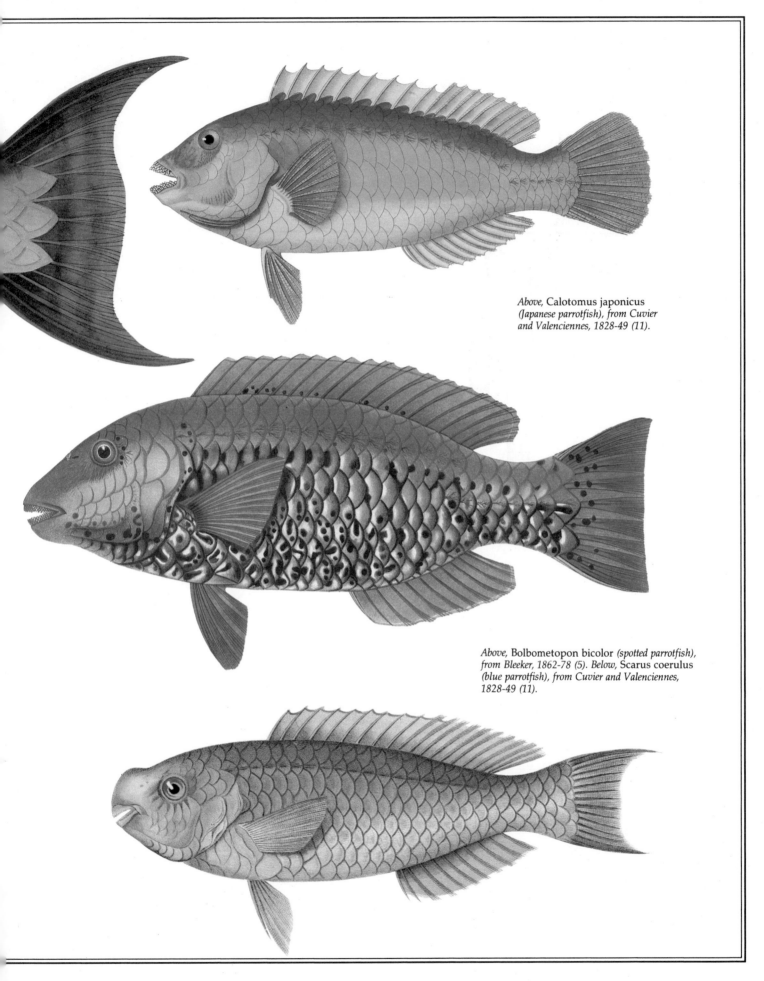

Above, Calotomus japonicus
*(Japanese parrotfish), from Cuvier
and Valenciennes, 1828-49 (11).*

Above, Bolbometopon bicolor *(spotted parrotfish),
from Bleeker, 1862-78 (5). Below,* Scarus coerulus
*(blue parrotfish), from Cuvier and Valenciennes,
1828-49 (11).*

Microcanthus strigatus *(footballer, convict fish, or stripey), from Yamamoto, date missing (65).*

Above left, Chaetodipterus goreensis *(spadefish); above right,* Microcanthus strigatus *(footballer, convict fish, or stripey); below left,* Chaetodipterus faber *(spadefish), all from Cuvier and Valenciennes, 1836-49 (13). Below right,* Drepane punctata *(concertina fish, spotted batfish or sticklefish), from Zoological Society of London, 1861-90 (66).*

Below, Scatophagus argus *(spotted scat), from Cuvier and Valenciennes, 1828-49 (11). Right,* Toxotes jaculator *(archerfish), from Cuvier, 1836-49 (13).*

Right, Ephippus orbis *(horseman), from Zoological Society of London, 1861-90 (66). Above right and left,* Scatophagus argus *(spotted scat), respectively from Schlosser and Boddaert, 1768-72 (55) and from Bennett, 1830 (4).*

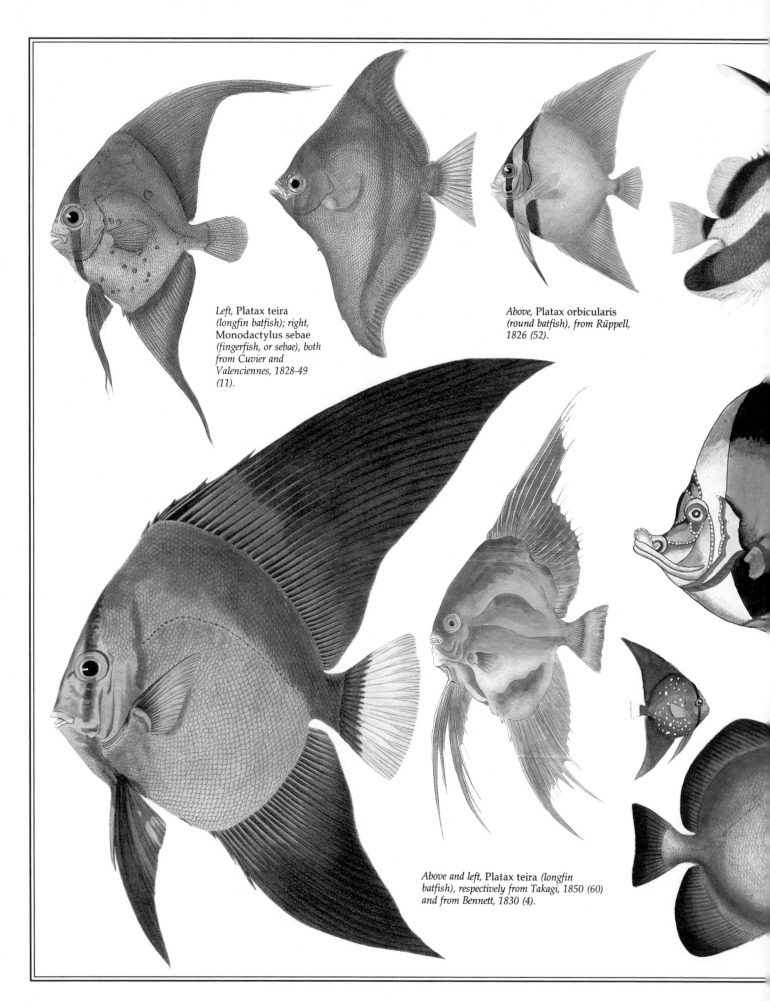

Left, Platax teira *(longfin batfish); right,* Monodactylus sebae *(fingerfish, or sebae), both from Cuvier and Valenciennes, 1828-49 (11).*

Above, Platax orbicularis *(round batfish), from Rüppell, 1826 (52).*

Above and left, Platax teira *(longfin batfish), respectively from Takagi, 1850 (60) and from Bennett, 1830 (4).*

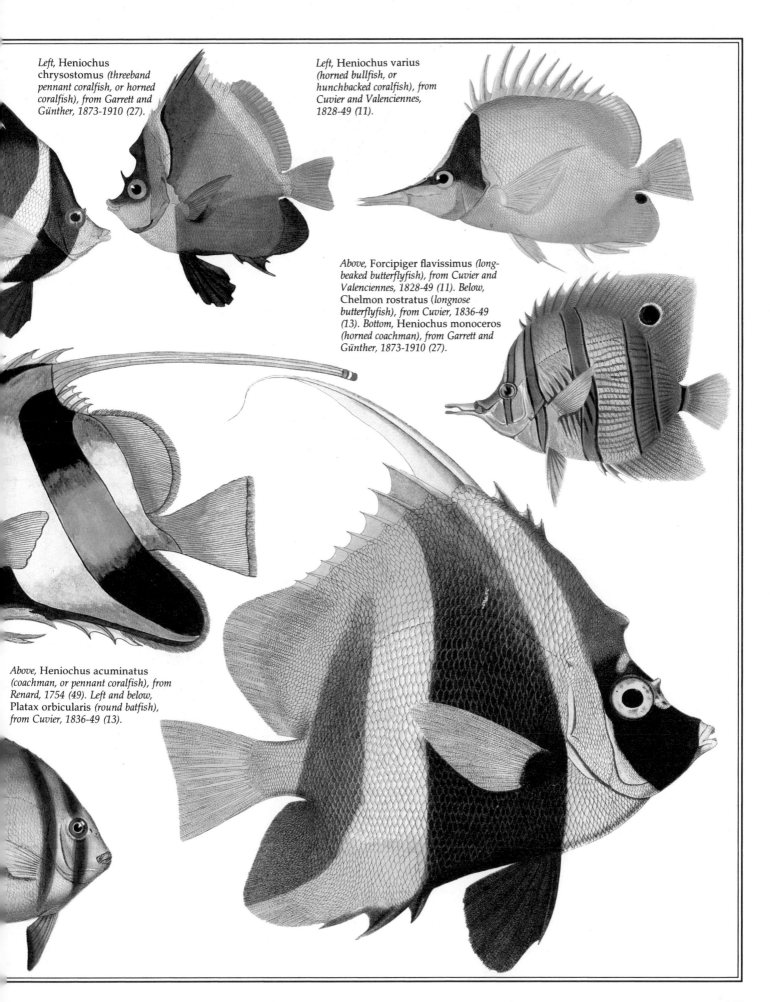

Left, Heniochus chrysostomus *(threeband pennant coralfish, or horned coralfish), from Garrett and Günther, 1873-1910 (27).*

Left, Heniochus varius *(horned bullfish, or hunchbacked coralfish), from Cuvier and Valenciennes, 1828-49 (11).*

Above, Forcipiger flavissimus *(long-beaked butterflyfish), from Cuvier and Valenciennes, 1828-49 (11). Below*, Chelmon rostratus *(longnose butterflyfish), from Cuvier, 1836-49 (13). Bottom*, Heniochus monoceros *(horned coachman), from Garrett and Günther, 1873-1910 (27).*

Above, Heniochus acuminatus *(coachman, or pennant coralfish), from Renard, 1754 (49). Left and below*, Platax orbicularis *(round batfish), from Cuvier, 1836-49 (13).*

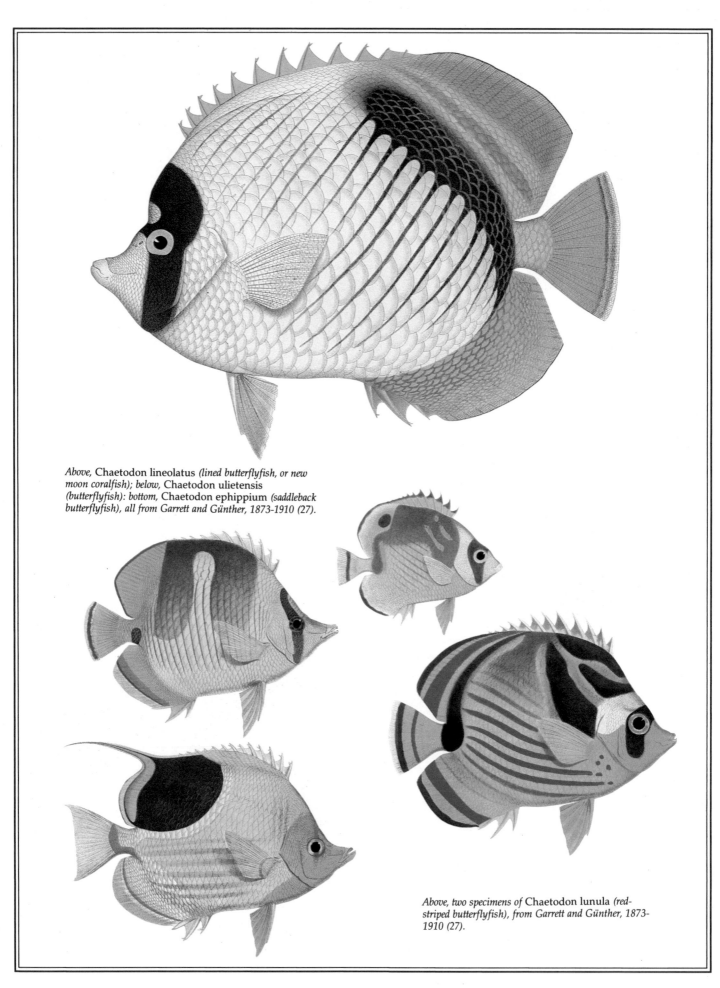

Above, Chaetodon lineolatus *(lined butterflyfish, or new moon coralfish); below,* Chaetodon ulietensis *(butterflyfish): bottom,* Chaetodon ephippium *(saddleback butterflyfish), all from Garrett and Günther, 1873-1910 (27).*

Above, two specimens of Chaetodon lunula *(red-striped butterflyfish), from Garrett and Günther, 1873-1910 (27).*

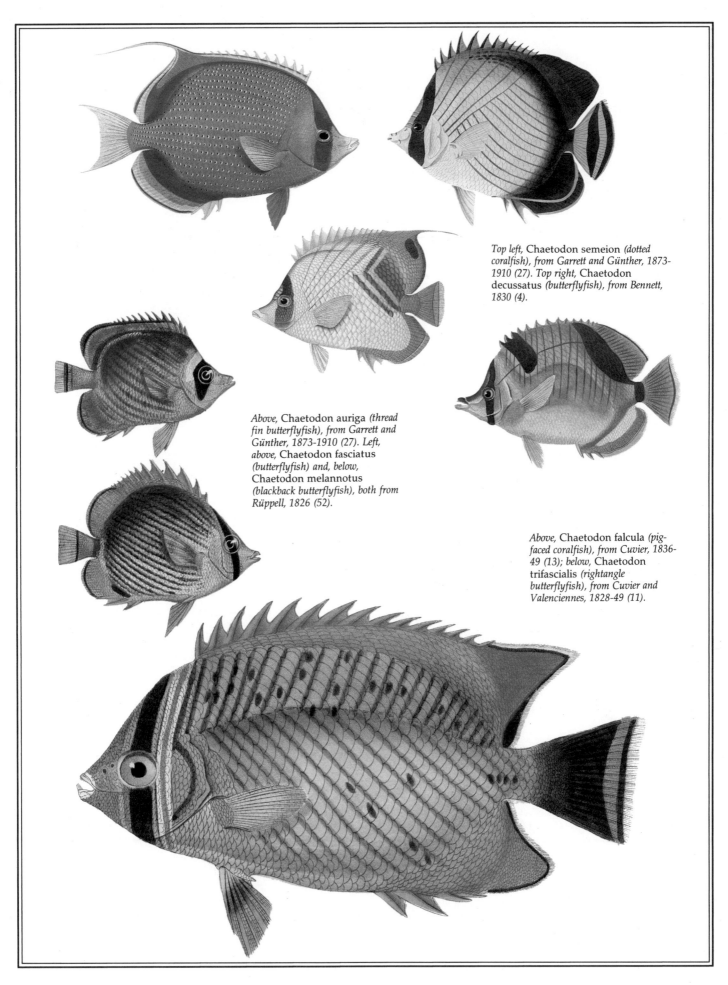

Top left, Chaetodon semeion *(dotted coralfish), from Garrett and Günther, 1873-1910 (27). Top right,* Chaetodon decussatus *(butterflyfish), from Bennett, 1830 (4).*

Above, Chaetodon auriga *(thread fin butterflyfish), from Garrett and Günther, 1873-1910 (27). Left, above,* Chaetodon fasciatus *(butterflyfish) and, below,* Chaetodon melannotus *(blackback butterflyfish), both from Rüppell, 1826 (52).*

Above, Chaetodon falcula *(pig-faced coralfish), from Cuvier, 1836-49 (13); below,* Chaetodon trifascialis *(rightangle butterflyfish), from Cuvier and Valenciennes, 1828-49 (11).*

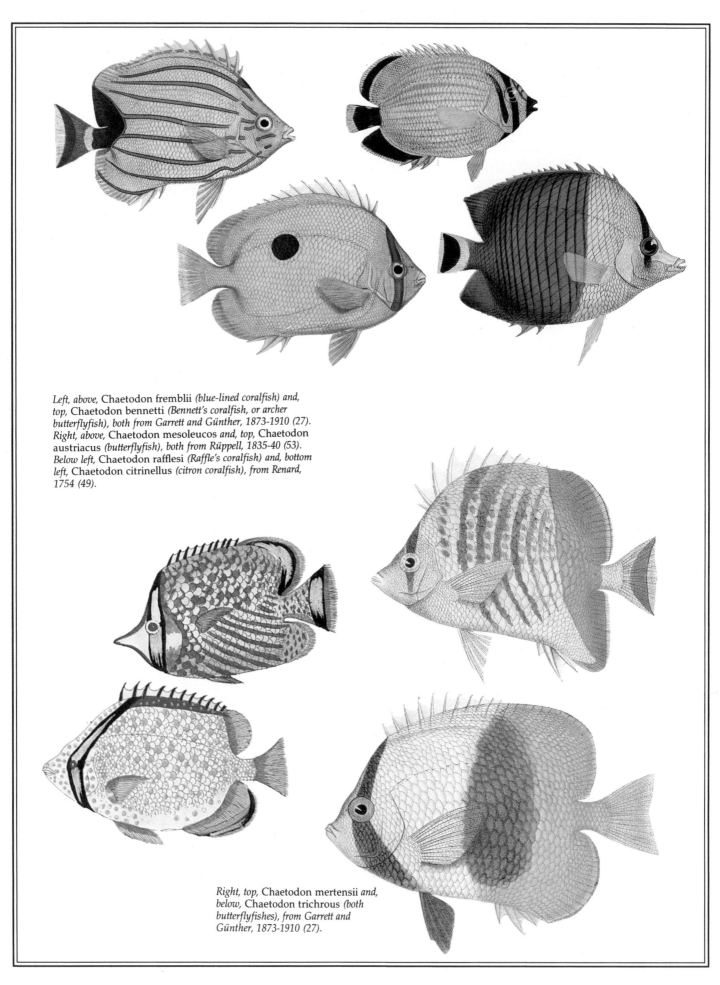

Left, above, Chaetodon fremblii *(blue-lined coralfish) and, top,* Chaetodon bennetti *(Bennett's coralfish, or archer butterflyfish), both from Garrett and Günther, 1873-1910 (27). Right, above,* Chaetodon mesoleucos *and, top,* Chaetodon austriacus *(butterflyfish), both from Rüppell, 1835-40 (53). Below left,* Chaetodon rafflesi *(Raffle's coralfish) and, bottom left,* Chaetodon citrinellus *(citron coralfish), from Renard, 1754 (49).*

Right, top, Chaetodon mertensii *and, below,* Chaetodon trichrous *(both butterflyfishes), from Garrett and Günther, 1873-1910 (27).*

Top left, Chaetodon pelewensis *(dot-and-dash coralfish); above,* Chaetodon reticulatus *(reticulated butterflyfish), both from Garrett and Günther, 1873-1910 (27). Below,* Chaetodon triangulum *(herring-bone butterflyfish, or triangular coralfish), from Renard, 1754 (49).*

Top right, Chaetodon ornatissimus *(ornate coralfish); above,* Chaetodon quadrimaculatus *(butterflyfish); left,* Chaetodon citrinellus *(citron coralfish); below,* Chaetodon miliaris *(millet-seed coralfish) and* Chaetodon rafflesi *(Raffle's coralfish), all from Garrett and Günther, 1873-1910 (27).*

Left, Zanclus cornutus (Moorish idol), from Cuvier and Valenciennes, 1828-49 (11). Right, Chaetodon modestus (brown-banded butterflyfish), from Illustrations of Fishes, 1868-1912 (33). Above, Chaetodon rafflesi (Raffle's coralfish), from Renard, 1754 (49).

Left, on the plate: top, Chaetodon austriacus *(butterflyfish),* Chaetodon auriga *(thread fin butterflyfish) and* Heniochus intermedius *(butterflyfish); center,* Pygoplites diacanthus *(blue-banded angelfish) and* Chaetodon fasciatus *(butterflyfish); bottom,* Pomacanthus imperator *(emperor angelfish), all from Cuvier, 1836-49 (13).*

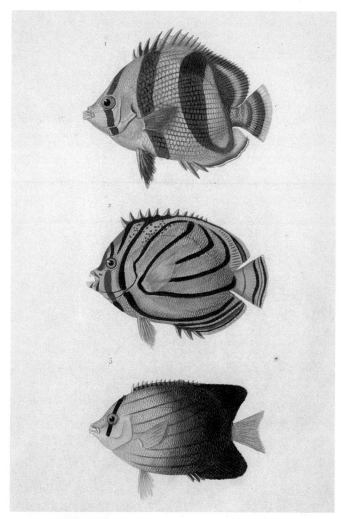

Right, on the plate: top, Chaetodon striatus *(banded butterflyfish); center,* Chaetodon meyeri *(Meyer's coralfish); bottom,* Chaetodon blackburnii *(butterflyfish), from Cuvier, 1836-49 (13). Below,* Chaetodon auripes *(Japanese butterflyfish), from National Museum of Tokyo, unpublished (45).*

Pomacanthus semicirculatus
*(zebra angelfish, or semicircle
angelfish), from Cuvier and
Valenciennes, 1828-49 (11).*

*Right and above, Pomacanthus imperator (emperor
angelfish), respectively from Renard, 1754 (49) and
from Garrett and Günther, 1873-1910 (27).*

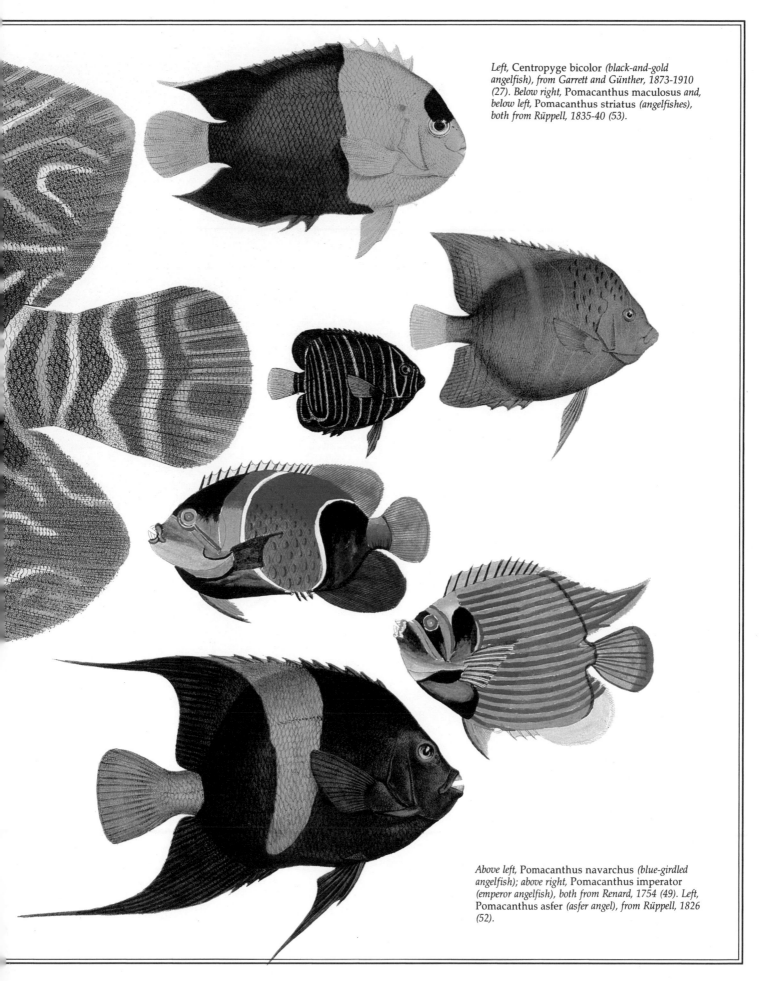

Left, Centropyge bicolor *(black-and-gold angelfish), from Garrett and Günther, 1873-1910 (27). Below right,* Pomacanthus maculosus *and, below left,* Pomacanthus striatus *(angelfishes), both from Rüppell, 1835-40 (53).*

Above left, Pomacanthus navarchus *(blue-girdled angelfish); above right,* Pomacanthus imperator *(emperor angelfish), both from Renard, 1754 (49). Left,* Pomacanthus asfer *(asfer angel), from Rüppell, 1826 (52).*

Top, Holacanthus tricolor *(rock beauty), from Cuvier, 1836-49 (13). Above,* Holacanthus ciliaris *(queen angelfish) and, left,* Holacanthus passer *(passer angelfish), both from Du Petit-Thouars, 1846 (22). Opposite page, top,* Genicanthus lamarcki *(freckletail angelfish, or swallow-tailed angelfish), two specimens from Renard, 1754 (49) and, center, from Cuvier and Valenciennes, 1828-49 (11). Bottom,* Pomacanthus arcuatus *(gray angelfish), from Cuvier and Valenciennes, 1828-49 (11).*

Ces deux poissons male et femelle ne s'abandonnent
jamais. Quand l'un est pris, l'autre suit le pêcheur
et s'offre à être pris aussi; et si on ne le prend
point, il se jette sur le rivage pour mourir.

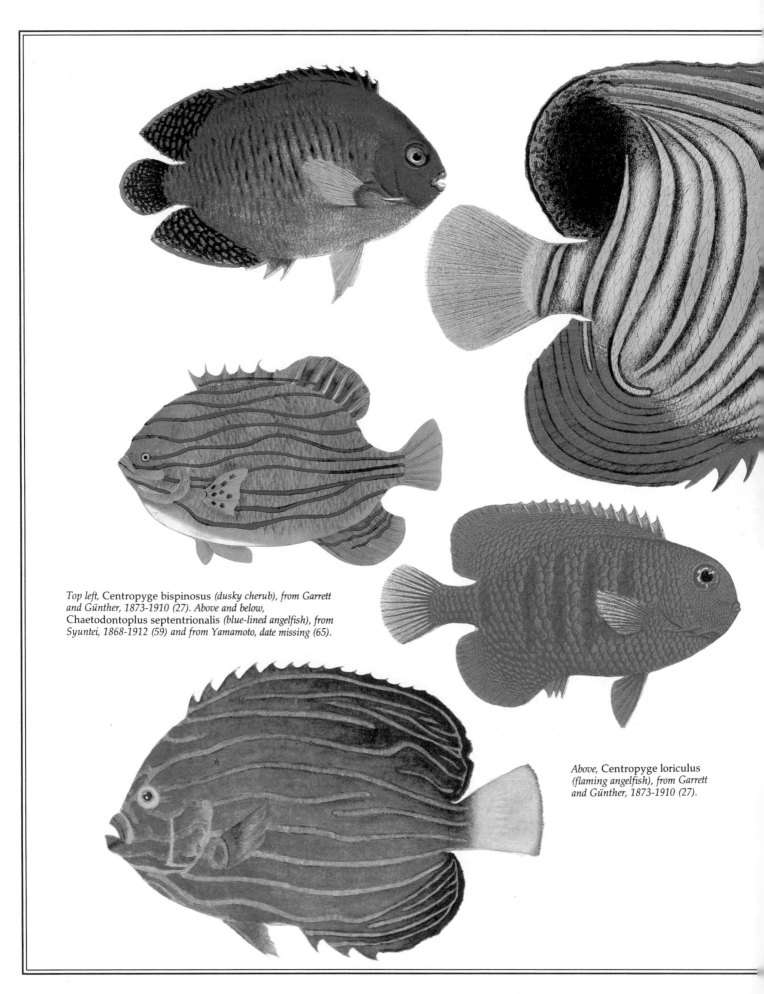

Top left, Centropyge bispinosus *(dusky cherub), from Garrett and Günther, 1873-1910 (27). Above and below,* Chaetodontoplus septentrionalis *(blue-lined angelfish), from Syuntei, 1868-1912 (59) and from Yamamoto, date missing (65).*

Above, Centropyge loriculus *(flaming angelfish), from Garrett and Günther, 1873-1910 (27).*

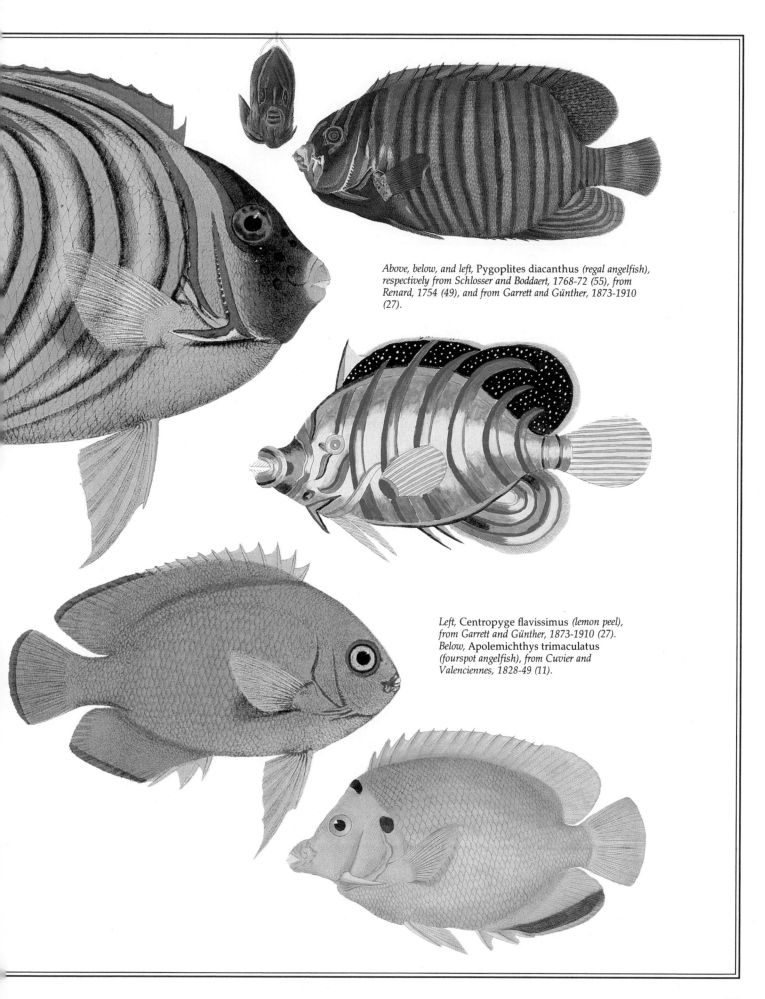

Above, below, and left, Pygoplites diacanthus *(regal angelfish), respectively from Schlosser and Boddaert, 1768-72 (55), from Renard, 1754 (49), and from Garrett and Günther, 1873-1910 (27).*

Left, Centropyge flavissimus *(lemon peel), from Garrett and Günther, 1873-1910 (27). Below,* Apolemichthys trimaculatus *(fourspot angelfish), from Cuvier and Valenciennes, 1828-49 (11).*

Top, Acanthurus dussumieri
(Dussumier's surgeonfish),
center, Acanthurus achilles
(Achilles tang), and bottom,
Acanthurus glaucopareius
(white-cheeked surgeonfish), all
from Garrett and Günther,
1873-1910 (27).

Right, Paracanthurus hepatus *(flagtail surgeonfish), from* Cuvier and Valenciennes, 1828-49 (11). *Below,* Acanthurus lineatus *(blue-lined surgeonfish), from Bennett, 1830 (4). Bottom,* Acanthurus triostegus *(fiveband surgeonfish), left, from Garman, 1899 (26) and, right, from Bennett, 1830 (4).*

Above and right, Naso vlamingii *(bignose unicorn, or Vlaming's unicornfish), respectively from Renard, 1754 (49) and from Garrett and Günther, 1873-1910 (27). Below left,* Zebrasoma veliferum *(purple sailfinned tang) and, bottom left,* Acanthurus nigrofuscus *(yellowfin surgeonfish), both from Rüppell, 1826 (52).*

Above, Zebrasoma veliferum *(purple sailfinned tang), from Gaimard, 1838-52 (25).*

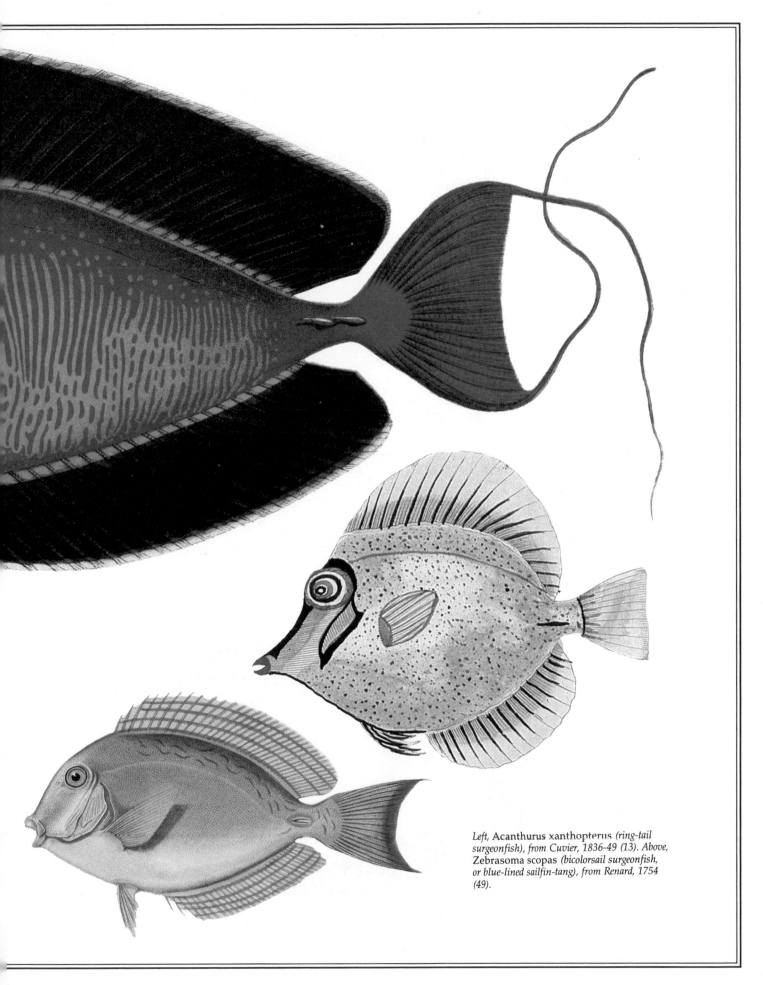

Left, Acanthurus xanthopterus *(ring-tail surgeonfish), from Cuvier, 1836-49 (13). Above,* Zebrasoma scopas *(bicolorsail surgeonfish, or blue-lined sailfin-tang), from Renard, 1754 (49).*

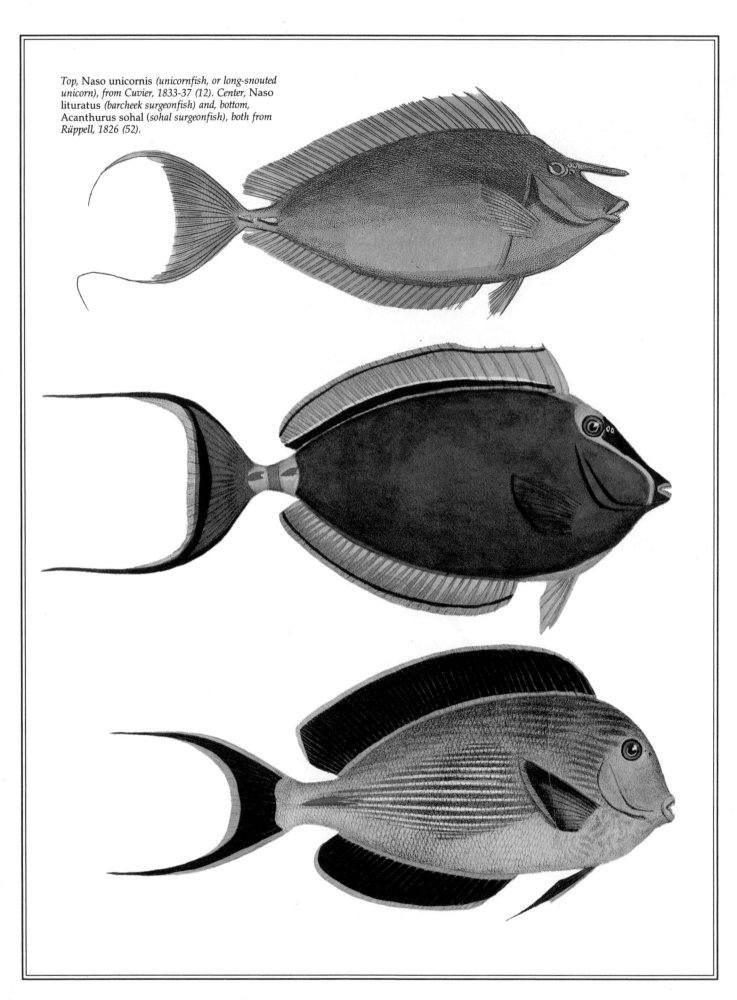

Top, Naso unicornis *(unicornfish, or long-snouted unicorn), from Cuvier, 1833-37 (12). Center,* Naso lituratus *(barcheek surgeonfish) and, bottom,* Acanthurus sohal *(sohal surgeonfish), both from Rüppell, 1826 (52).*

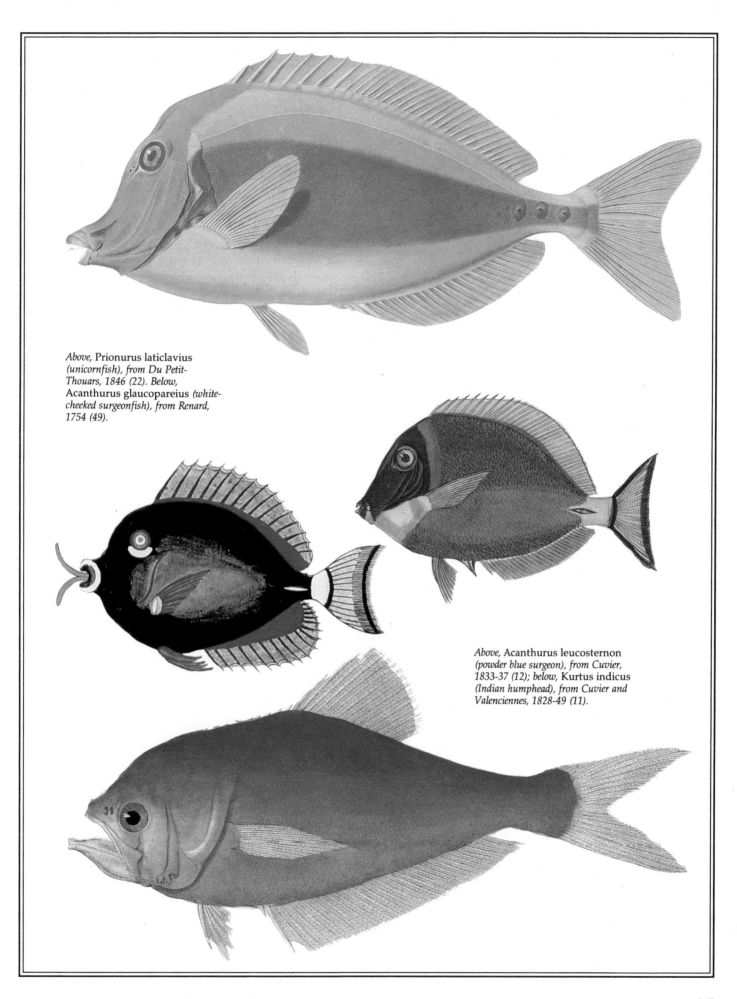

Above, Prionurus laticlavius *(unicornfish), from Du Petit-Thouars, 1846 (22). Below,* Acanthurus glaucopareius *(white-cheeked surgeonfish), from Renard, 1754 (49).*

Above, Acanthurus leucosternon *(powder blue surgeon), from Cuvier, 1833-37 (12); below,* Kurtus indicus *(Indian humphead), from Cuvier and Valenciennes, 1828-49 (11).*

165

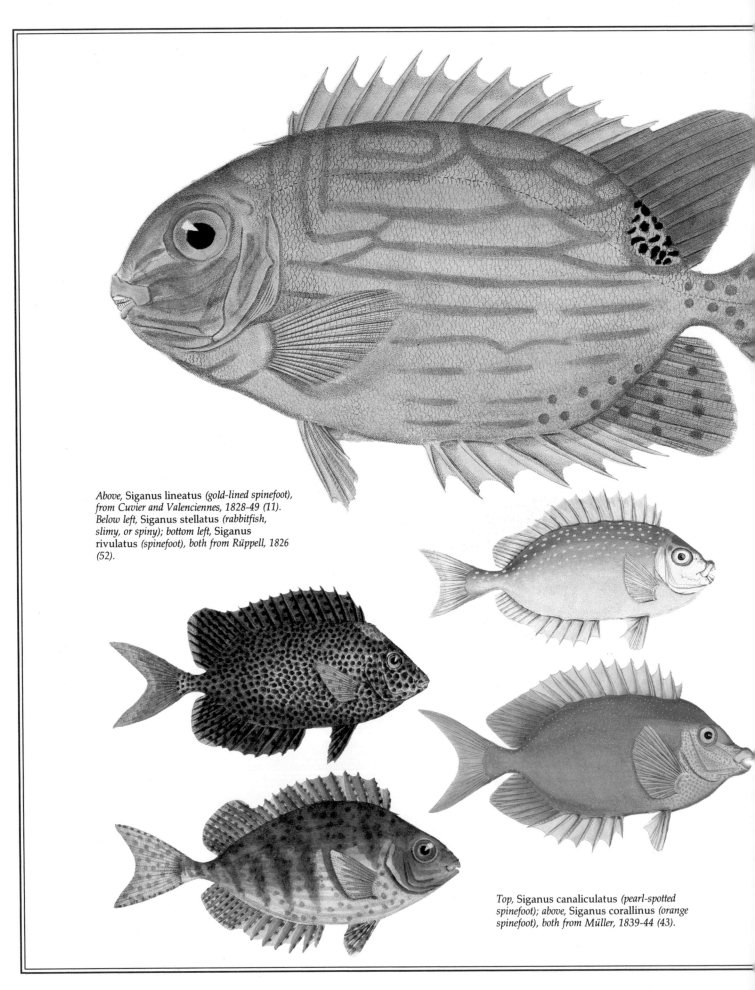

Above, Siganus lineatus *(gold-lined spinefoot),
from Cuvier and Valenciennes, 1828-49 (11).
Below left,* Siganus stellatus *(rabbitfish,
slimy, or spiny); bottom left,* Siganus
rivulatus *(spinefoot), both from Rüppell, 1826
(52).*

Top, Siganus canaliculatus *(pearl-spotted
spinefoot); above,* Siganus corallinus *(orange
spinefoot), both from Müller, 1839-44 (43).*

Top, Siganus virgatus *(blue-lined spinefoot); above right,*
Siganus vermiculatus *(vermiculated spinefoot), both from*
Müller, 1839-44 (43). Left, Siganus doliatus *(pencil-streaked*
spinefoot), from Cuvier, 1836-49 (13). Below, left and right,
Siganus vulpinus *(fox-face, or fox-fish), from Renard, 1754*
(49).

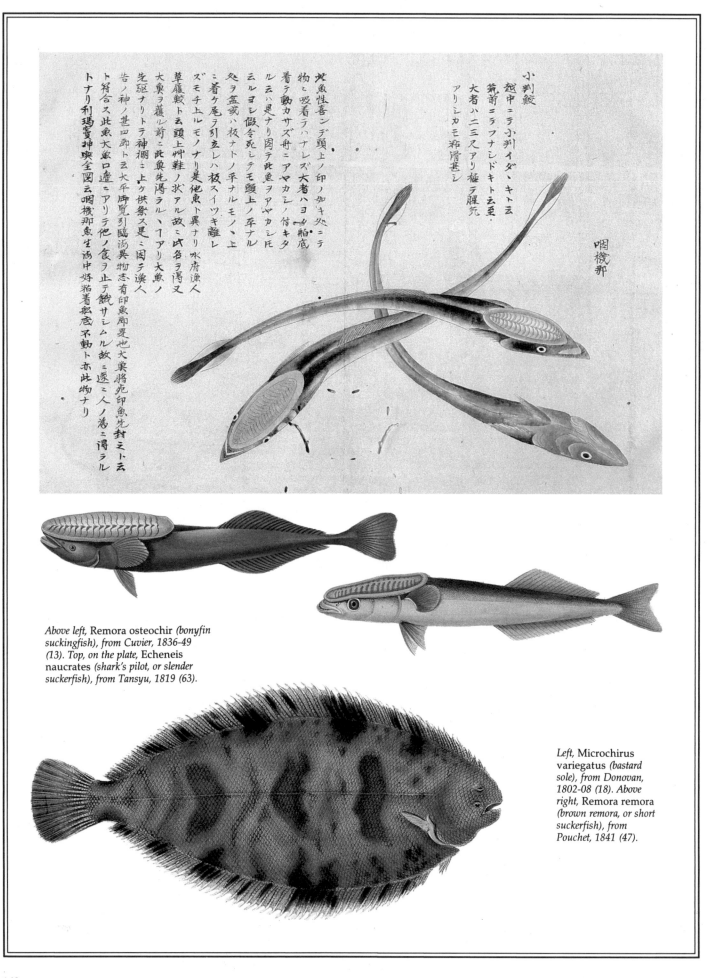

小判鮫
越中ニテ小判イダ、キト云
筑前ニテフナシドキト云至
大者ハ二三尺アリ極テ腥気
アリシカモ粘滑甚シ

咽微那

Above left, Remora osteochir *(bonyfin suckingfish), from Cuvier, 1836-49 (13). Top, on the plate,* Echeneis naucrates *(shark's pilot, or slender suckerfish), from Tansyu, 1819 (63).*

Left, Microchirus variegatus *(bastard sole), from Donovan, 1802-08 (18). Above right,* Remora remora *(brown remora, or short suckerfish), from Pouchet, 1841 (47).*

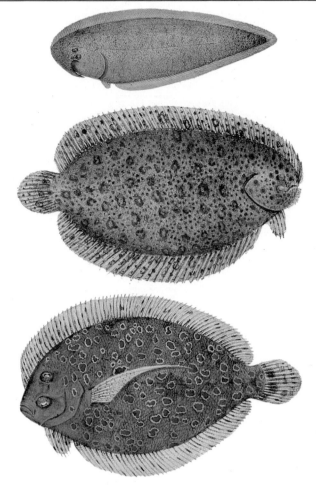

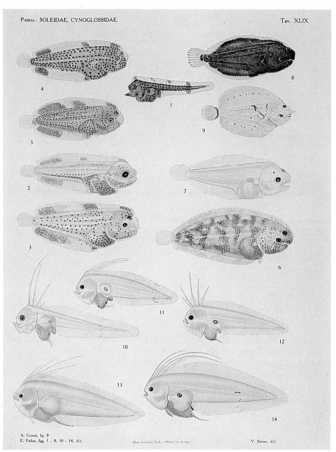

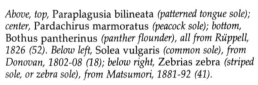

Above, top, Paraplagusia bilineata *(patterned tongue sole); center,* Pardachirus marmoratus *(peacock sole); bottom,* Bothus pantherinus *(panther flounder), all from Rüppell, 1826 (52). Below left,* Solea vulgaris *(common sole), from Donovan, 1802-08 (18); below right,* Zebrias zebra *(striped sole, or zebra sole), from Matsumori, 1881-92 (41).*

On the plate, ill. 1-6, Solea impar; *ill. 7-8* Solea nasuta *(all Soleids); ill. 9* Monochirus ispidus; *ill. 10-14* Symphurus nigrescens *(all Cynoglossids), from Lo Bianco, date missing (40).*

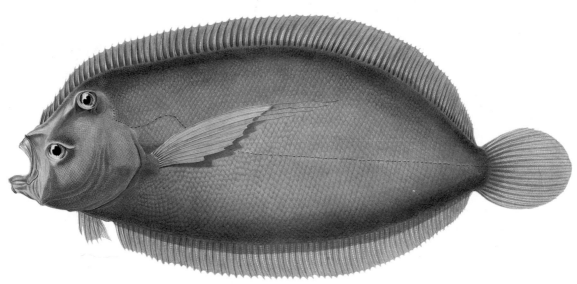

Above, Bothus pantherinus *(panther flounder), from Du Petit-Thouars, 1846 (22). Right, on the plate: ill. 1-3* Arnoglossus kessleri *(Kessler's scaldfish); ill. 4-7* Arnoglossus rueppelli *(Rüppell's scaldfish); ill. 8-10* Bothus podas *(lefteye flounder), from Lo Bianco, date missing (40).*

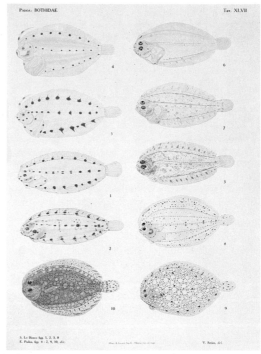

Above, Pleuronichthys cornutus *(fine-spotted flounder); right,* Paralichthys olivaceus *(Japanese flounder), both from Ohno, 1937-44 (46).*

Left, above, Psetta maxima *(turbot); below,* Scophthalmus rhombus *(brill, or pearl), both from Donovan, 1802-08 (18).*

On the plate, ill. 1-4 Psetta maxima *(turbot); ill. 5-10* Scophthalmus rhombus *(brill, or pearl), from Lo Bianco, date missing (40).*

Top left, Pleuronectes platessa *(plaice); top right,* Hippoglossus hippoglossus *(halibut); above,* Platichthys flesus *(flounder), all from Donovan, 1802-08 (18).*

Below, Synanceia horrida *(stonefish), from Gray, 1830-34 (29).*

Top left, Scorpaenodes kelloggi *(Guam stingfish); above right,* Pterois radiata *(radial firefish), from Garrett and Günther, 1873-1910 (27). Below,* Pterois volitans *(ornate butterfly-cod), from Bennett, 1830 (4).*

On the plate above, top left, Pterois lunulata *(butterflyfish, or lion fish); top right,* Hypodytes rubripinnis *(redfin velvetfish); bottom,* Sebastes trivittatus *(snowy rockfish), from* Illustrations of many kinds of Fishes, *late 18th C. (34). On the plate left,* Pterois lunulata *(butterflyfish, or lion fish), from Takagi, 1850 (60). Below,* Scorpaenopsis gibbosa *(scorpionfish), from Cuvier, 1836-49 (13).*

Above right, Taenianotus triacanthus *(paperfish); left, above,* Gymnapistes marmoratus *(South Australian cobbler) and, below,* Blepsias bilobus *(crested sculpin), all from Cuvier, 1836-49 (13).*

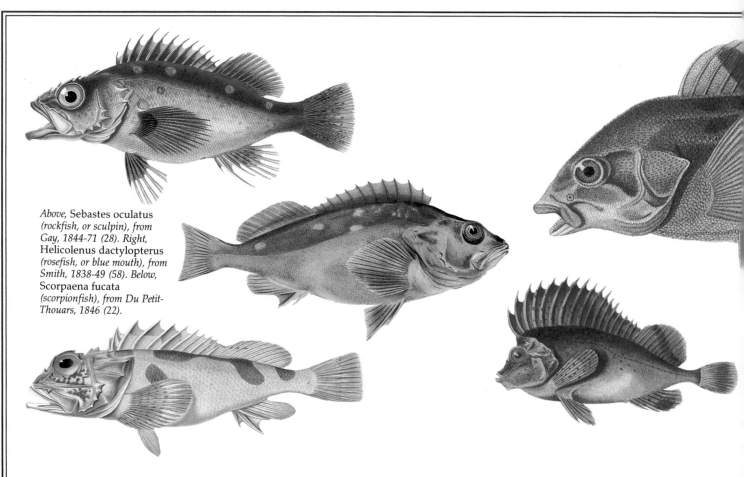

Above, Sebastes oculatus *(rockfish, or sculpin), from Gay, 1844-71 (28). Right,* Helicolenus dactylopterus *(rosefish, or blue mouth), from Smith, 1838-49 (58). Below,* Scorpaena fucata *(scorpionfish), from Du Petit-Thouars, 1846 (22).*

On the plate below: ill. 1-9 Scorpaena porcus *(sea scropion);* ill.10-20 Scorpaena scrofa *(large-scaled scorpionfish), from Lo Bianco, date missing (40). Left, on the plate, from top:* Sebastes capensis; Scorpaenopsis novaeguineae; Sebastapistes strongia; Paracentropogon longispinis *(all scorpionfishes);* Apistus carinatus *(bearded waspfish) and* Dendrochirus zebra *(zebra firefish), from Dumont d'Urville, 1830-35 (21).*

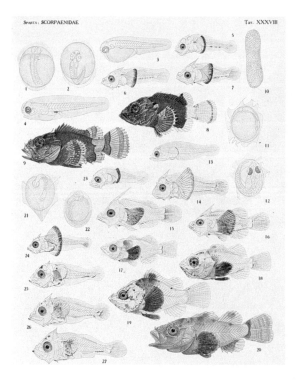

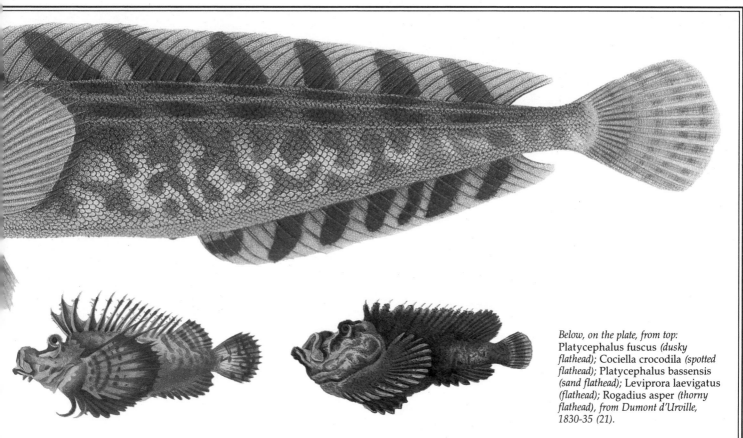

Below, on the plate, from top:
Platycephalus fuscus (dusky
flathead); Cociella crocodila (spotted
flathead); Platycephalus bassensis
(sand flathead); Leviprora laevigatus
(flathead); Rogadius asper (thorny
flathead), from Dumont d'Urville,
1830-35 (21).

Top, Hexagrammos stelleri (white-spotted greenling); above, far left,
Congiopodus peruvianus (Congiopodid), left, Inimicus filamentosus
(ghoul), and right, Synanceia verrucosa (poison scorpionfish), all from
Cuvier, 1836-49 (13). Below, Platycephalus indicus (flathead fish), from
Ohno, 1937-44 (46).

Die Roßkolbe

Das Scelet.

von unten.

Das Scelet von unten.

Left and below, Cottus gobio (river bullhead), from Meyer, 1752 (42) and from Donovan, 1802-08 (18).

クロハゼ

Myoxocephalus scorpius *(bullrout, or short-spined sea scorpion), from Bloch, 1785-89 (6).*

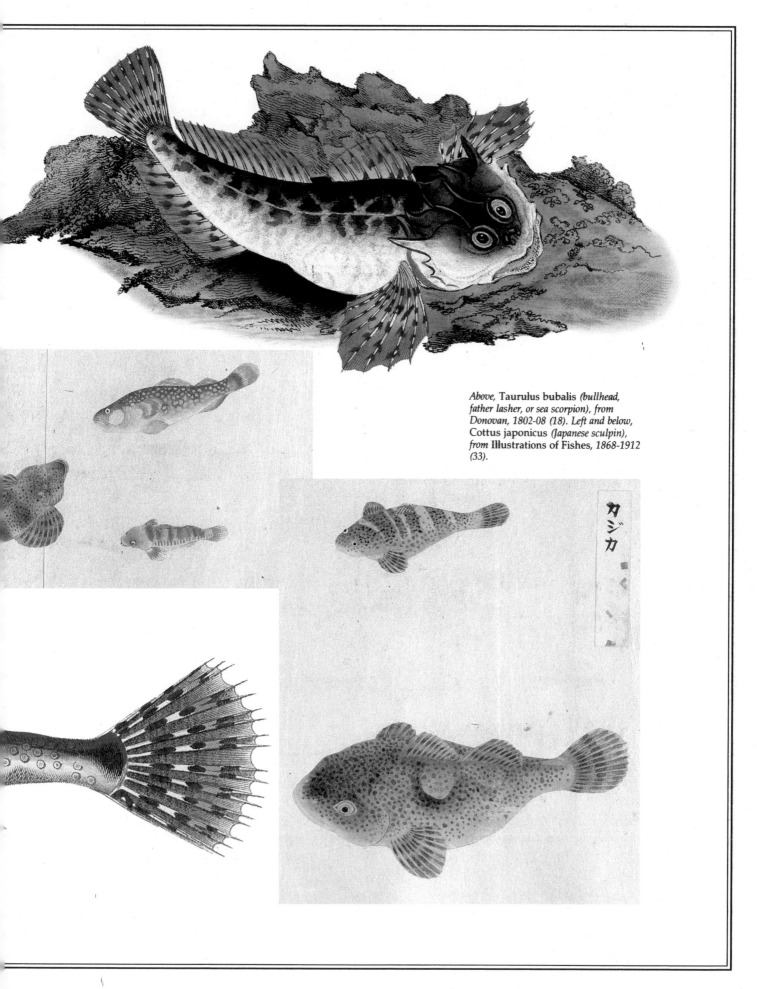

Above, Taurulus bubalis *(bullhead, father lasher, or sea scorpion), from* Donovan, *1802-08 (18). Left and below,* Cottus japonicus *(Japanese sculpin), from* Illustrations of Fishes, *1868-1912 (33).*

カジカ

Right, Dactylopterus volitans *(flying gurnard), from Pouchet, 1841 (47).*

Left, from the top, Lepidotrigla cavillone; Prionotus lineatus *(both gurnards);* Peristedion cataphractum *(armed gurnard);* Dactylopterus volitans *(flying gurnard), all from Cuvier, 1836-49 (13).*

Above, Trigloporus lastoviza *(streaked gurnard), from Donovan, 1802-08 (18).*

Above, Dactyloptena orientalis *(purple flying gurnard), from Takagi, 1850 (60).*

Above and left, Trigla lucerna *(tub, or yellow gurnard), respectively from Lo Bianco, date missing (40) and from Donovan, 1802-08 (18). Right,* Dactyloptena *sp. (flying gurnard), from Renard, 1754 (49).*

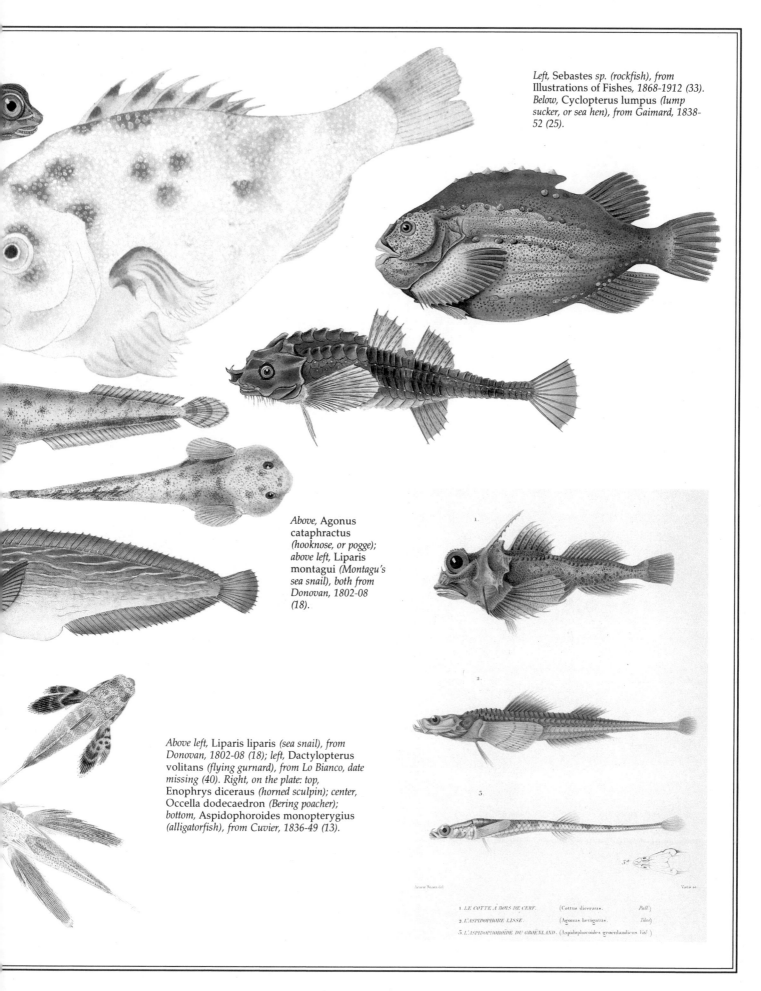

Left, Sebastes *sp. (rockfish), from* Illustrations of Fishes, *1868-1912 (33).* *Below,* Cyclopterus lumpus *(lump sucker, or sea hen), from Gaimard, 1838-52 (25).*

Above, Agonus cataphractus *(hooknose, or pogge); above left,* Liparis montagui *(Montagu's sea snail), both from Donovan, 1802-08 (18).*

Above left, Liparis liparis *(sea snail), from Donovan, 1802-08 (18); left,* Dactylopterus volitans *(flying gurnard), from Lo Bianco, date missing (40). Right, on the plate: top,* Enophrys diceraus *(horned sculpin); center,* Occella dodecaedron *(Bering poacher); bottom,* Aspidophoroides monopterygius *(alligatorfish), from Cuvier, 1836-49 (13).*

1. LE COTTE À BOIS DE CERF. (Cottus diceraus. *Pall.*)
2. L'ASPIDOPHORE LISSE. (Agonus lævigatus. *Tiles.*)
5. L'ASPIDOPHOROÏDE DU GROENLAND. (Aspidophoroides groenlandicus *Val.*)

Top and center, Callionymus lyra *(dragonet), from Donovan, 1802-08 (18); bottom, from Cuvier, 1836-49 (13).*

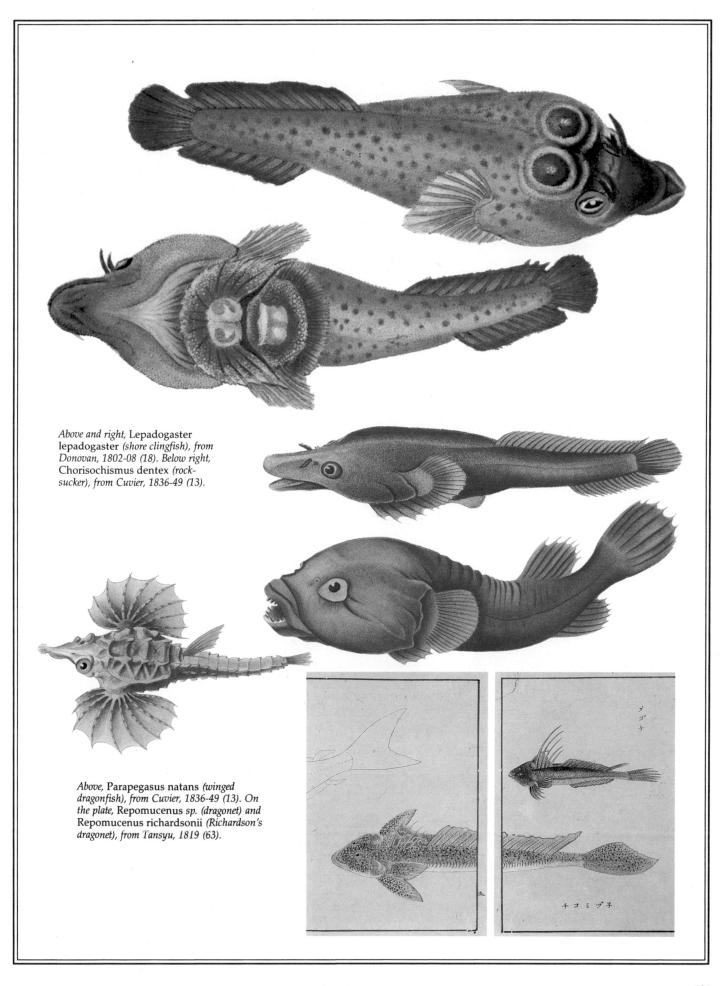

Above and right, Lepadogaster lepadogaster *(shore clingfish), from Donovan, 1802-08 (18). Below right,* Chorisochismus dentex *(rocksucker), from Cuvier, 1836-49 (13).*

Above, Parapegasus natans *(winged dragonfish), from Cuvier, 1836-49 (13). On the plate,* Repomucenus *sp. (dragonet) and* Repomucenus richardsonii *(Richardson's dragonet), from Tansyu, 1819 (63).*

メゴチ

チコミヅ子

Right, Meuschenia australis *(Southern filefish), from Donovan, 1802-08 (18). Below,* Navodon modestus *(black scraper, or filefish), from Risyun, 1771 (51). Bottom,* Monocanthus chinensis *(fanbelly leatherjacket), from Richardson, 1843 (50).*

Above, Psilocephalus barbatus = Anacanthus barbatus *(beardie, or tape-fish), from Gray, 1830-34 (29). Below,* Triacanthus biaculeatus *(ankatillah), from Bennett, 1830 (4). On the plate,* Stephanolepis cirrhifer *(threadsail filefish, or porky), from Ohno, 1937-44 (46).*

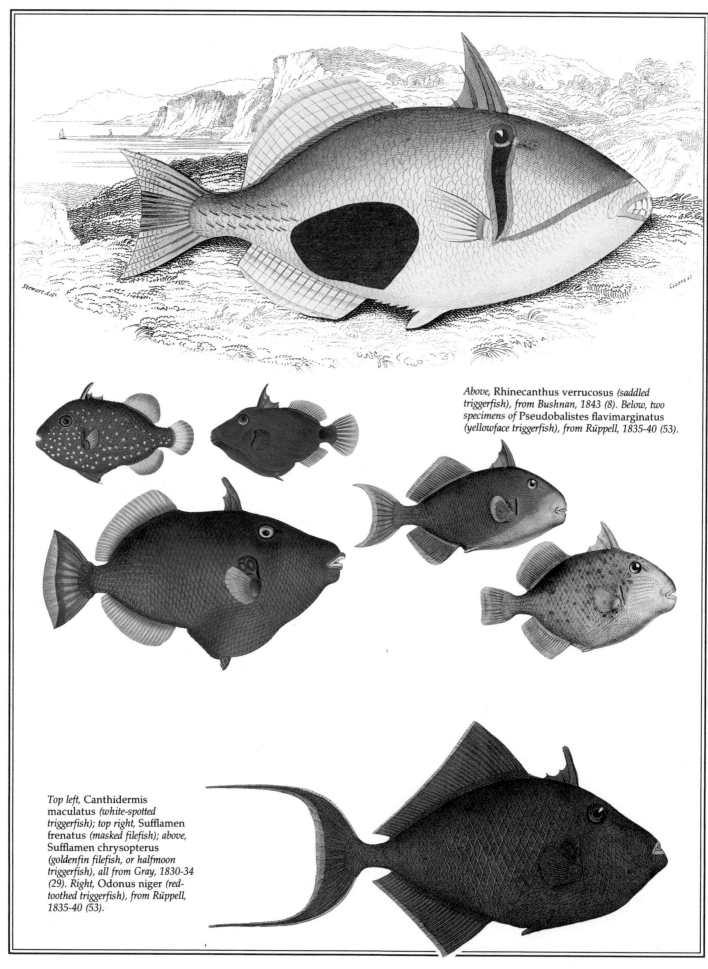

Above, Rhinecanthus verrucosus *(saddled triggerfish), from Bushnan, 1843 (8). Below, two specimens of* Pseudobalistes flavimarginatus *(yellowface triggerfish), from Rüppell, 1835-40 (53).*

Top left, Canthidermis maculatus *(white-spotted triggerfish); top right,* Sufflamen frenatus *(masked filefish); above,* Sufflamen chrysopterus *(goldenfin filefish, or halfmoon triggerfish), all from Gray, 1830-34 (29). Right,* Odonus niger *(red-toothed triggerfish), from Rüppell, 1835-40 (53).*

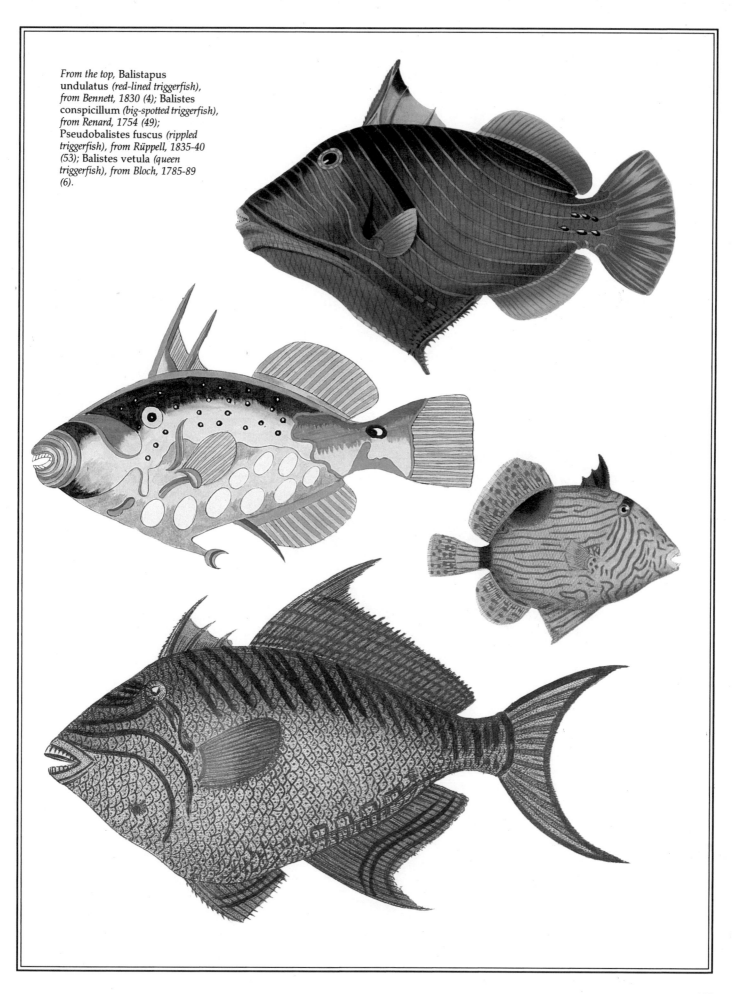

From the top, Balistapus undulatus *(red-lined triggerfish), from Bennett, 1830 (4);* Balistes conspicillum *(big-spotted triggerfish), from Renard, 1754 (49);* Pseudobalistes fuscus *(rippled triggerfish), from Rüppell, 1835-40 (53);* Balistes vetula *(queen triggerfish), from Bloch, 1785-89 (6).*

HORNED OSTRACION

Lizars sc

From the top, Aracana aurita
*(Ostraciid), from Donovan, 1802-08
(18); Tetrosomus concatenatus
(triangular boxfish), from Smith,
1838-49 (58); Lactoria sp. (cowfish),
from Renard, 1754 (49); Lactoria
cornuta (longhorn cowfish), from
Bushnan, 1843 (8).*

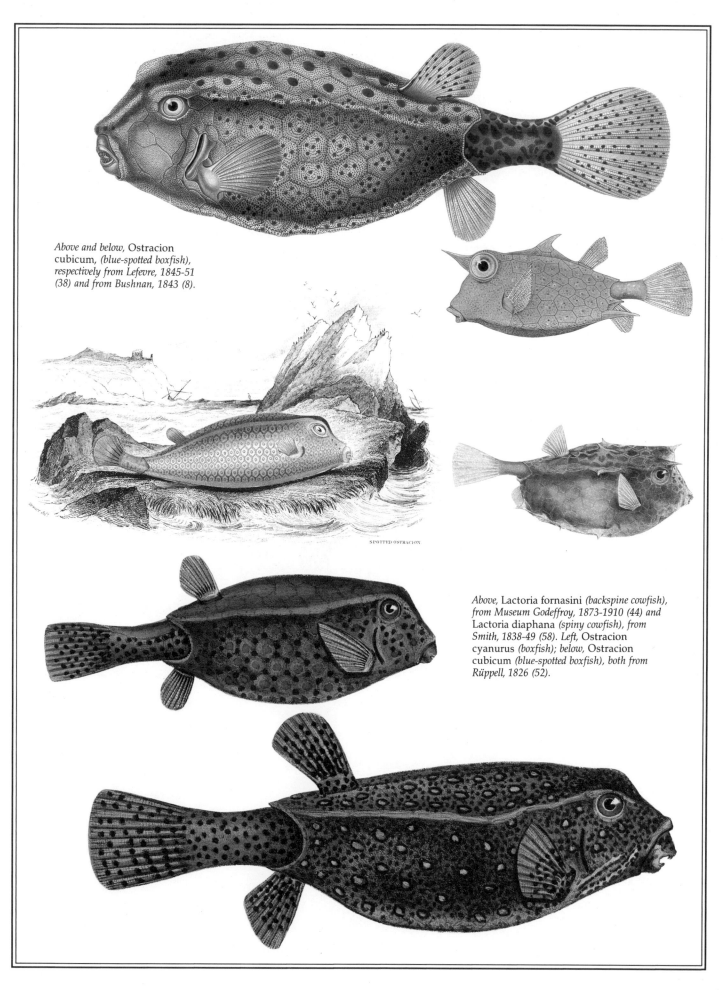

Above and below, Ostracion cubicum, *(blue-spotted boxfish), respectively from Lefevre, 1845-51 (38) and from Bushnan, 1843 (8).*

SPOTTED OSTRACION

Above, Lactoria fornasini *(backspine cowfish), from Museum Godeffroy, 1873-1910 (44) and* Lactoria diaphana *(spiny cowfish), from Smith, 1838-49 (58). Left,* Ostracion cyanurus *(boxfish); below,* Ostracion cubicum *(blue-spotted boxfish), both from Rüppell, 1826 (52).*

Top left, Arothron immaculatus
(narrow-lined toadfish); top right,
Arothron viridipunctatus
*(toadfish), both from Day, 1865
(15). On the plate,* Takifugu
rubripes *(tiger puffer), from Ohno,
1937-44 (46).*

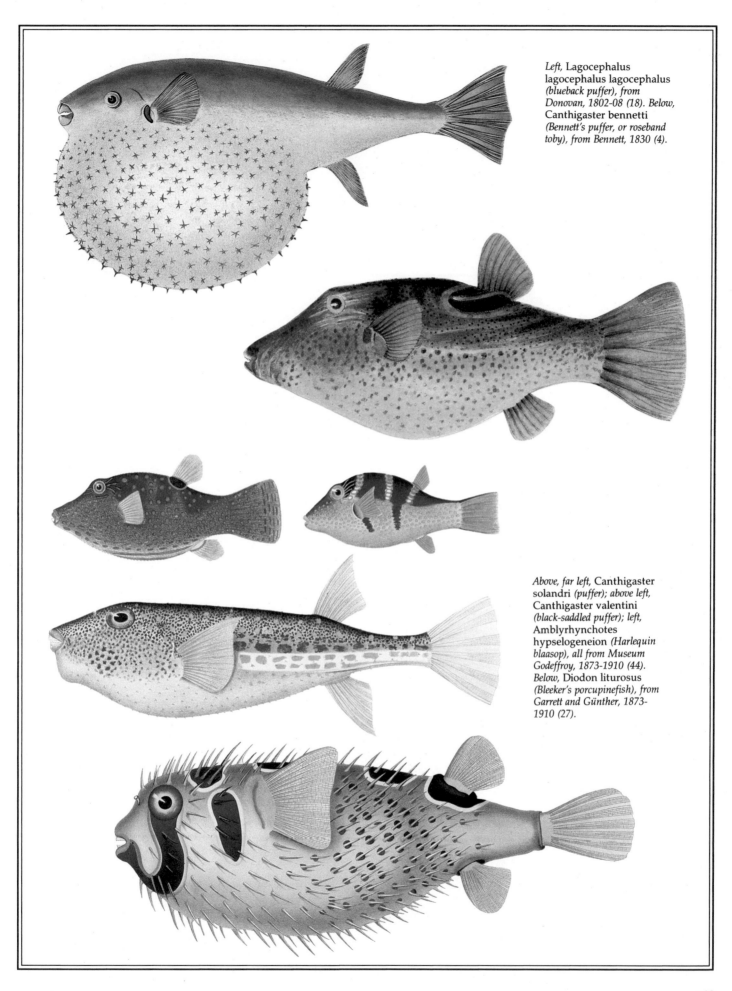

Left, Lagocephalus lagocephalus lagocephalus *(blueback puffer), from Donovan, 1802-08 (18). Below,* Canthigaster bennetti *(Bennett's puffer, or roseband toby), from Bennett, 1830 (4).*

Above, far left, Canthigaster solandri *(puffer); above left,* Canthigaster valentini *(black-saddled puffer); left,* Amblyrhynchotes hypselogeneion *(Harlequin blaasop), all from Museum Godeffroy, 1873-1910 (44). Below,* Diodon liturosus *(Bleeker's porcupinefish), from Garrett and Günther, 1873-1910 (27).*

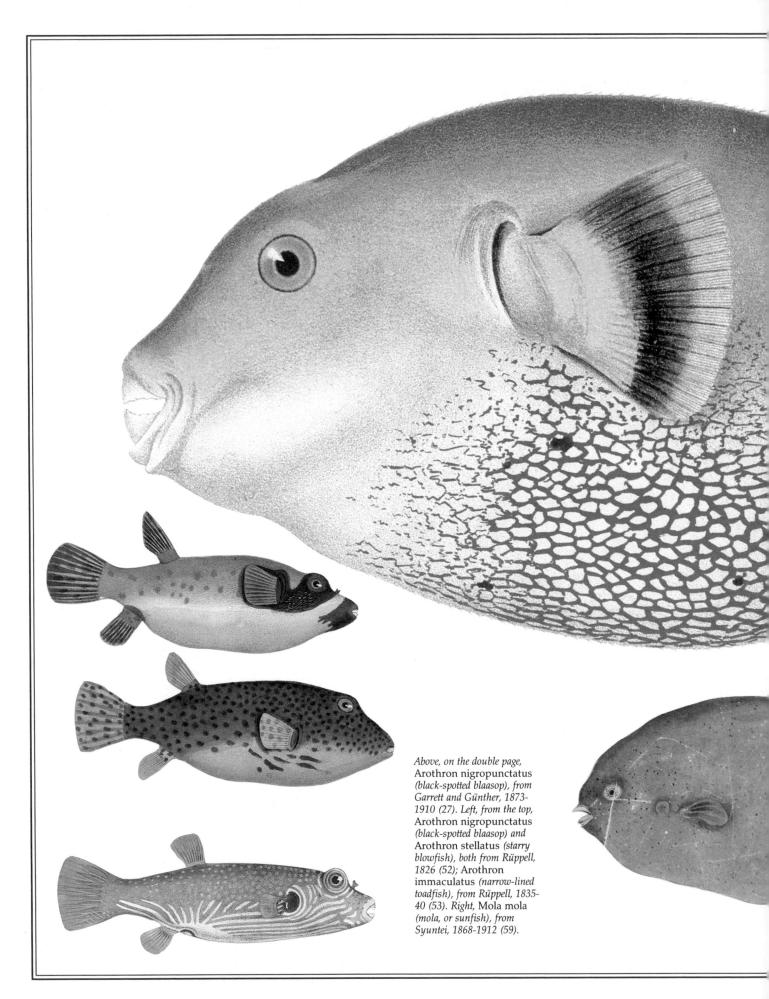

Above, on the double page, Arothron nigropunctatus *(black-spotted blaasop), from Garrett and Günther, 1873-1910 (27). Left, from the top,* Arothron nigropunctatus *(black-spotted blaasop) and* Arothron stellatus *(starry blowfish), both from Rüppell, 1826 (52);* Arothron immaculatus *(narrow-lined toadfish), from Rüppell, 1835-40 (53). Right,* Mola mola *(mola, or sunfish), from Syuntei, 1868-1912 (59).*

Top right, Arothron hispidus *(toby, blaasop, or toadfish), from Rüppell, 1835-40 (53). Above*, Arothron stellatus *(starry blowfish), from Museum Godeffroy, 1873-1910 (44). Left*, Triodon macropterus *(three-tooth puffer), from Iinuma, 19th C. (32).*

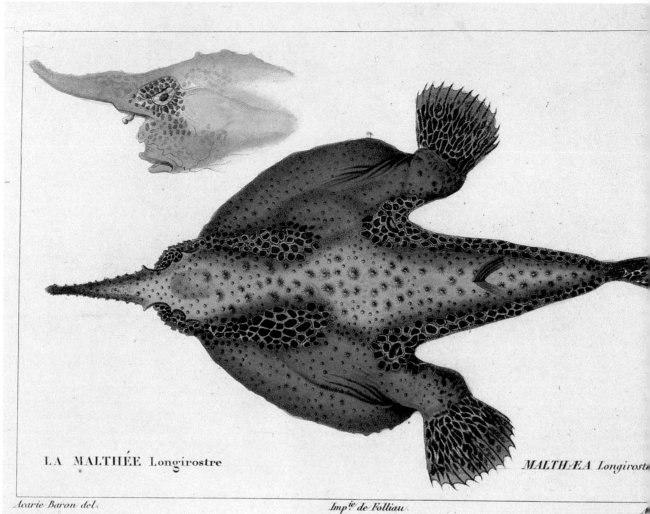

LA MALTHÉE Longirostre

MALTHÆA Longirostr

Acarie Baron del.

Imp.ie de Folliau.

On the plate, Ogcocephalus vespertilio *(longnose batfish) and, below left,* Antennarius pictus *(roughskin frogfish), both from Cuvier and Valenciennes, 1828-49 (11). Below right,* Histrio histrio *(Sargassumfish), from Tansyu, 1811 (62).*

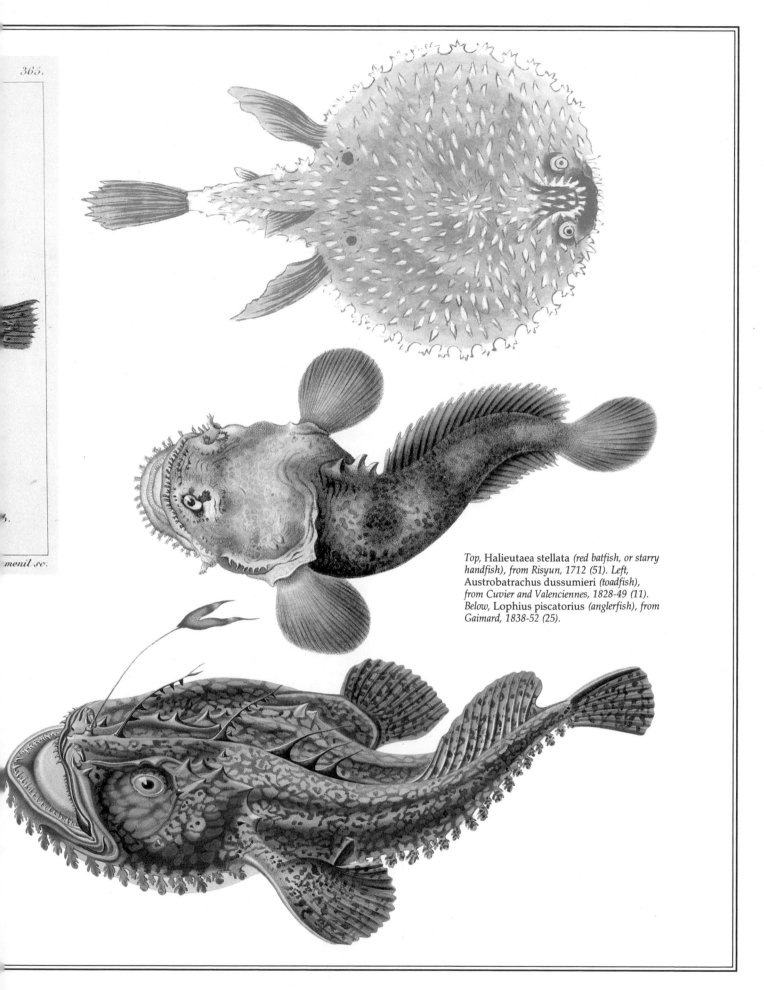

Top, Halieutaea stellata *(red batfish, or starry handfish), from Risyun, 1712 (51).* Left, Austrobatrachus dussumieri *(toadfish), from Cuvier and Valenciennes, 1828-49 (11).* Below, Lophius piscatorius *(anglerfish), from Gaimard, 1838-52 (25).*

Above, Antennarius sarasa *(calico frogfish), from* Illustrations of Fishes, *1868-1912 (33). Top,* Antennarius pardalis *(leopard frogfish), from Cuvier and Valenciennes, 1828-49 (11).*

Top, Antennarius sp. (frogfish), from Takagi, 1850 (60). Center, Ogcocephalus vespertilio (longnose batfish) and, bottom, Batrichthys apiatus (toadfish), both from Cuvier, 1836-49 (13).

Lights in the great darkness

In a twilight that turns gradually into perennial darkness, the fishes of the marine depths, embellished by gorgeous displays of bioluminescence, live under the weight of an enormous blanket of water. This is the thrilling story of a knowledge acquired, among thousands of obstacles, in the course of two centuries of oceanographic research.

Port of Plymouth, August 28, 1768. George III's H.M.S. *Endeavour* weighs anchor to venture on the circumnavigation of the globe, having as its main scientific aim (together with the political aim of asserting the British presence in the austral hemisphere) the observation of the planet Venus on its passage in front the sun. But the eyes of Captain James Cook and his traveling companions were going to observe not only the sky, but also — with an interest, sharpness, and thoroughness until then unknown — the sea they were going to plough for four long years of navigation. They had prepared for this undertaking very thoroughly and with great financial soundness. John Ellis, a merchant with an inclination for natural history — he had been accepted among the members of the prestigious Royal Society — wrote to the great Linnaeus, who had been one of the main promoters of the expedition, as follows: "No people ever went to sea better fitted out for the purpose of Natural History, nor more elegantly. They have got a fine library of Natural History; they have all sorts of machines for catching and preserving insects; all kinds of nets, drags, and hooks for coral fishing; they have even a curious contrivance of a telescope, by which, put into water, you can see the bottom to a great depth, where it is clear. They have many cases of bottles with ground stoppers, of several sizes, to preserve animals in spirits... besides there are many people whose sole business is to attend them for this very purpose. There are two painters and draughtsmen, several volunteers who have a tolerable notion of Natural History." This description by Ellis is an astonishing anticipation of what would be later called an "oceanographic ship," that is, a ship designed and equipped for the purpose of studying the sea: instruments for observation and sampling, well-equipped laboratories, a specialized library, scientists and technicians with appropriately differentiated functions,

young apprentices. And even the "sponsor" was not missing in the expedition of the *Endeavour*, in the person of Joseph Banks, a rich young man — his properties were bringing him an income of six thousand pounds per year — who had studied at Harrow, Eton, and Oxford and had later specialized in botany. Today we know (thanks to the indiscretion of Solander, his assistant-secretary) that the financial support he offered the expedition amounted to ten thousand pounds: but more than in this enlightened generosity, the merits of this brilliant young man of 25 years of age — who was later president of the Royal Society for forty years — consist in his contribution to the progress of botanic sciences: the discovery of over 1,300 new plant species, collected, studied, and portrayed in the course of the voyage.

So, thanks to Cook and the *Endeavour*, an entirely new way to navigate was then starting — for the conquest of knowledge and not only, as in the past, of new colonies. Of course, politics did not cease to assert their usual rights, and from its beginning the "science of the sea" was the scene of hazardous competitions to which the great powers entrusted their reputation. It was not by chance that the most important expedition, after Cook's expedition, carried out in the austral waters was French; in those years, the Napoleonic wind was blowing strongly on the fire of the historic hostility between France and England (over 40 years of war in the course of 140 years), and the First Consul himself had been interested in the choice of the 23 *savants* (botanists, zoologists, mineralogists, geographers, hydrographers, astronomers, horticulturists, painters) destined to journey on the *Géographe*, a 350-ton corvette, and on the *Naturaliste*, of a slightly smaller tonnage. However, not many of them were destined to complete their voyage, which, having started in 1800 at Le Havre, concluded after three years: some of them died of various illnesses, others — young civilians —

disembarked in the course of the voyage because they couldn't stand the military discipline enforced by the 46-year-old Captain Nicholas Baudin, who lost his life on September 16, 1802, within sight of Mauritius. Nevertheless, the expedition brought about over forty thousand marvellous scientific findings; and the observations of 22-year-old François Péron on sea water (the measurements were effected at six-hour intervals in the course of the whole voyage) are probably the first example of conscientiously and accurately programmed research carried out in the field of physical oceanography. One more aspect must be pointed out about that great adventure: the great friendliness that marked all the meetings between the Frenchmen of Captain Baudin and the British ships cruising over those remote austral waters, at the very moment when, in the battlefields, the armies of the two countries were fighting ferociously; and this — as the Institut National wrote from Paris to the Royal Society, requesting a safe-conduct for the two ships that were about to set sail — because at "the very moment war again overwhelms the world, the friends of mankind must act with the purpose of making arts progress thanks to enterprises such as those that have immortalized the great navigators of our two nations and the renowned scientists that have roamed the seas and the earth to observe nature. "A noble call, true at all times, that solemnly ratifies the supremacy of intellect and harmony over the force of arms and hate.

In the following decades the young science of oceanography underwent a literally explosive development, to which both Europe and North America offered contributions. The harvest of data and information was rich, in spite of the fact that the original professional training of the protagonists of those scientific cruises was often quite different from what we might expect today, devoted as we are, no one excepted, to the cult of overspecialization. Thus Karl Ernst von Baer, best known as the founder of embriology, was the first to lead an expedition, in 1837, in the cold waters of Novaya Zemlya and later, repeatedly, in the warmer water of the Caspian Sea; William B. Carpenter, who with Wyville Thomson organized in 1868 the cruise of the *Lightning* and in the following year the cruise of the *Porcupine*, had been interested at first in physiology (his book became widely known and was published four times from 1839 to 1854), then in microscopy, attaining also in this field a large publishing success (as many as eight editions from 1856 to 1901). But most remarkable is the strange case of Adalbert von Chamisso who, leaving temporarily aside his pen (his works in prose and verse occupy an outstanding position in early romantic German literature), took part as a naturalist, beginning in 1815, on a Russian scientific expedition led by Otto von Kotzbue; and apparently with success, as on his return he was entrusted with the direction of the Berlin Botanical Gardens.

In this roughly sketched story of very early oceanographic research, the year 1872 appears particularly bright, as it is marked by two equally essential events in the development of the new discipline. It is marked on one side by the foundation of the Zoological Station of Naples by Anton Dohrn; on the other, by the beginning of the *Challenger* expedition. The first was a scientific institution destined to be the model (as to size, organization, equipment, financial soundness, international communication) for many more, founded later with similar purposes all over the world. As for the cruise of the *Challenger*, it is unanimously considered the beginning of modern oceanography, thanks to its accurate planning, the enormous amount of collected data, the integration of physics and marine biology, and the collaboration of experts belonging to many countries that characterized it. Actually the fated year 1872 is the culminating point of a process of intellectual, technological, and methodological ripening that had started many years before under the pressure of several heterogeneous factors: the formidable power of intellectual provocation and stimulus of Charles Darwin's works; the reconstruction, on the part of zoologists, of the complex evolution cycles characterizing many marine invertebrates; the fully deserved insertion of hydrobiology among university course subjects, requiring — in addition to theoretical classes — "open-air" practicing near the sea and other aquatic environments; the growing public interest in all that concerned the sea, increased besides by the creation of the first public aquariums and by the publication of the first popular works concerning the wonders and mysteries of the sea.

The actual transformation of this great effervescence of ideas and enthusiasms would certainly not have been possible without the plentiful harvest of discoveries and technological innovations consequent to the Industrial Revolution. First of all, we must obviously mention the replacement of sail navigation by steam navigation, which was of primary importance not only for covering great distances over the seas but also, and especially, for carrying out regularly and accurately all the measurement operations and collection of samples usually performed by an oceanographic ship. As to the other technological innovations of those years, they were of such importance and so numerous that it is certainly not possible to list them here. Just think — as a single example — of the innovations in glass manufacturing: without them it would not have been possible to manufacture large glass sheets strong enough to bear the pressure of the great mass of water of an aquarium and at the same time so transparent as to allow a clear vision of the organisms inside; microscopes, as well, would not have become those incomparable means of research — including hydrobiological research — without the creation of lenses with no serious "aberrations."

Mentioning again briefly the *Challenger*, she weighed anchor from the port of Plymouth on December 21, 1872 — it was a Saturday — to start a circumnavigation of the oceans of 68,980 marine miles that concluded at Spithead on May 24, 1876. Professor Wyville Thomson, the scientist leading the expedition, had the help of naturalists H.N. Moseley, John Murray, and Rudolf von Willemoes-Suhm, of the chemist and physician J.Y. Buchanan, and of his secretary J.J. Wild, who was in charge of the pictorial documentation. The observation area of the expedition included 362 stations, where depth and temperature measurements were carried out, water samples were collected, meteorological observations were effected, the speed and direction of surface currents were measured, and biologic materials of all kinds were collected with the help of drags and nets of various designs. One of the main characteristics of this expedition, which is greatly admired by experts still today, is its remarkable working efficiency. In the course of three and a half years of dredgings on the sea floor, only eleven accidents were suffered by the equipment used for such a delicate operation, and only twenty-eight thermometers were lost in the course of the very frequent temperature measurements effected from the surface down to a depth of several hundred meters. Sir Edwin Ray Lankester, director of the section of natural history of the British Museum and promoter of the marine zoology department in Plymouth, is right when he writes about the *Challenger*: "Never did an expedition cost so little and produce such momentous results for human knowledge."

The extension of the ocean waters covers seven tenths of the earth's surface, and they go down to depths unequalled by the height of any mountain rising above their level. Along this vertical dimension of theirs, such elements as temperature, salinity, light, and oxygen, which are of vital importance for marine life, undergo changes that are often quite remarkable but are impossible to detect from the surface. This makes oceanography a perfectly three-dimensional science, characterized in its progress by the ability, acquired by scientists in the course of the years, to ascertain more and more accurately and quickly conditions and phenomena occurring at a depth of tens, hundreds, thousands of meters. Because direct exploration — until recently — was totally excluded to man, such knowledge was necessarily acquired through the mediation of properly conceived and manufactured instruments, which became therefore, so to speak, the eyes and hands of the oceanographer.

Setting up instruments for such special tasks was of no little difficulty. Until then, in the course of navigation man had taken soundings only along the coastal waters by means of a rope with a weight to prevent the danger of running aground or even of wrecking in shallow waters. But when the thought occurred that a thermometer or a water sampler could be fastened to a ballasted rope and plunged to a depth not of tens but of hundreds or thousands of meters, it was immediately realized that too many obstacles hindered such an operation. In fact, because of the force exerted by the current, the rope was displaced from its vertical position or it even deteriorated and then was torn by the joined action of tension and pressure; furthermore, the pressure crushed organic materials such as wood and deformed the glass of the thermometers of traditional design used initially, making their operation quite unreliable. The manual heaving up of the rope required quite a large number of the ship's personnel, and it often took them several hours to get the rope back on board, not to mention the fact that very

often in the course of the operation the capstan went out of use because of the terrible effort it had to bear for such a long time.

For these reasons, in the second half of the 17th century, Robert Hooke, who was in charge of the experimental section of the Royal Society, had tried to solve the problem of taking depth soundings without depending on a rope. He created a ropeless sounding apparatus that consisted essentially of a weight that was released on touching the sea floor, allowing a float to come up to the surface: in the perfected version of this instrument the float could measure the distance from the surface to the bottom by means of a revolution indicator. This was clearly a very original and "modern" instrument, but it was never actually used, neither during Hooke's times nor later, because the materials then available were totally inadequate (the sounding apparatus was made mainly of wood, and the float consisted of a animal bladder). In the following century Luigi Ferdinando Marsili, an ingenious Italian scientist, also had to face the problem of materials: thanks to his work *Histoire physique de la mer*, which was published in 1725, he is often called "the father of oceanography." In the second half of the 19th century the Industrial Revolution provided at last the long-awaited solution in the form of very thin but extremely strong wires and mechanical capstans that were operated by an engine that could wind up the wires very quickly without the assistance of man. Furthermore, new materials became available for the production of research instruments, such as rubber, ebonite, and celluloid, not to mention metal alloys providing extraordinary performances. In short, thanks to all these innovations, the oceanography of the last decades of the 19th century was transformed and improved to such an extent that it offered at last an univocal and definite answer to the most fascinating and intriguing questions that were asked of it: is there some sort of life, and of what kind, in the great depths of the sea?

Some people had already found an answer to such questions: Sicilian and Calabrian fishermen were accustomed to finding small fishes with surreal shapes pushed ashore, there to die, by the impetuous tidal waters of the Strait of Messina. In the opinion of those simple men, it was obvious that such fantastic creatures had been taken away from the abysses of the sea, a sea as deep as hell; they well deserved, therefore, the name of "Devil's fishes." When Cocco, the Italian naturalist, examined them — first in 1829, and later in 1838 — he turned his attention to the luminous organs spread all over their bodies; so did Verany in the same years at Nice — another important place in the Mediterranean where living organisms from the deep were pushed ashore — observing the extraordinary luminescence phenomena shown by the squid *Histioteuthis bonnelliana.*

As far as we know, the first man to ascertain in those years the presence of ichthyofauna at great depths was Risso, a French zoologist who, describing for the first time such fishes as *Alepocephalus rostratus, Trachyrhynchus trachyrhynchus,* and *Coelorhynchus coelorhynchus,* located their habitat between 450 and 640 meters under the surface. Also, R.T. Lowe and J.Y. Johnson, working on the island of Madeira between 1835 and 1866, described a great number of abyssal fishes that had been caught by local fishermen by depth fishing lines or that had reached the surface by chance. This valuable material, including among other things some voracious predators such as *Alepisaurus ferox, Chiasmodon niger,* and *Melanocetus johnsoni,* became part of the British Museum's collections, thus allowing Albert Günther to single out the anatomical features that most characterize the fishes of the deep: extremely thin muscles of the body and tail, very fragile tissues, a scarce minera-lization of the skeleton, eyes of either enlarged or reduced size, presence of luminous organs, black pigmentation of pharynx and peritoneum, and many more.

Every science must complain about a negative balance of "ignored discoveries": the intuitions of perspicacious men ahead of their times that would have greatly accelerated scientific development had they not met the indifference — sometimes even the hostility — of most people. Oceanography was not an exception to such behavior: in the years 1817 to 1818, in fact, Sir John Smith, master of the ships *Isabella* and *Alexander* in Baffin Bay, while looking for the "Northwest Passage," had collected some samples from the sea floor by means of a drag of his own design. This instrument, after being immersed at a depth of 820, 1,130, 1,830, and 1,920 meters, had brought back to the surface, together with slime, some crustaceans, worms, hydroids, and starfishes. Later his nephew, Sir James Clark Ross, led an expedition exactly at the antipodes, reaching the antarctic waters with two ships, *Erebus* and *Terror;* he successfully collected some samples of animals living on the sea floor, at a depth of 730 meters, and was surprised to discover that many of such organisms were exactly the same as those that had been found at the same latitudes in the northern hemisphere. In 1841, strongly underlining this surprising homogeneity of the fauna living in the deep, he wrote, "Although contrary to the general belief of naturalists I have no doubt that from however great a depth we may be able to bring the mud and stones of the bed of the ocean, we shall find them teeming with animal life; the extreme pressure at the greatest depth does not appear to affect these creatures." These were extraordinarily "modern" words, disregarded, however, by official science, as it was still under the influence of the theses of Edward Forbes, one of its most brilliant, authoritative, and leading protagonists. The latter, in fact, in the course of an expedition in the Aegean Sea aboard the ship *Beacon* had come to the conclusion — which he fully described in 1843 to the British Association at Cork — that animal life was no longer present at a depth of about 550 meters, below which started what he had called the "Azoic Region." "It was almost as difficult to believe that creatures comparable with those of which we have experience in the upper world could live at the bottom of the deep sea, as they could live in a vacuum, or in fire."

If science represents the fuel that feeds the technical progress of man, the latter, through ever changing requirements and questions asked of science, contributes to its continuous progress. Therefore, the laying of the submarine cable from France to England in 1850, the beginning of the era of transoceanic telegraphy, marks also the beginning of a time in which oceanography showed growing interest in the deep-sea environment. In effect, the laying of over 5,000 kilometers of submarine cable across the Atlantic Ocean to connect the American and British telegraph networks meant acquiring a very accurate knowledge of the topography of the sea floor, sometimes under 5,000 meters of water, as well as of the chemical and physical characteristics that existed there. Therefore, the problem of the possible existence of an "abyssal" fauna had to be faced more systematically and urgently. The first positive answers to this question were given by the submarine cables themselves when they were lifted up to the surface for necessary periodic maintenance. In 1860, for instance, the Mediterranean Telegraph Company, checking the cable laid between Sardinia and North Africa, found it to be abundantly covered — down to a depth of over 2,000 meters — by gastropod and lamellibranch mollusks, corals and Cephalopods' eggs. Their presence was estimated by Professor Wyville Thompson to be one of the first

unquestionable proofs that rather complex organisms such as these could live at a depth of thousands of meters.

The full blossoming of oceanography, which had in the *Challenger* expedition its origin and also one of its most remarkable moments, starts in this climate of great interest for "what lives down there," thanks also to the awareness — as Wyville Thomson wrote in 1868 in a letter to his friend M.D. W.B. Carpenter, vice-president of the Royal Society — that many of the essential questions about life conditions in the ocean depths had been given at last that final answer that they had hitherto lacked.

It would be impossible, if not rather boring, to give here a detailed list of the oceanographic ships that, starting with the *Challenger*, greatly contributed to increasing knowledge of the biology of the deep marine habitat. As brief examples, we can mention the U.S.S. *Blake*, which, under the scientific guidance of Alexander Agassiz, effected systematic dredgings at great depths, beginning in 1877, in the Caribbean Sea; the French ships *Travailleur* and *Talisman*, which from 1880 to 1883 carried out comparative studies of the bottom fauna of the Atlantic and the Mediterranean that revealed a more scarce presence of life in the latter. The Mediterranean was explored in the same years down to a depth of about 3,700 meters by Giglioli, an Italian aboard the ship *Washington*. The *Albatross*, also owned by the United States, examined in particular the tropical Pacific Ocean, at first with Agassiz and later with Charles S. Townsend, catching a large number of deep-sea fishes, which was rather unusual at the time. The *Investigator*, of the Royal Indian Navy, analyzed very accurately the fauna of the deep while navigating the Indian waters.

One of the most remarkable persons in the field of oceanography between the two centuries was certainly the Prince of Monaco Albert I, thanks to his unusually high social standing and much more to his vast and very important scientific work. He started cruising aboard the yacht *Hirondelle* in 1885; then aboard the *Princesse Alice I*, and finally aboard the splendid *Princesse Alice II*. In the years 1905 to 1910, which represent the most active and successful period of his research, he took a long summer cruise each year, sailing in the Atlantic from the Azores to Spitzbergen, without neglecting, however, examination of the marine habitat of the Mediterranean. Prince Albert was awarded several university doctorates *honoris causa*, and he was often cited by other marine biologists who mentioned his family (the Grimaldi family) in the scientific denomination of some new species of invertebrates and fishes of the deep. He certainly deserved the honors conferred on him in the course of his life and afterward. He is widely known thanks to the creation of the Musée Oceanographique in Monaco, which was started in 1895, but he should be even more popular thanks to his apostolate effort in favor of science — and of oceanography in particular — all over the world. His belief was clearly expressed in his autobiographic work *La carrière d'un navigateur*, translated later into several languages (the Italian edition was edited by the Nobel Prize novelist Grazia Deledda). It is worth underlining, in the technical field, the creation by Prince Albert and his collaborators of some new and more effective methods for sample collecting. In fact, the faster-moving depth organisms — especially fishes — tended to elude the capturing equipment that had hitherto been used: therefore nets of an entirely new design were perfected to work on the sea floor and in mid-water; large traps equipped with natural baits and even with luminous decoys electrically fed; automatically closing nets to collect samples only at the desired depth; and the like.

Returning to our brief and incomplete list of oceanographic expeditions, we would like to mention the German *Valdivia*, which sailed in the Atlantic and Indian oceans in the years 1898 to 1899 under the leadership of Carl Cuhn, carrying out a series of excellent studies on the eyes and luminescent organs of fish and Cephalopods of the deep; the Norwegian expedition of the *Michael Sars*, which described clearly for the first time a vertical sequence of marine "regions," each of which was characterized by specific fish schools and invertebrates; the cruises of the Danish ship *Dana* (from 1920 to 1922, and then again from 1928 to 1930), during which Johannes Schmidt discovered, among other things, the area of reproduction of European and American eels in the deep waters of the Sargasso Sea; the research of the Dutch ship *Willebrord Snellius*, which in the years 1925 to 1930 sailed in the southeastern regions of the Indian Ocean and discovered several fish species (especially Macrura) never caught anywhere else.

In the course of the terrible years of the Second World War quite different ships from the oceanographic ones navigated the seas of our planet with an utterly different purpose. But as early as 1947, the Swedish ship *Albatross*, making use of sample collectors of a new design, collected a large amount of data on the nature and distribution of slime in the abysses, followed by the English ship *Discovery II* (1950 to 1951), which operated in the antarctic seas, and by the Danish *Galathea* (1950 to 1952), which, under the leadership of Anton Fr. Bruun, explored the deepest oceanic areas, catching fish at a depth of 7,000 meters and bringing to the surface from a depth of over 10,000 meters — in the Philippines Trench — rocks covered with sea anemones. This was from a depth that nearly reaches the maximum depth ever found in the oceans (10,863 meters), that of the Marianas Trench.

Nothing could be imagined more different than these two realities because of their different environments: the "other space" that enfolds us and the "liquid space" that surrounds us. Two antithetical realities made similar by the fact that both, the universe and the sea, are totally extraneous to us and impossible for us to live in; hence the largely parallel course in this century of the exploration of outer space and of oceans along the tracks of the same technological progress. Therefore both studies — thanks to a host of materials of entirely new design, including powerful sensors of every kind, faster and faster, more and more reliable calculation means, more and more perfect "miniaturizations," more and more efficient automatic devices — have achieved once unimaginable goals in the field of direct investigation, — investigation through the mediation of instruments. And in the same years, both sciences contributed together to make man the direct protagonist of natural research. Remarkably, Auguste Piccard, a physicist and civil engineer who was a true pioneer in the exploration of the atmosphere (in 1934 his balloon reached a height of 17,500 meters), was at the same time very interested in the study of ocean depths, and to this purpose he designed in 1938, together with M. Cosyns, the first of a long series of bathyscaphes.

But there is a name that is still present in the minds and hearts of those people — white-haired today — who were very keen in their youth on learning about this "new frontier" of human knowledge and human enterprise: William Beebe. This American zoologist can be proud of many scientific achievements that do not concern oceanography: for instance, his four-volume monograph about a pheasant living in the mountains of Nepal, *Catreus wallichi,* published in 1922, is considered a monument to ecology, such as very seldom has been dedicated to a single animal species. But for the majority of the people who are not specialized but symply very fond of all that concerns the sea, his memory is connected to an epoch-making book: *Half Mile Down.*

The book was translated into several languages and was written with maximum scientific competence and also with a deep human warmth and a great sense of humor: it fascinated and excited millions of people, who felt as if they were true participants of the extraordinary adventure Beebe described. It had started one winter morning in 1928, when Otis Barton knocked at the door of William Beebe's workroom — he was the director of the tropical research department of the New York Zoological Society — and showed him, all in a flutter, a design of his for a bathysphere for undersea exploration. Never before was a proposal accepted with such enthusiasm. In 1930, it had already materialized into a steel sphere with a weight of 2,275 kilograms, locked by a watertight door with a weight of 182 kilograms tightly fixed by ten bolts, and equipped with three windows made of molded quartz cylinders, 20 cm wide and 7 cm thick, inserted into special projections of the sphere. The bathysphere was lowered vertically from a tender ship by means of a steel wire with a diameter of about 22 mm (it could support a weight of 25 tons), along which ran electric wires and telephone wires for communication with the surface. Dives were limited to a depth of about 500 meters during the period of research in 1930, but in 1934 they reached a maximum depth of 923 meters — off Nonesuch Island in the Bermuda Islands — thanks to the remarkable technical improvements of those years.

Revealed by the beam of the floodlights or by their own luminescence, crustaceans, jellyfish, Ctenophora, Cephalopods — fishes until then trapped in the nets of oceanographic ships and brought to the surface either dead or dying — passed by slowly or with a sudden jerk before the experienced but nonetheless fascinated eyes of Beebe and Barton, who were so mesmerized as not to feel the torture of that icy prison of hardly one meter and a half in diameter. "The light of the lamp revealed several small hatchet fishes." "It was a network of luminescence, of a very delicate, wide-mesh fabric, all in motion." "It was an almost round fish, with long vertical fins of moderate height; large eyes, a mouth of normal size and small pectoral fins. The color was brown. The bathysphere turned around a few degrees, leaving the fish in the dim blue shade of the light beam; and it was then that I contemplated all its rare beauty. Along the sides it revealed five lines of unbelievably beautiful lights: one was equatorial, two were arranged above and two below it. The pale-yellow bright spots were half-circled by small photophores of a deep purple color... I named it *Bathysidus pentagrammus*... All my life I will keep the memory of it, as one of the most beautiful creatures I have ever seen." So, remark after remark, page after page, an extraordinary "diary of the abysses" was composed, and after its publication it fascinated readers and made them experience an emotion that, on rereading the book over half a century later, remains unaltered.

After the long period of forced interruption caused by the Second World War, Auguste Piccard started his underwater exploration, in 1948, by testing the bathysphere *FNRS II* without crew off Cape Verde. An improved version of this bathysphere, with G. Huot and P. Willon aboard, reached in 1954, off Dakar, a depth of 4,050 meters. No longer hanging from a wire, as was the case of Beebe's glorious bathysphere, the new underwater craft now available are self-propelled and can move either vertically or horizontally and, as a logical consequence, acquire suitably hydrodynamic shapes. Taking advantage of previous experience, Piccard designed a new bathysphere called *Trieste* as a tribute to the Italian city where it was built. His son, Jacques Piccard, performed several dives in the Mediterranean aboard this bathysphere, reaching in 1956, off the island of

Ponza, a depth of 3,700 meters. Four years later, aboard the same craft, it was possible to accomplish a record dive in the Marianas Trench (Pacific Ocean), reaching a depth of nearly 11,000 meters.

It would be rather difficult, as it was for the oceanographic expeditions on the surface, to give a complete list of all the underwater craft that in the last thirty years have allowed man to carry out underwater exploration. These craft acquired gradually the look of real miniature submarines, as is the case of the craft designed by Captain J.Y. Cousteau (*SP 350, SP 500, Deep Star, Cyana*), the *Deep Quest* by Lockeed, the *Dowb* by General Motors, the *Beaver* by North American Rockwell, the *Star II* by General Dynamics. The diving system composed of the tender ship *Aloha* and the research submarine *Mermaid II* was highly sophisticated. In the summer of 1980, fifty years after the first experiment of William Beebe and Otis Barton, it dived in the same Caribbean waters that had been the theater of those enterprises to honor these pioneers and at the same time to underline the enormous progress made since then in oceanographic exploration.

Another name deserves mention for the large and systematic research this underwater craft effected and for the importance of the information attained in the course of its dives: the *Alvin*. Derived from a prototype that had been designed in 1956 — the *Aluminaut* — this had a highly sophisticated aluminium shell that was the result of collaboration between the United States Navy and some of the most prestigious marine research institutions of the United States, first of all the Woods Hole Oceanographic Institution of Woods Hole, Massachusetts. Among the various achievements of the *Alvin*, one deserves particular mention: direct knowledge — a close and detailed view — of the sea floor at great depths. This was also reached by another very important American research institution (Scripps

Institution of the University of California) from the sea surface, through very sensitive equipment: high and multiple frequency echo sounders, lateral scanning echo sounders, gravity and magnetism gauges, etc. Down there, under thousands of meters of water, it is possible to detect very clearly the barely perceptible but uninterrupted movements that huge clods of the earth's crust make by sliding, like rafts, on the underlying mass of semifluid material, sometimes getting so close to one another as to generate very slow but enormous collisions, or else getting so far apart as to create cracks that let out incandescent lava, which, after solidifying, brings the earth's crust back to its original condition. This phenomenon — "volcanism" — takes place on the ocean floor and is particularly active along some very long "ridges," such as those that stretch along the bottom in the middle of the Atlantic Ocean and in an area of the Pacific Ocean included between the South American coast and the Galapagos Islands. It is exactly along this ridge that in the 1970s researchers from Stanford University ascertained and carefully studied the presence of a phenomenon closely related to underwater volcanism — "hot springs." Lava, on contacting sea water, cools and shrinks, while water flows inside the ensuing cracks and then, on contacting the rocks, gets hot and flows out again through other cracks. An exploration carried out by the *Alvin* in that area — at a depth of about 2,500 meters — ascertained that these hot springs are usually clearly visible because of their opaque waters; this is caused by the precipitation of soluble elements — such as sulphides and carbonates — which takes place when the water of the springs cools while mixing with the surrounding water. But the greatest surprise of a biological nature was another phenomenon: the sea floor, where the temperature of the springs did not exceed 25 °C (in some cases it can reach a temperature of even 400 °C), was literally packed with crabs, polychaete worms, siphonophora, bivalve mollusks, and other invertebrates, among which a few fishes still unknown to science. It was a real oasis of life — in an environment usually deprived of it — whose existence was made possible by the great quantities of sulphides and methane dissolved in the hot springs: in fact, these compounds, used as energy sources by bacteria, contribute to a massive development of microorganisms that in turn feed, either directly or indirectly, animals of many sorts.

What contribution do data collected in the course of over a century concerning the sea floor and particularly its fishes make, nowadays, to oceanographic research? The reader should know by now that a satisfactory answer would mean filling a large library up to the ceiling. Therefore, we must necessarily condense here some concise and simple information. So let's start by tracing the boundaries of what is called the deep sea, making them coincide with the external edges of the continental shelf, the underwater extension of dry land located at a depth of about 110 to 150 meters. The continental shelf shows an average depth increase slightly over two meters per kilometer. However, in some cases, for instance where the coast is particularly steep, its external border can be noticed at a distance of a few tens of meters from the shore; on the contrary, in other cases — as in the case of the coasts of Siberia facing the Arctic Ocean — it may be necessary to move 1,000 to 1,500 kilometers off the coast to find it. An increase of the slope indicates that the continental shelf is gradually turning into the "continental slope," where there is an average depth increase of about 40 to 50 meters per kilometer. The continental slope, which can extend as far as nearly 200 kilometers, is crossed by very steep "canyons" and ends up in the "abyssal plane," an immense shelf located at an average depth of about 4,000 meters, made uneven by several mountain groups (there are hundreds of volcanoes in the Pacific Ocean, for instance, with typically flat tops, which sometimes rise up to less than 1,000 meters from the surface) and of abyssal trenches, whose depth exceeds 10,000 meters.

Excluding the waters of the continental shelf, which form the so-called neritic region, the remaining waters constitute the oceanic region (about nineteen-twentieths of the total oceanic volume). So, with the exception of its more superficial or epipelagic area — which is the realm of tunny fish, dolphins, mackerels, swordfish, squids, sharks, flying fish, and sea turtles — the largest portion of this enormous liquid mass, from about 150 to 200 meters downward, represents what we generally call the deep sea, the oppressive perennial realm of darkness, pressure, and cold.

In the more limpid oceanic waters, typical of tropical and subtropical areas, even at a depth of 100 meters the intensity of sunlight is so strong that it allows chlorophyllian photosynthesis of the plant organisms, which is already impossible at much lower depths in less clear waters, such as temperate and cold waters. Going farther down toward the bottom, sunlight turns gradually into twilight, until even the most powerful components of the sun's radiation — blue and green — are completely absorbed and total darkness begins.

If we locate the fading out of the last light gleam at an average depth of 1,000 meters and if we assume — as before — the average depth of the oceans to be of about 4,000 meters, we can calculate the relative importance — considering the total volume of the oceanic zone — of well-lighted (euphotic) layers, scarcely lighted (dysphotic) layers, and un-lighted (aphotic) layers, with the relevant percentages of 2.5, 22.5, and 75 percent.

With depth, also the heat of the sun, though efficiently distributed by the powerful mixing action of the wind, finds it more and more difficult to penetrate the water. Hence there is a condition of very low temperatures, which below 2,000 meters tend to the same homogeneous and steady values in all the oceans, included between 0.6 and 3.6 °C (the same applies to salinity, which has a value of about 34 per thousand practically everywhere).

However, the most important and unique characteristic of the deep-sea environment is represented by a very high hydrostatic pressure together with the total absence of light. In fact, a liquid blanket, with a thickness and weight that increase with depth, gravitates on the organisms living down there; and this gradual pressure increase — one atmosphere every ten meters — reaches a value that at the maximum oceanic depth corresponds to a thousand times the pressure to which we are subjected. The animals of the abyss have reacted to these prohibitive conditions with such efficient anatomical and physiological modifications that they survive them perfectly, so much so that many of them cannot live without them or need them to perform their vital functions properly. Therefore fishes can reach depths that exceed 7,000 meters (at this depth it was possible to catch *Bassogigas profundissimus*, of the Brotulidae family, and *Careproctus amblystomopsis*, of the Liparidae family), and various species of invertebrates (actiniarides, polychaetes, bivalve mollusks, and gastropods, isopod and amphipod crustaceans, holothurians and many more) reach even greater depths, down to the bottom of the abyssal oceanic trenches. Among these animals — called by marine biologists ultraabyssal or adalii — crinoids and pogonophorans apparently bear the greatest depths (over 10,000 meters); pycnogonids, cirriped, and decapod crustaceans have never been caught until now at depths exceeding 6,860, 6,840, and 4,430 meters respectively; as to sea urchins, starfishes, and ophiuroids, it appears that they are no longer present at depths between 7,000 and 8,000 meters.

At depths from 200 to 1,000 meters — in the layer characterized by a twilight that fades out gradually — we find the so-called mesopelagic ichthyofauna, composed by rather heterogeneous families (Alepocephalida, Argentinida, Bathylagida, Gonostomatida, Sternoptichida, Melanostomatida, Cauliodontida, Stomiatida, Chlorophtalmida, Paralepidida, Anopterida, Michtiophida, Nemictida, Bregmacerotida, Gempilida). They are of a rather small size, of a blackish or reddish color, and feed on planktonic invertebrates, which they often follow in the course of their long nightly migrations toward more superficial waters. There are also some voracious predators, of a size of less than 20 cm for Stomiatida and over one meter for *Anotopterus* and *Alepisaurus*; their aggressiveness is clearly demonstrated by their very large mouths equipped with scimitar-shaped teeth and extraordinarily dilatable stomachs (*Chiasmodon*, for instance, can swallow prey of a size exceeding its own).

Below 1,000 meters, where total darkness begins, there is the bathypelagic zone, where the ichthyofauna is more dispersed due to the ever increasing scarcity of food, all of it coming, either directly or indirectly, from the very distant epipelagic zone. This ichthyofauna consists of a smaller number of fish species, characterized among other things by a remarkable reduction of the skeleton and often by the disappearance of the swim bladder. This is the realm of Evermanellida, Giganturida, Saccopharyngida, and, especially, Ceratida, the grotesque "deep-sea angler," living at great depths. These — about eighty known species until now — attract their prey by moving in front of their huge mouths a sticklike appendage (illicium) equipped with a luminous gland at the end that works as bait. This is a behavior typical only to females, due to the following extraordinary reason: males are of much smaller size (the male of *Ceratias holboei*, for instance, is less than 10 cm long, whereas the female is over one meter long), and after living on their own for a short time, they cling firmly with their mouths to the skin of their "brides" and become real parasites whose unique, entirely autonomous physiological function is to fecundate the eggs laid by females.

N.B. Marshall, one of the most important and brilliant experts on the subject, makes a distinction between the bathypelagic fishes proper, which move constantly suspended in the water, never touching the bottom, and benthospelagic fishes, which, on the contrary, swim or remain suspended very near the sea floor and sometimes touch it. For benthonic fishes this is instead the natural life condition, as they lie almost constantly on the sea floor, from which they also get their food, consisting of organic materials coming from the upper layers of water or organisms — including fish — that they feed on. Whereas on the upper part of the continental slope the benthonic ichthyofauna includes species well known to us because we are used to catching them — codfish, scorpion fish, halibut, and "flat fishes," sharks, rays, etc. — there where the slope sinks gradually into deeper and deeper darkness, many new and peculiar species begin to appear. Among them, some families deserve to be mentioned, such as Gadoids (the same order to which codfish belong), including Morida and Macrura. The latter are unmistakable because of the gradual tapering of the body into a long and sharp tail, with no caudal fin at its end, and because of a head that protrudes into a large rostrum below which the mouth opens. Whereas "rat's tails" — this is the common name for Macrura — that live at depths exceeding 600 meters (*Coelorhynchus, Macrourus*) have very large eyes, the species living at greater depths (*Gadomus* and *Bathygadus*, for instance) have much smaller eyes. Such a reduction of the visual organs — probably due to their increasing "uselessness" — is extreme in those families that, like the already mentioned Brotulidae and Liparidae, reach depths of 6,000 to 7,000 meters.

As our towns, at sunset, glimmer with lights, so the twilight and then the night of the deep sea are continuously dotted and streaked by thousands of lights, either steady or flickering, emitted by crustaceans, mollusks, polychaete worms, ctenophora, ophiuroids, and, especially, fishes. About forty families of these vertebrates display the phenomenon of bioluminescence, and the great majority of them can be found in the sea at depths exceeding 200 meters. Mesopelagic fishes, at depths between 300 and 1,000 meters, include most of the luminescent species, so that over 60 percent of the species and 90 percent of the individuals that are caught show this characteristic. The Mychtophidae family — it is not a coincidence that they are called "lantern fishes" — includes the largest number of luminescent genera and species, but the Opistoproctida, Macrura, Ogcocephalida, Ceratiodes, and Stomiatoides include plenty of them.

The light emitted by fishes, produced by the action of an enzyme (luciferase) on a phenolic compound called luciferin, may be generated by some special bacteria living inside special tube-shaped structures, or by the fishes themselves by means of light-emitting organs — or photophores — usually consisting of a "photogenic gland," a transparent lens that concentrates light and an internal surface of pigmented cells that reflect it, to which some colored "filters" are frequently added, giving light a special tonality.

The variety of "luminous signs" that characterize the various fish species is unbelievable: there are continuous or flickering lights, quite different as to number, size, location, or color, from the "necklaces" of photophores that spread along the sides of many Mychtophida to the large ocular photophores, emit-ting a deep blue light, of Stomiatoides; from the already mentioned "luminous baits" of Ceratiodes to the "pyrotechnic fires" produced by Searsida by emptying toward the outside the luminous contents of a gland located at the base of the pectoral fins.

The functions that can be ascribed to the phenomenon of bioluminescence of depth fishes are just as various: the signaling of their presence to other individuals of the same species, in particular individuals of the opposite sex; the attraction of prey; a warning to possible antagonists and adversaries to remain at a distance; camouflage; the lighting, though very faint, of the surrounding environment, which allows extremely sensitive eyes (such as the eyes of meso- and bathypelagic fishes) to detect contours; and many more.

Freshwater fishes

Osteoichthyes appeared at the beginning of the Devonian period, therefore earlier than Chondroichthyes, with primitive forms suited to fresh water that later gave origin to not only 96 percent of the fish species living today, but also all terrestrial vertebrates.

Already at that time it was possible to recognize Osteoichthyes because they had an ossified exoskeleton, at least partially — hence their name — gills enclosed in a branchial chamber covered by a scale called an operculum, and one or two air bags, deriving from a ventral diverticulum of the pharynx, that helped facilitate branchial breathing through a sort of pulmonary breathing.

Since their first appearance, Osteoichthyes have been divided into two groups, Sarcopterygoids, so called because their paired fins have muscles and endoskeletal elements, and Actinopterygoids, whose fins are simple cutaneous folds supported by dermal beams. Sarcopterygoids include Dipnoans and Crossopterygoids; the latter are believed to be the direct ancestors of terrestrial vertebrates.

Nowadays, Dipnoans are represented only by three surviving genera, scattered over three continents as a consequence of continental drift: the genus Neoceratodus with one species in Australia, Lepidosiren (page 212) with one species in South America, and Protopterus (page 212), with four species in Africa. All of them live in dry, tropical areas, breathing air when waters stagnate, and, except Neoceratodus aestivating when waters dry up; that is, they remain asleep inside a cocoon of a hardened secretion, sunk deep into the mud but provided with a tiny hole to allow breathing. Dipnoans, in addition to gills, have one or two dorsal lungs, ventrally connected to the pharynx through a pneumatic duct, and Protopterus depends on air to such an extent that it will drown if prevented from surfacing from time to time.

Crossopterygoids were believed to have been extinct for at least 65 million years until, on December 23, 1938, not far off the coast of South Africa, a specimen was caught that belonged to a surviving species of the coelacanths group, Latimeria chalumnae. From that moment, about two hundred have been caught in the deep waters around the Comoro Islands in the Indian Ocean, where the German zoologist Hans Fricke has been able to examine them. An extraordinary feature of these rather stout fishes, of a blue-purplish color, is the fact that when swimming they move front fin and counterlateral back fin in the same direction, exactly like tetrapods.

Whereas the descendants of Crossopterygoids chose to become adapted to terrestrial life and abandoned water except in cases, such as Sirenians or Cetaceans, in which then chose to return to it, the evolutionary history of Actinopterygoids has entirely developed in the water. They are usually divided into three groups, called Chondrosteans, Olosteans, and Teleosteans, corresponding respectively to three subsequent specialization waves in the course of which the more evolved new group replaced the previous one in dominating over the water. Chondrosteans have dwindled today to three families only, all characterized by a cartilaginous endoskeleton.

The first family, Polypterii, consists of eleven species, ten of which belong to the genus Polypterus (page 212), which is definitely one of the most primitive. Polypterii live in African fresh waters, in areas subject to recurrent drought periods, and when the water has entirely dried out, they begin a sort of latent life, breathing air through two ventral pulmonary bags, exactly like Dipnoans.

Then there is the family of Acipensera, or sturgeons, which numbers 23 species scattered in the cold and temperate areas of the boreal hemisphere. Sturgeons have an elongate body, along which run five longitudinal series of ossified dermal plates, and they have an extendible lower jaw with no teeth in adult individuals. The air bag has evolved into a large dorsal swim-bladder, connected to the pharyngeal vault by a pneumatic duct, but it no longer has a breathing purpose, and serves to control hydrostatic balance and pressure.

The third family, Polyodontes, consists of two species only, the best-known of which, Polyodon spathula (page 216), has a very elongate snout, but neither dorsal plates nor an extendible mouth.

During the 100 million years of the Mesozoic period, Olosteans replaced Chondrosteans, from which they had evolved, and expanded in the internal waters and especially in the oceans. Then the whole group became extinct, except seven species of the genus Lepisosteus (page 217), one of which is about 3 m long, and one species only of the whole Amiiforms order, Amia calva (page 216), which may be considered a true living fossil. These aggressive and voracious fishes live in the eastern fresh waters of North and Central America, where they are considered dangerous for the local ichthyofauna.

Teleosteans, with a mainly ossified endoskeleton, evolved from Olosteans in the late Mesozoic period and went on expanding, leading to an unbelievable variety of forms. Their success must be largely ascribed to their enormous reproduction capacities, thanks to the production of an enormous number of telo-lecithal eggs (the gilthead can lay as many as a million eggs per kg of body weight in one season), to their amazing swimming abilities, obtained through the sophisticated controlling organs of the muscular muscles and fin movements, and thanks to the complicated mobility of the mouth and therefore a much wider feeding range. According to Nelson (1984), the superorder of Teleosteans consists of 35 orders, 109 families, 3,876 genera and 20,812 species. Fresh-water species make up 40 percent of these, though continental waters are only one small fraction of the waters of the whole world. This means that, in the course of their passage from the ocean to the continental waters, Teleosteans have undergone a remarkable process of adaptational differentation caused by the more restricted isolation of these environments and by the more variable and less stable conditions of their ecosystem.

From a systematic point of view, fresh-water fishes are a rather homogeneous unity: just two orders of the Ostariophyses super order, Cyprinids and Siluroids, number 57 families with about 5,600 species, which means 75 percent of fresh-water Telosteans and 31 percent of the Teleosteans of the whole world. These are comparatively underdeveloped species, spread all over the continents, Antarctica and Greenland excluded.

Unlike most fishes, Ostariophyses have a highly developed sense of hearing, as the acoustic vibrations brought from the outside into contact with the gases inside the swim-bladder can be transmitted to the endolymph of the internal ear through a series of ossicleds deriving from the first four or more skull vertebrae. Another characteristic of Ostariophyses is that when wounded certain special skin cells release a pheromonal substance that alerts the other members of the group, in a sort of altruistic connection.

The Cypriniforms order includes 2,422 species grouped into six families and is therefore the largest order of Telosteans after Perciforms. As to families, we can mention the quiet Cyprinids, such as the carp, Cyprinus carpio (pages 229, 231) and the goldfish Carassius auratus (pages 229, 232), or Characins, including the terrible piranha of the genus Serrasalmus (page 224), or Gymnotides, which can emit electric discharges, like Gymnotus carapo (page 225). Siluroids are composed of thirty-one families, with 2,111 species, 1,300 of which live in South America, and only fifty have adapted to the sea environment. Their mouth is surrounded by one to four pairs of barbels with a tactual and chemosensorial purpose. The first beam of the dorsal fin and of the pectoral fin is often transformed into a hard stinger with poisonous glands. The three best-known families are Siluroids, including the giant Silirus glanis (page 244), which, thanks to its size, 3 m, and weight, 250 kg, can be considered the largest Telostean of the European internal waters; Ichtalurides, originating from North America, some of which are the subject of intense breeding; and Clarides, which breathe atmospheric oxygen through para-branchial organs that sometimes entirely replace gills.

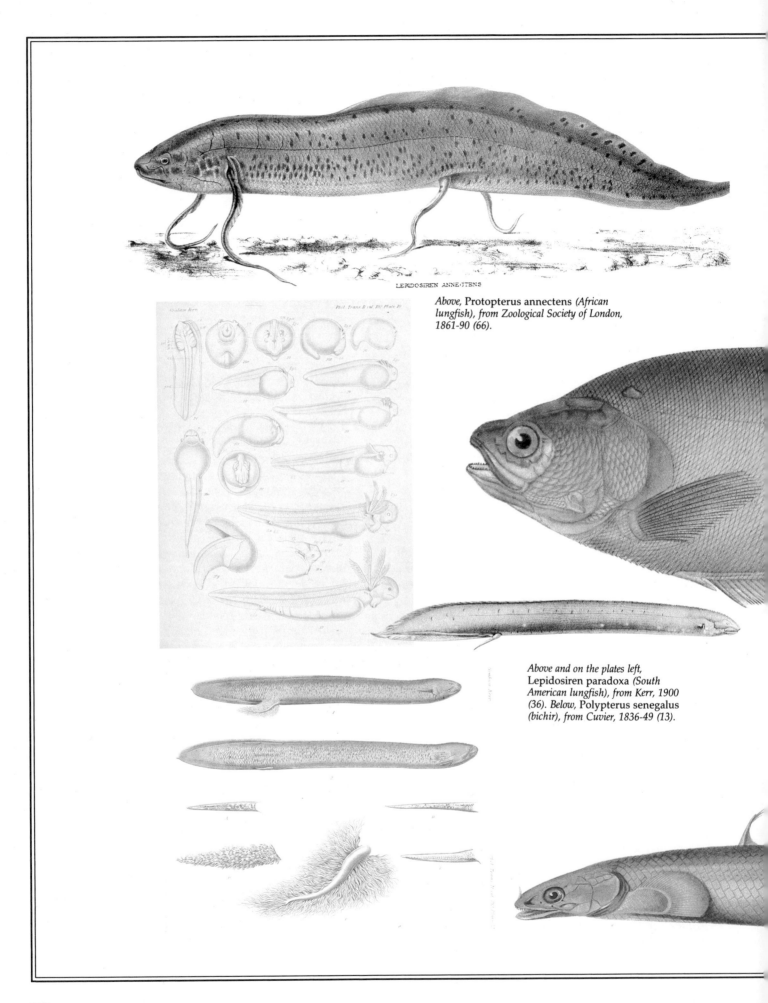

LEPIDOSIREN ANNECTENS

Above, Protopterus annectens *(African lungfish), from Zoological Society of London, 1861-90 (66).*

Above and on the plates left, Lepidosiren paradoxa *(South American lungfish), from Kerr, 1900 (36). Below,* Polypterus senegalus *(bichir), from Cuvier, 1836-49 (13).*

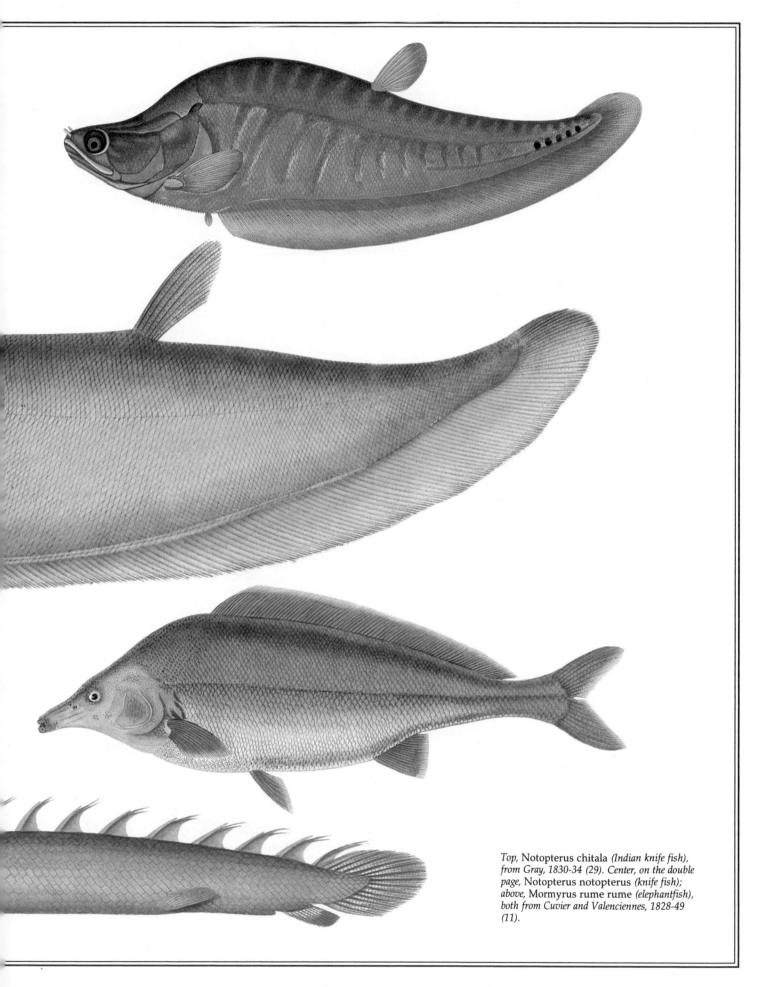

Top, Notopterus chitala *(Indian knife fish),* from Gray, 1830-34 *(29). Center, on the double page,* Notopterus notopterus *(knife fish); above,* Mormyrus rume rume *(elephantfish), both from Cuvier and Valenciennes, 1828-49 (11).*

213

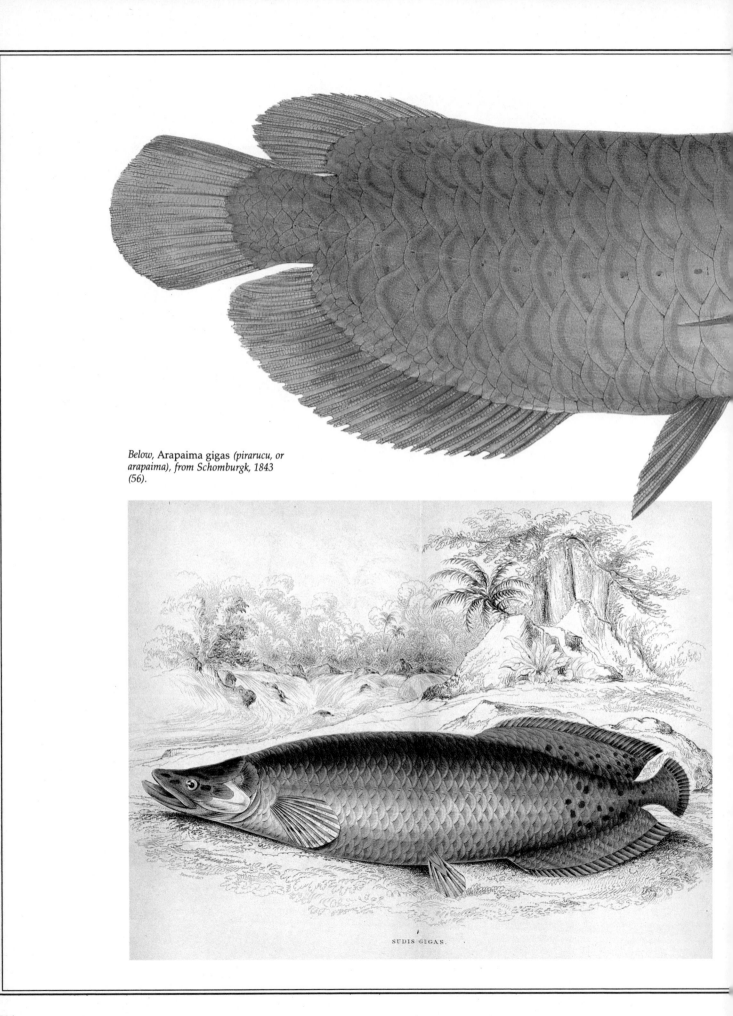

Below, Arapaima gigas *(pirarucu, or arapaima), from Schomburgk, 1843 (56).*

SUDIS GIGAS.

214

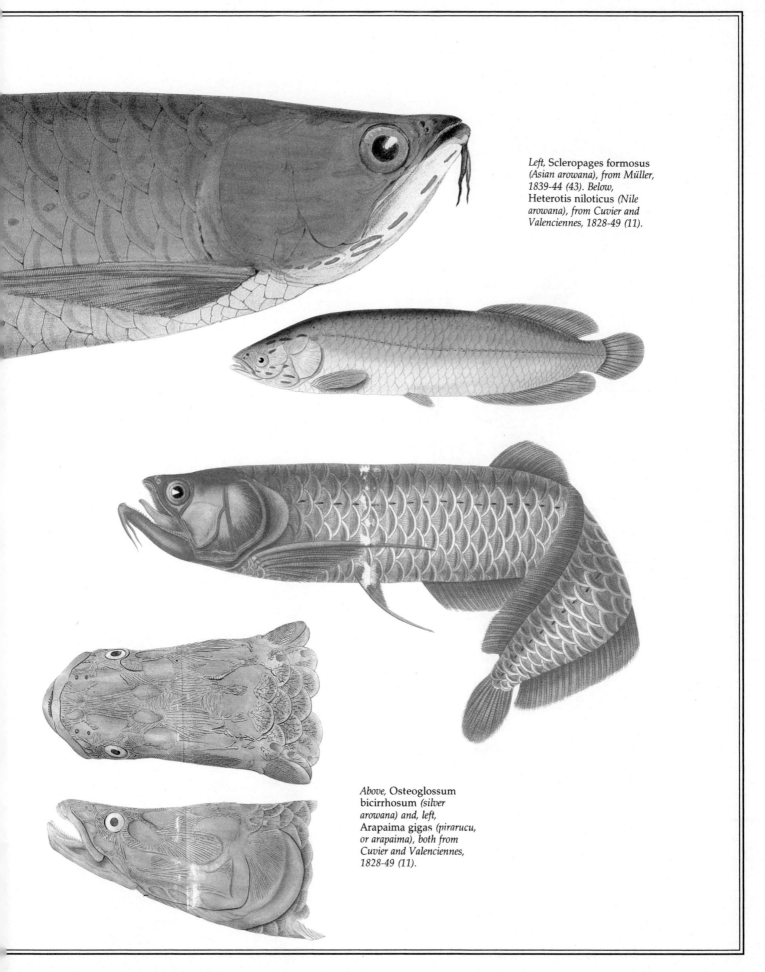

Left, Scleropages formosus *(Asian arowana), from Müller, 1839-44 (43).* Below, Heterotis niloticus *(Nile arowana), from Cuvier and Valenciennes, 1828-49 (11).*

Above, Osteoglossum bicirrhosum *(silver arowana) and, left,* Arapaima gigas *(pirarucu, or arapaima), both from Cuvier and Valenciennes, 1828-49 (11).*

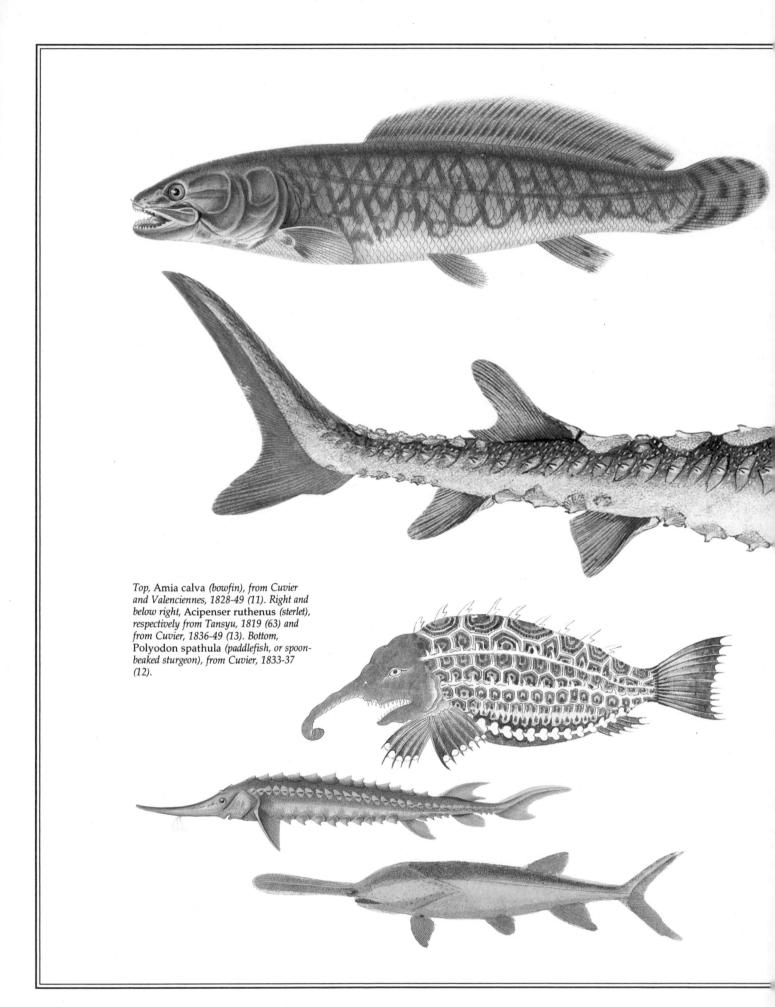

Top, Amia calva *(bowfin), from Cuvier and Valenciennes, 1828-49 (11). Right and below right,* Acipenser ruthenus *(sterlet), respectively from Tansyu, 1819 (63) and from Cuvier, 1836-49 (13). Bottom,* Polyodon spathula *(paddlefish, or spoon-beaked sturgeon), from Cuvier, 1833-37 (12).*

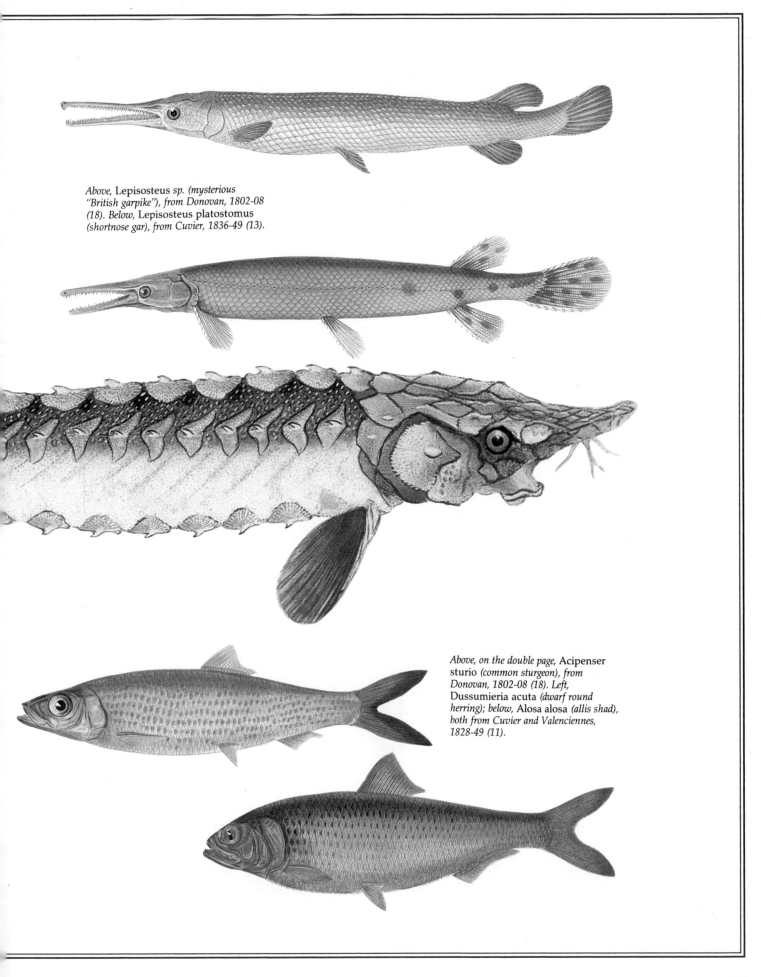

Above, Lepisosteus *sp. (mysterious "British garpike"), from Donovan, 1802-08 (18). Below,* Lepisosteus platostomus *(shortnose gar), from Cuvier, 1836-49 (13).*

Above, on the double page, Acipenser sturio *(common sturgeon), from Donovan, 1802-08 (18). Left,* Dussumieria acuta *(dwarf round herring); below,* Alosa alosa *(allis shad), both from Cuvier and Valenciennes, 1828-49 (11).*

Left, Alosa fallax *(twaite shad), from Donovan, 1802-08 (18). Below,* Ilisha elongata *(slender shad), from Gray, 1830-34 (29).*

Above, Microstoma microstoma *(deep-sea smelt); right,* Glossanodon leioglossus *(Argentine or herring smelt), both from Cuvier and Valenciennes, 1828-49 (11).*

Above, Salmo trutta *(brown trout, or brooktrout), from Zoological Society of London, 1861-90 (66). Left,* Salvelinus *sp. (brown trout, or brooktrout), from Donovan, 1802-08 (18). Below,* Hucho perryi *(hucho trout), from Cuvier, 1836-49 (13).*

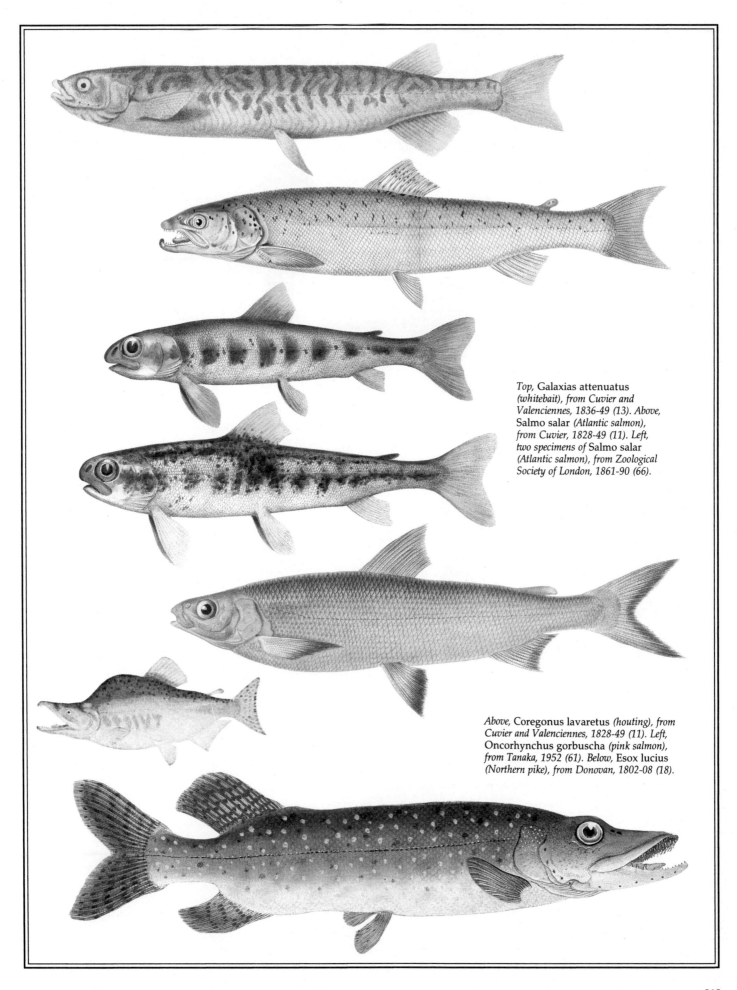

Top, Galaxias attenuatus
*(whitebait), from Cuvier and
Valenciennes, 1836-49 (13). Above,*
Salmo salar *(Atlantic salmon),
from Cuvier, 1828-49 (11). Left,*
two specimens of Salmo salar
*(Atlantic salmon), from Zoological
Society of London, 1861-90 (66).*

Above, Coregonus lavaretus *(houting), from
Cuvier and Valenciennes, 1828-49 (11). Left,*
Oncorhynchus gorbuscha *(pink salmon),
from Tanaka, 1952 (61). Below,* Esox lucius
(Northern pike), from Donovan, 1802-08 (18).

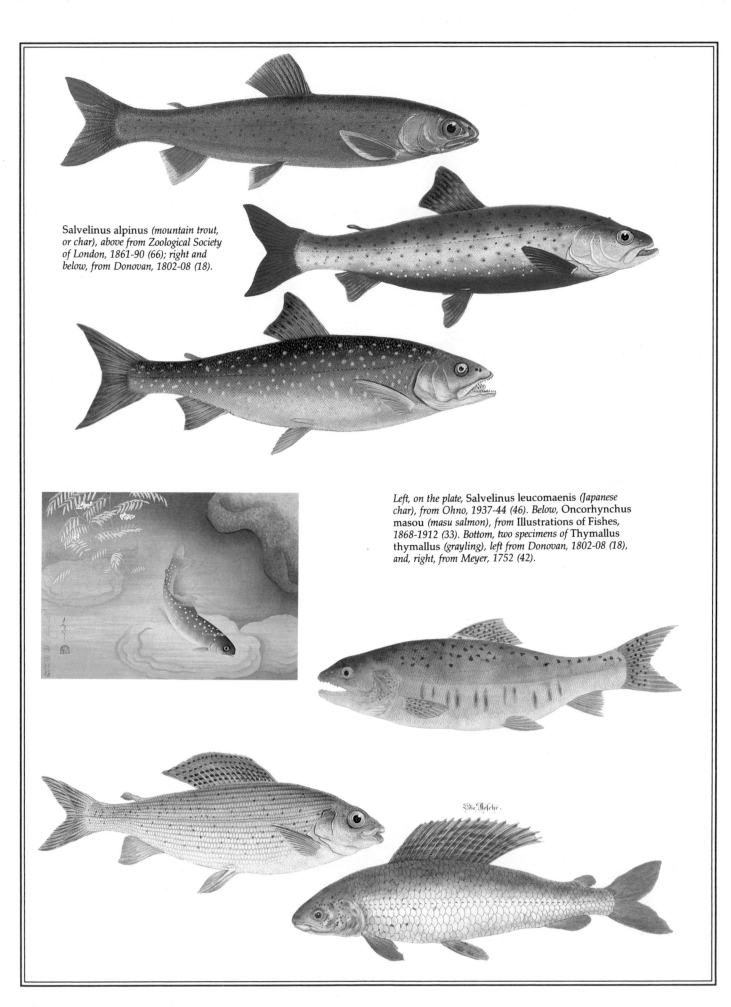

Salvelinus alpinus *(mountain trout, or char), above from Zoological Society of London, 1861-90 (66); right and below, from Donovan, 1802-08 (18).*

Left, on the plate, Salvelinus leucomaenis *(Japanese char), from Ohno, 1937-44 (46). Below,* Oncorhynchus masou *(masu salmon), from Illustrations of Fishes, 1868-1912 (33). Bottom, two specimens of* Thymallus thymallus *(grayling), left from Donovan, 1802-08 (18), and, right, from Meyer, 1752 (42).*

On the plate, Plecoglossus altivelis *(ayu, or sweetfish), from Ohno, 1937-44 (46). Below, top,* Osmerus eperlanus eperlanus *(smelt, or sparling); center,* Coregonus albula *(vedance); bottom,* Umbra krameri *(European mudminnow), all from Cuvier and Valenciennes, 1828-49 (11).*

Left, Potamorhina laticeps *(Curimatid); below, left,* Lebiasina bimaculata *(two-spot lebiasina), both from* Cuvier and Valenciennes, 1828-49 (11). *On the plate below,* Pristella maxillaris *(water goldfinch), from* Aqualium, *1932-66 (1).*

Above left, Anisitsia notata *(Anostomid); above right,* Pyrrhulina filamentosa *(pirrhulina), both from Cuvier and Valenciennes, 1828-49 (11).*

Above, Hoplias malabaricus *(Erythrinid); right,* Leporinus leschenaulti *(three-spotted leporinus), both from Cuvier and Valenciennes, 1828-49 (11).*

On the plate above, Chalceus macrolepidotus *(pink-tail characin), from Schomburgk, 1843 (56). Above,* Ctenolucius hujeta *(pike characin, or blunt-nosed gar), from De Spix and Agassiz, 1829 (17). Below,* Charax gibbosus *(glass headstander) and, left,* Distichodus niloticus *(Citharinid), both from Cuvier and Valenciennes, 1828-49 (11).*

Right, Anostomus fasciatus *(banded anostomus); above,* Prochilodus insignis *(flag-tailed prochilodus), both from Schomburgk, 1843 (56).*

SCHIZODON FASCIATUS.

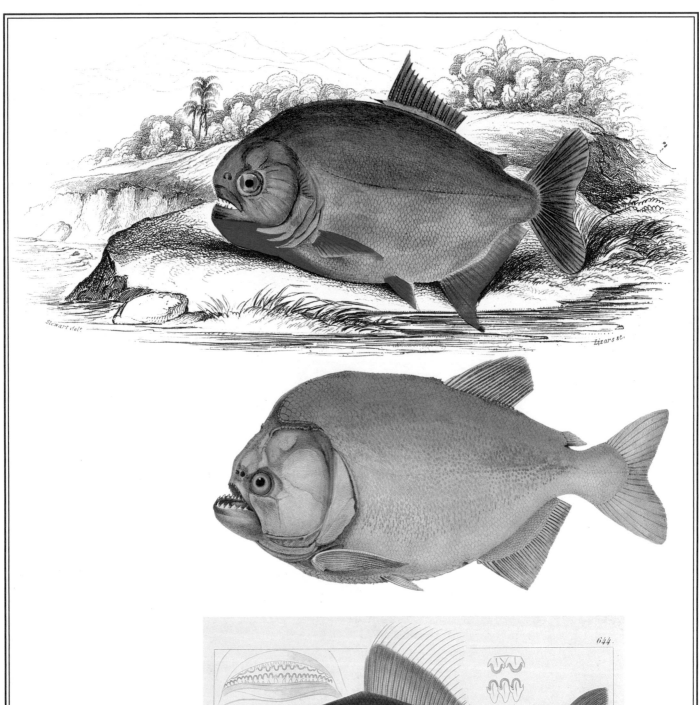

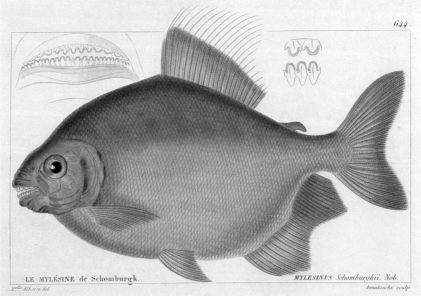

Top, Serrasalmus nattereri
*(piranha), from Schomburgk, 1843
(56). Center*, Serrasalmus piraya
*(black piranha), from De Spix and
Agassiz, 1829 (17). Bottom*,
Myleus sp. *(Characid), from
Cuvier and Valenciennes, 1828-49
(11).*

LE MYLÉSINE de Schomburgk.

MYLESINUS Schomburgkii. Nob.

Melle Alberts del.

Annedouche sculp.

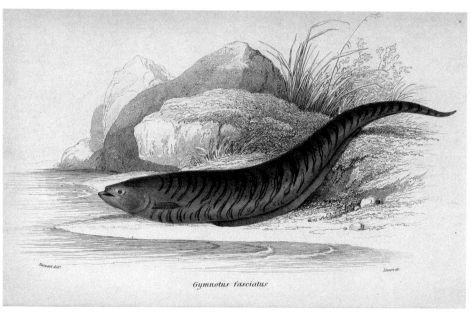

Gymnotus fasciatus

Top, Myleus schomburgkii
(Characid); Gymnotus carapo
(banded knife fish), both from
Schomburgk, 1843 (56). Center,
Myleus altipinnis *(Characid),*
from Cuvier and Valenciennes,
1828-49 (11).

Above and left, Tinca tinca *(tench), respectively from Donovan, 1802-08 (18), and from Houghton, 1879 (31). Below, from top, Cyprinus alburnus = Alburnus alburnus (bleak); Cyprinus gobio = Gobio gobio (gudgeon); Leuciscus leuciscus (dace), all from Donovan, 1802-08 (18). Below left, Carassius carassius (crucian carp), from Meyer, 1752 (42).*

Top left, Rutilus rutilus *(roach)*; top right,
Leuciscus cephalus *(chub)*; above left,
Barbus barbus *(barbel)*; above right, Abramis
brama *(bream)*, all from Donovan, 1802-08
(18). Left above, Chondrostoma nasus *(nase)*,
from Meyer, 1752 *(42)*; left below, Gobio
gobio *(gudgeon)*, from Cuvier and
Valenciennes, 1828-49 *(11). Below*, Barbus tor
(tor mahseer), from Gray, 1830-34 *(29). Right,
on the plate: top*, Balitora brucei; *center*,
Balitora maculata *(both loaches); bottom*,
Garra gotyla *(Cyprinid), from Gray, 1830-34
(29)*.

Opposite page, from the top, Labeo angra, *from Gray, 1830-34 (29);* Puntius melanampyx *and* Puntius denisonii, *both from Day, 1865 (15);* Labeo dussumieri *(all Cyprinids), from Cuvier and Valenciennes, 1828-49 (11).*
Left, top, Hampala macrolepidota *(hampala), from Cuvier and Valenciennes, 1828-49 (11); center,* Barilius bendelisis *(Cyprinid), from Gray, 1830-34 (29); bottom,* Notemigonus crysoleucas *(golden shiner), from Cuvier and Valenciennes, 1828-49 (11). Below,* Cyprinus carpio *(carp), from D'Orbigny, 1837 (20).*
Right, on the plate, Carassius auratus *(goldfish), from Ohno, 1937-44 (46).*

Left, Labeo calbasu, *from Cuvier, 1836-49 (13). Above,* Labeo angra *(both Cyprinids), from Gray, 1830-34 (29). Right,* Cyprinus carpio *(carp), from Donovan, 1802-08 (18).*

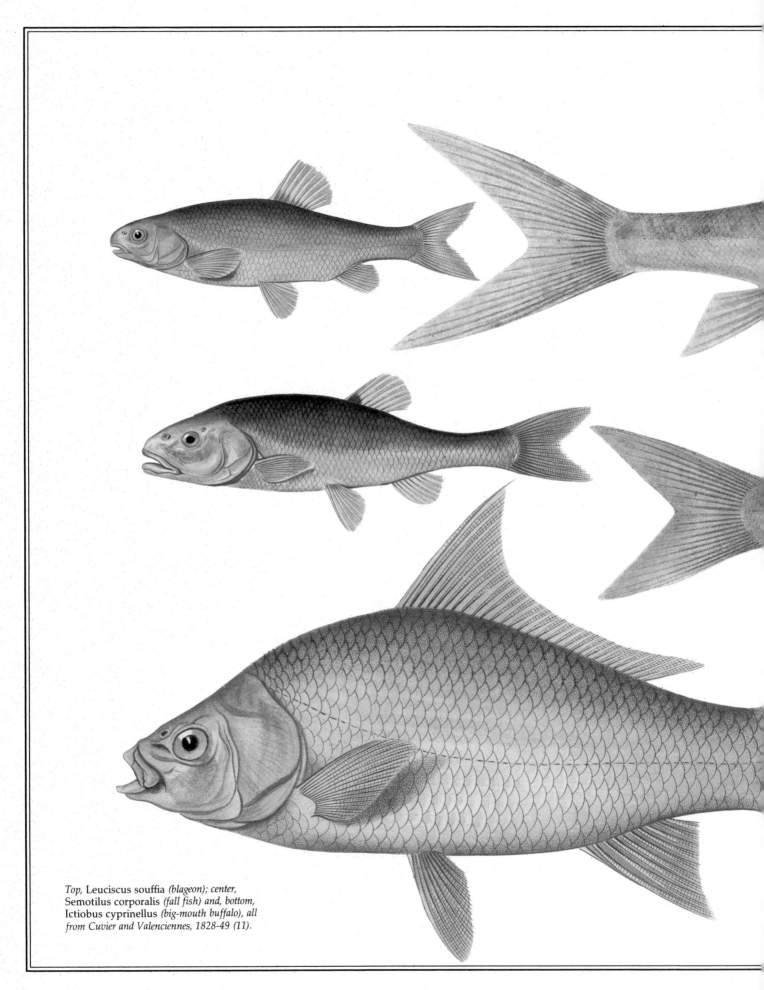

Top, Leuciscus souffia *(blageon); center,*
Semotilus corporalis *(fall fish) and, bottom,*
Ictiobus cyprinellus *(big-mouth buffalo), all
from Cuvier and Valenciennes, 1828-49 (11).*

Top, Labeo umbratus, *and center,* Labeo capensis *(Cyprinids), both from Smith, 1838-49 (58); bottom,* Cyprinus carpio *(red carp), from National Museum of Tokyo, unpublished (45).*

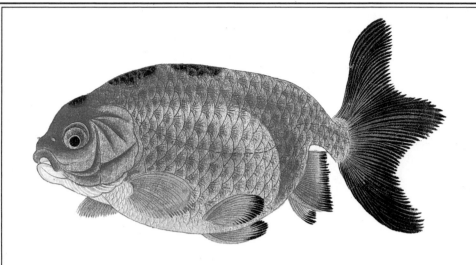

Left, Carassius auratus (goldfish),
from National Museum of Tokyo,
unpublished (45). Below, right and left,
Carassius auratus (goldfish),
respectively from Ohno, 1937-44 (46),
and Tansyu, 1819 (63).

On the plate and below, Carassius auratus (goldfish),
respectively from Tansyu, 1819 (63), and from Takagi,
1850 (60).

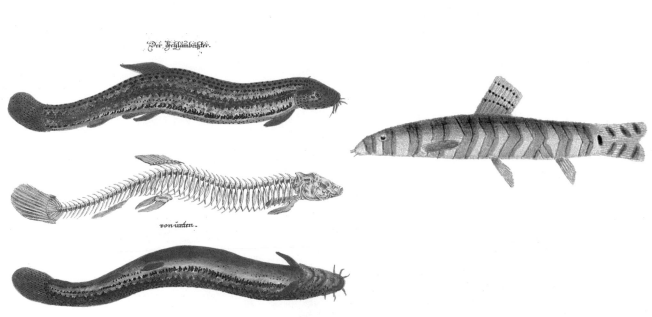

Der Schlammbeißer.

von unten.

Above left, Misgurnus fossilis *(pond loach), from Meyer, 1752 (42); above right*, Lepidocephalichthys thermalis *(loach), from Day, 1865 (15). On the plates: right*, Misgurnus anguillicaudatus *(Japanese weatherfish, Asian pond loach, or dojo); below*, Rhodeus *sp. (bitterling), both from Ohno, 1937-44 (46). Below right*, Noemacheilus barbatulus *(stone loach), from Donovan, 1802-08 (18).*

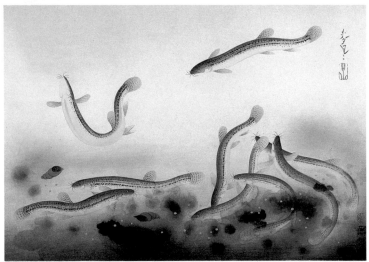

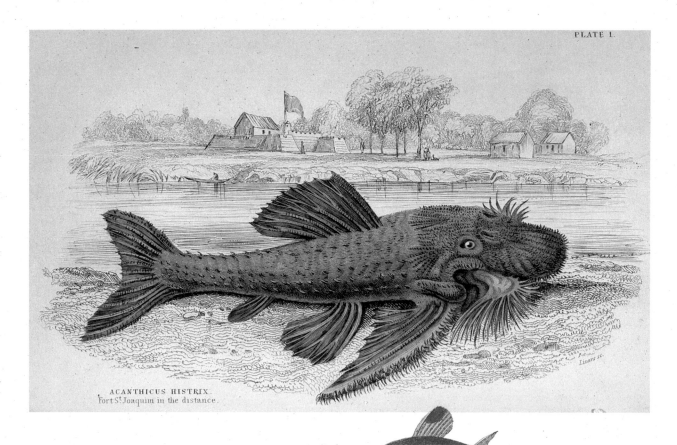

ACANTHICUS HISTRIX.
Fort St. Joaquim in the distance.

PLATE I.

LORICARIA

1—The Cataphracted Cuirassier.   2—Variety of the same.
3—The Yellow Cuirassier.   4—Variety of the same.

Top, on the plate, Acanthicus histrix *(bristlenose catfish), from Schomburgk, 1843 (56).* Above, *Pterygoplichthys duodecimalis (armored catfish), from Cuvier and Valenciennes, 1828-49 (11), and, above top,* Corydoras paleatus *(peppered corydoras), from Bloch, 1785-89 (6). On the plate left, top,* Loricariichthys maculatus *(armored catfish); center,* Loricaria sp. *(armored catfish), and* Hypostomus plecostomus *(sucker catfish); bottom,* Plecostomus sp. *(catfish), all from Bloch, 1785-89 (6).*

Opposite page, top, Aspredo filamentosus *(banjo catfish); center,* Hoplosternum thoracatum *(atipa, or port holpo), from Cuvier and Valenciennes, 1828-49 (11); bottom,* Loricaria cataphracta *(armored catfish), from Cuvier, 1836-49 (13).*

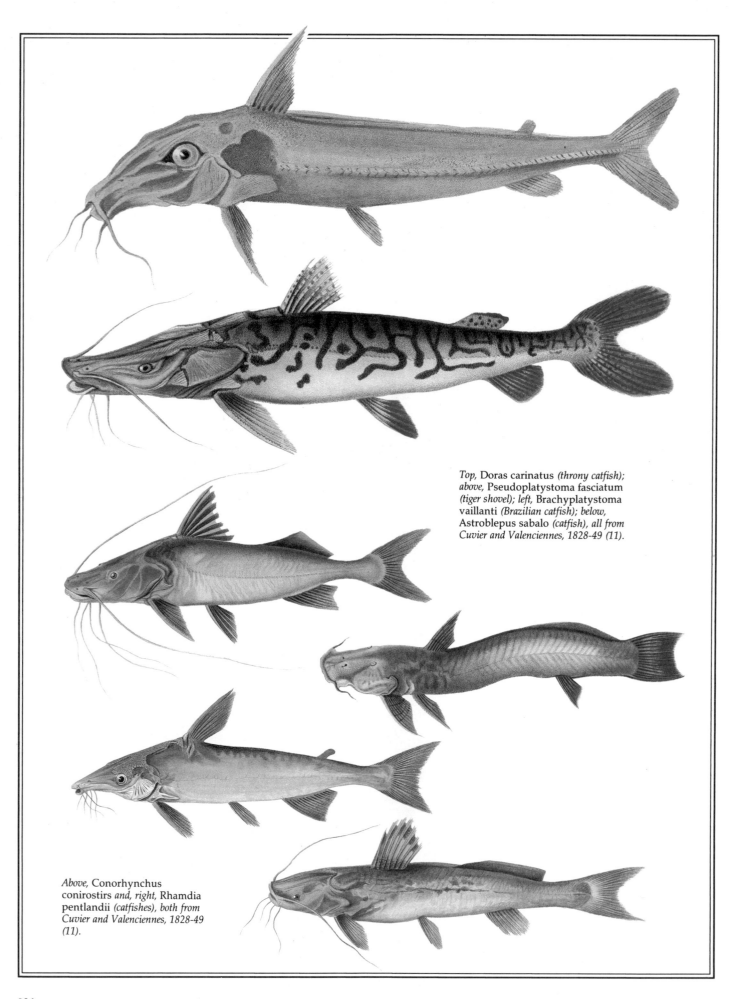

Top, Doras carinatus *(throny catfish);*
above, Pseudoplatystoma fasciatum
(tiger shovel); left, Brachyplatystoma
vaillanti *(Brazilian catfish); below,*
Astroblepus sabalo *(catfish), all from*
Cuvier and Valenciennes, 1828-49 (11).

Above, Conorhynchus
conirostirs *and, right,* Rhamdia
pentlandii *(catfishes), both from*
Cuvier and Valenciennes, 1828-49
(11).

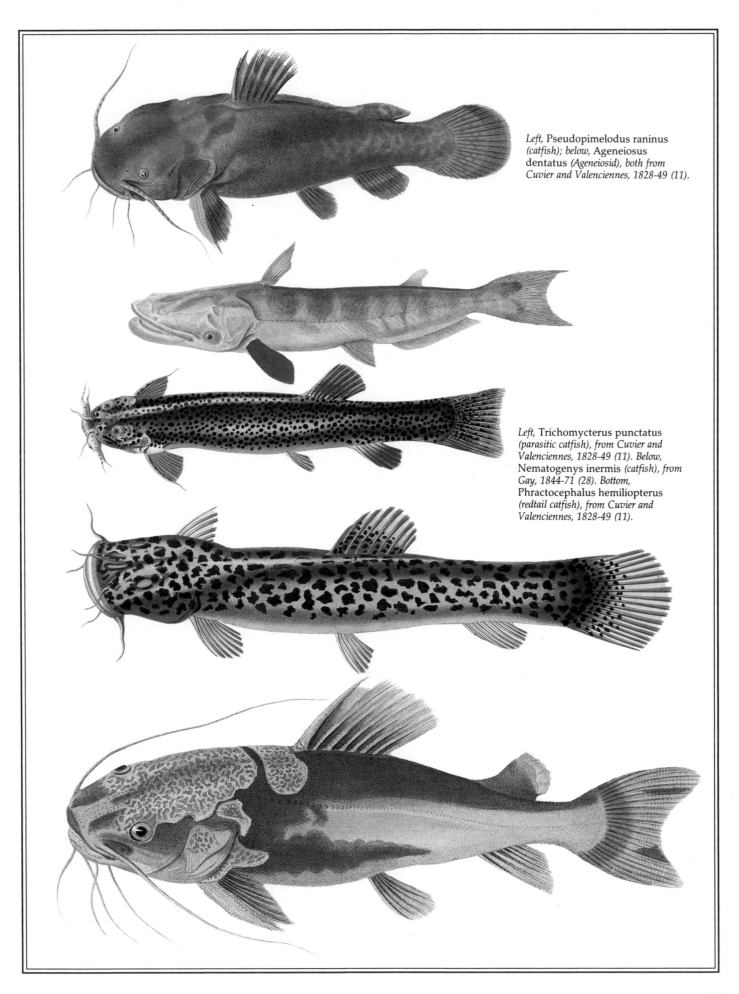

Left, Pseudopimelodus raninus *(catfish); below,* Ageneiosus dentatus *(Ageneiosid), both from Cuvier and Valenciennes, 1828-49 (11).*

Left, Trichomycterus punctatus *(parasitic catfish), from Cuvier and Valenciennes, 1828-49 (11). Below,* Nematogenys inermis *(catfish), from Gay, 1844-71 (28). Bottom,* Phractocephalus hemiliopterus *(redtail catfish), from Cuvier and Valenciennes, 1828-49 (11).*

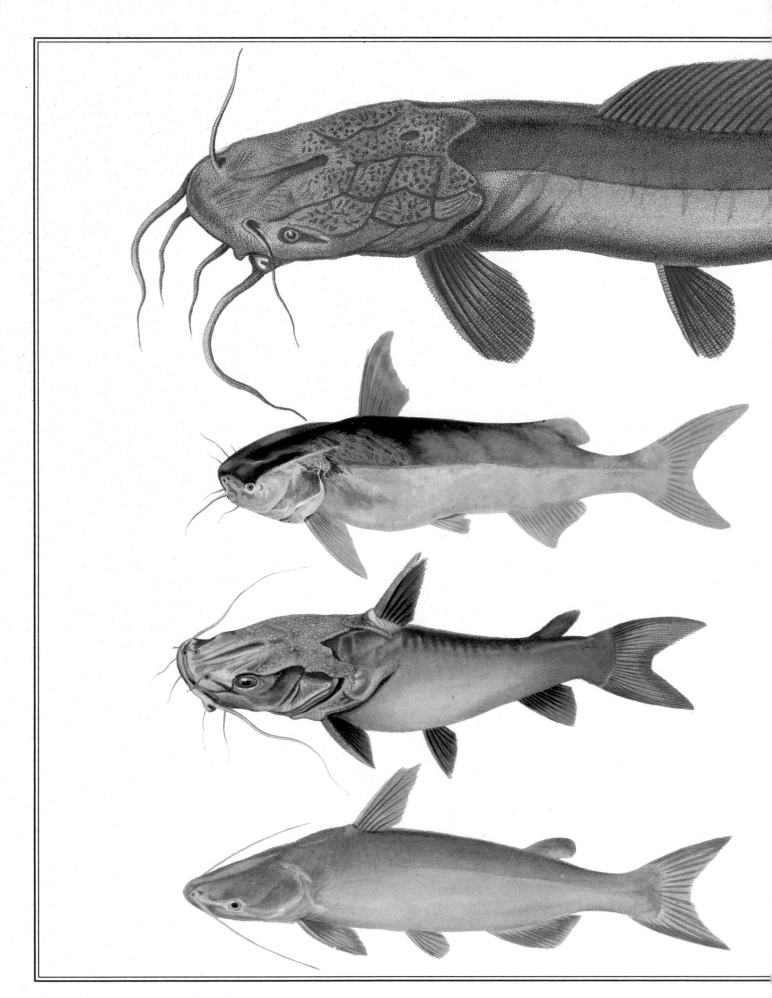

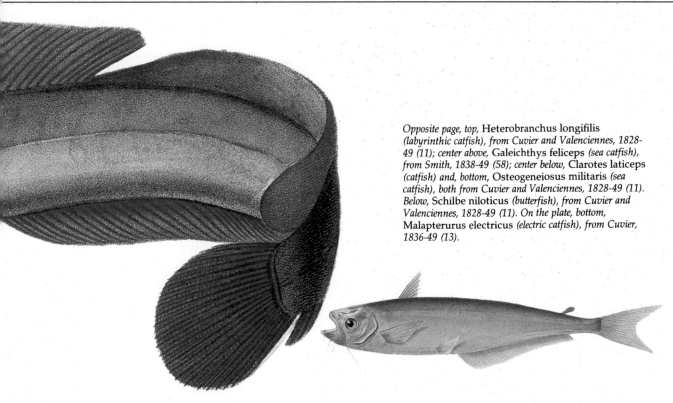

Opposite page, top, Heterobranchus longifilis *(labyrinthic catfish), from Cuvier and Valenciennes, 1828-49 (11); center above,* Galeichthys feliceps *(sea catfish), from Smith, 1838-49 (58); center below,* Clarotes laticeps *(catfish) and, bottom,* Osteogeneiosus militaris *(sea catfish), both from Cuvier and Valenciennes, 1828-49 (11). Below,* Schilbe niloticus *(butterfish), from Cuvier and Valenciennes, 1828-49 (11). On the plate, bottom,* Malapterurus electricus *(electric catfish), from Cuvier, 1836-49 (13).*

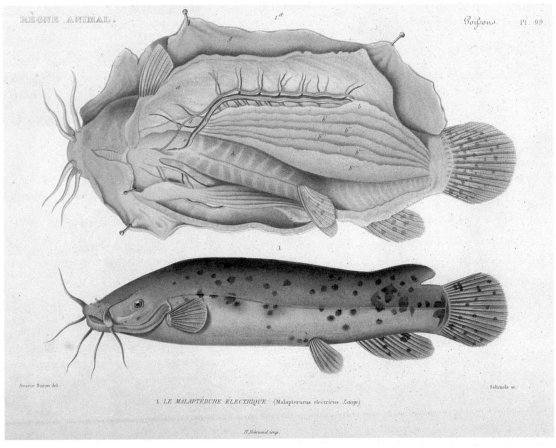

RÈGNE ANIMAL.   Poissons   Pl. 99

Acarie Baron del.   Schmelz sc.

1. *LE MALAPTÉRURE ÉLECTRIQUE.* (Malapterurus electricus. *Lacép.*)

N.Rémond imp.

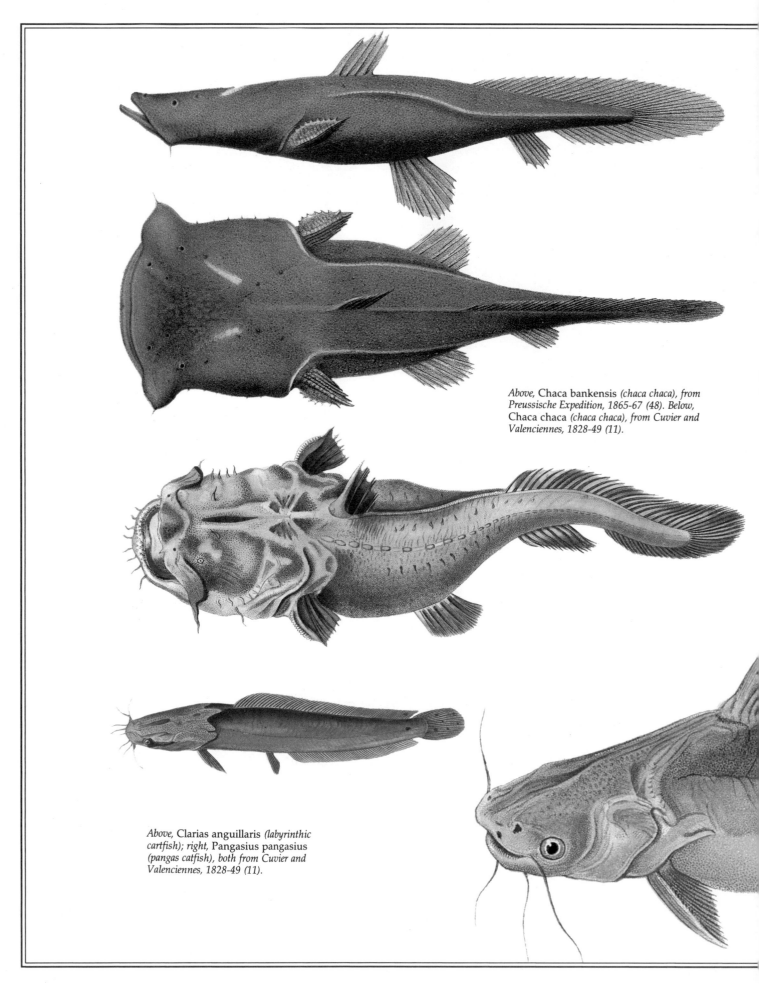

Above, Chaca bankensis *(chaca chaca), from Preussische Expedition, 1865-67 (48). Below,* Chaca chaca *(chaca chaca), from Cuvier and Valenciennes, 1828-49 (11).*

Above, Clarias anguillaris *(labyrinthic cartfish); right,* Pangasius pangasius *(pangas catfish), both from Cuvier and Valenciennes, 1828-49 (11).*

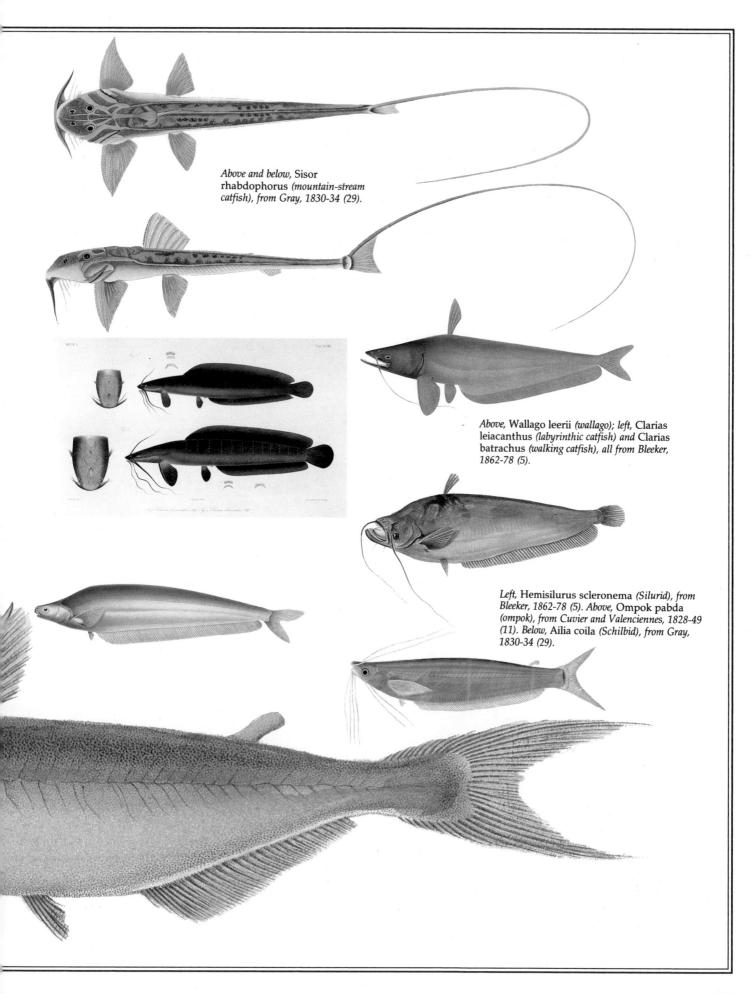

Above and below, Sisor rhabdophorus *(mountain-stream catfish), from Gray, 1830-34 (29).*

Above, Wallago leerii *(wallago); left,* Clarias leiacanthus *(labyrinthic catfish) and* Clarias batrachus *(walking catfish), all from Bleeker, 1862-78 (5).*

Left, Hemisilurus scleronema *(Silurid), from Bleeker, 1862-78 (5). Above,* Ompok pabda *(ompok), from Cuvier and Valenciennes, 1828-49 (11). Below,* Ailia coila *(Schilbid), from Gray, 1830-34 (29).*

Top, Bagarius yarrelli *(mountain-stream catfish), from Bleeker, 1862-78 (5). Center,* Rita rita *and* Aorichthys seenghala *(both Bagrids), both from Cuvier and Valenciennes, 1828-49 (11). Above,* Bagrichthys hypselopterus *(mountain-stream catfish), from Bleeker, 1862-78 (5).*

Above, Arius thalassinus *(sea catfish), from Cuvier and Valenciennes, 1828-49 (11). Below,* Arius sagor *and, bottom,* Arius macrocephalus *(sea catfish), both from Bleeker, 1862-78 (5).*

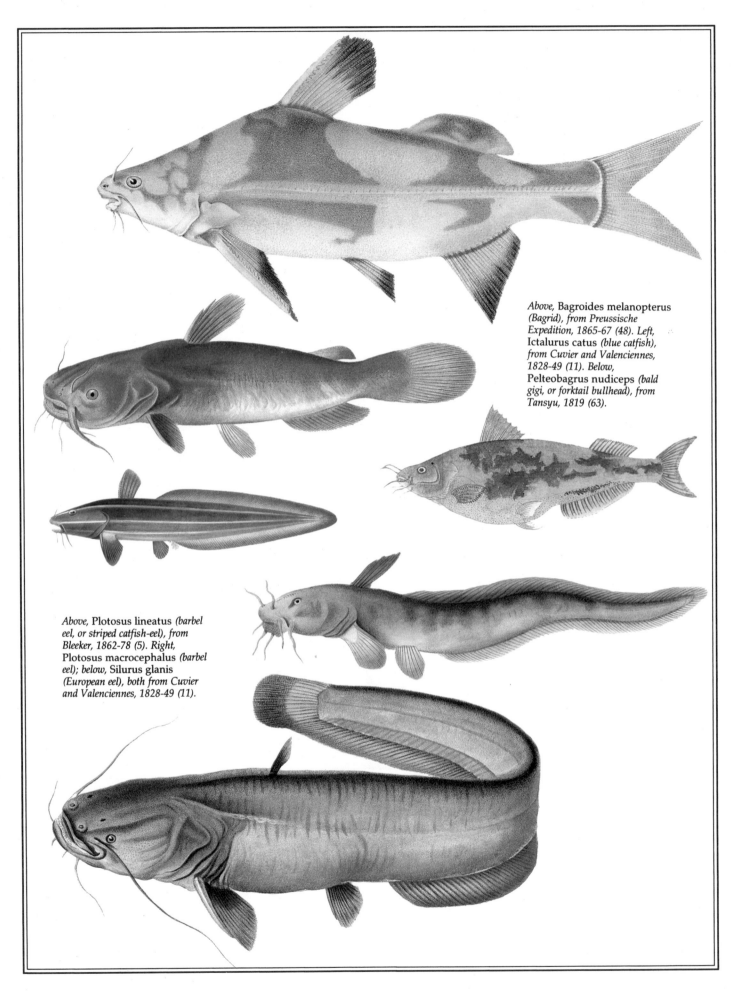

Above, Bagroides melanopterus *(Bagrid), from Preussische Expedition, 1865-67 (48). Left,* Ictalurus catus *(blue catfish), from Cuvier and Valenciennes, 1828-49 (11). Below,* Pelteobagrus nudiceps *(bald gigi, or forktail bullhead), from Tansyu, 1819 (63).*

Above, Plotosus lineatus *(barbel eel, or striped catfish-eel), from Bleeker, 1862-78 (5). Right,* Plotosus macrocephalus *(barbel eel); below,* Silurus glanis *(European eel), both from Cuvier and Valenciennes, 1828-49 (11).*

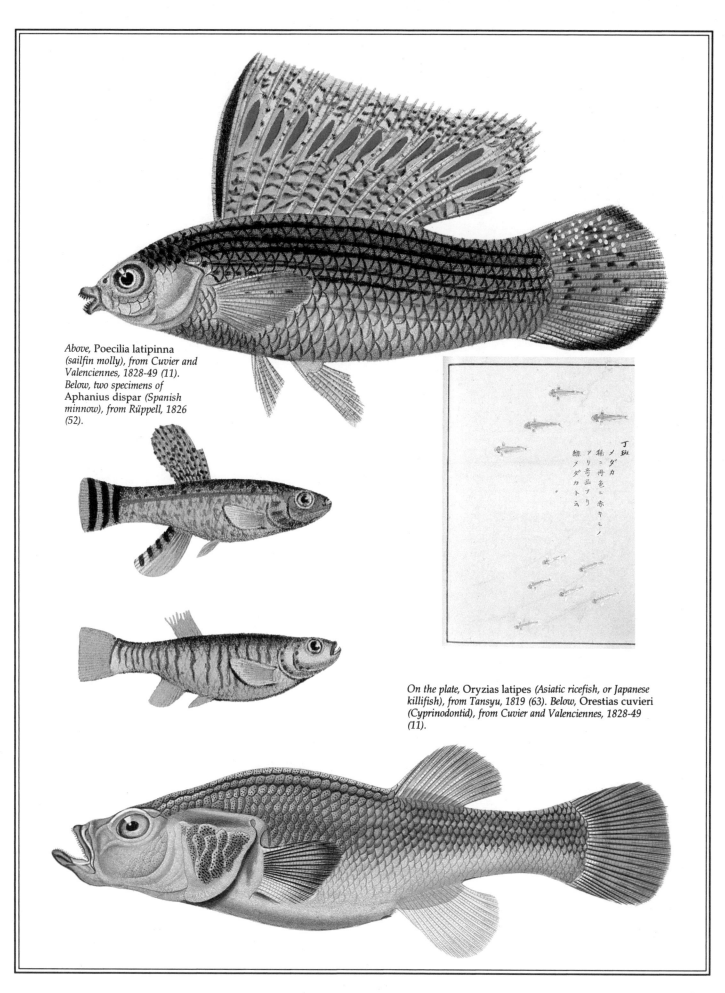

Above, Poecilia latipinna
*(sailfin molly), from Cuvier and
Valenciennes, 1828-49 (11).
Below, two specimens of*
Aphanius dispar *(Spanish
minnow), from Rüppell, 1826
(52).*

丁班
メ
ダ
カ
稀
ニ
丹
色
ニ
赤
キ
モ
ノ
ア
リ
奇
品
ナ
リ
雛
メ
ダ
カ
ト
云

On the plate, Oryzias latipes *(Asiatic ricefish, or Japanese
killifish), from Tansyu, 1819 (63). Below,* Orestias cuvieri
*(Cyprinodontid), from Cuvier and Valenciennes, 1828-49
(11).*

On the plate, top left, Cynolebias bellotti *(argentine pearl fish); right,* Aplocheilus lineatus *(striped panchax); bottom left,* Xiphophorus helleri *(green swordtail); right,* Aphyosemion australe *(lyretail), from* Aqualium, *1932-66 (1).*

Below, top, Fundulus heteroclitus *(zebra killi); center,* Anableps microlepis *(foureye fish); bottom,* Anableps *sp. (foureye fish), all from Cuvier and Valenciennes, 1828-49 (11).*

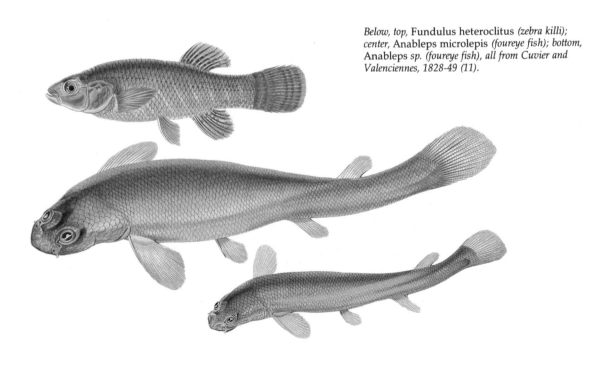

Above, Spinachia spinachia *(fifteen-spined stickleback), from Cuvier, 1836-49 (13). Left,* Gasterosteus aculeatus microcephalus *(three-spined stickleback), from Yamamoto, date missing (65).*

Above, Spinachia spinachia *(fifteen-spined stickleback), from Jardine, 1843 (35). Below, left,* Gasterosteus aculeatus aculeatus *(three-spined stickleback); right,* Pungitius pungitius *(minor stickleback), all from Donovan, 1802-08 (18).*

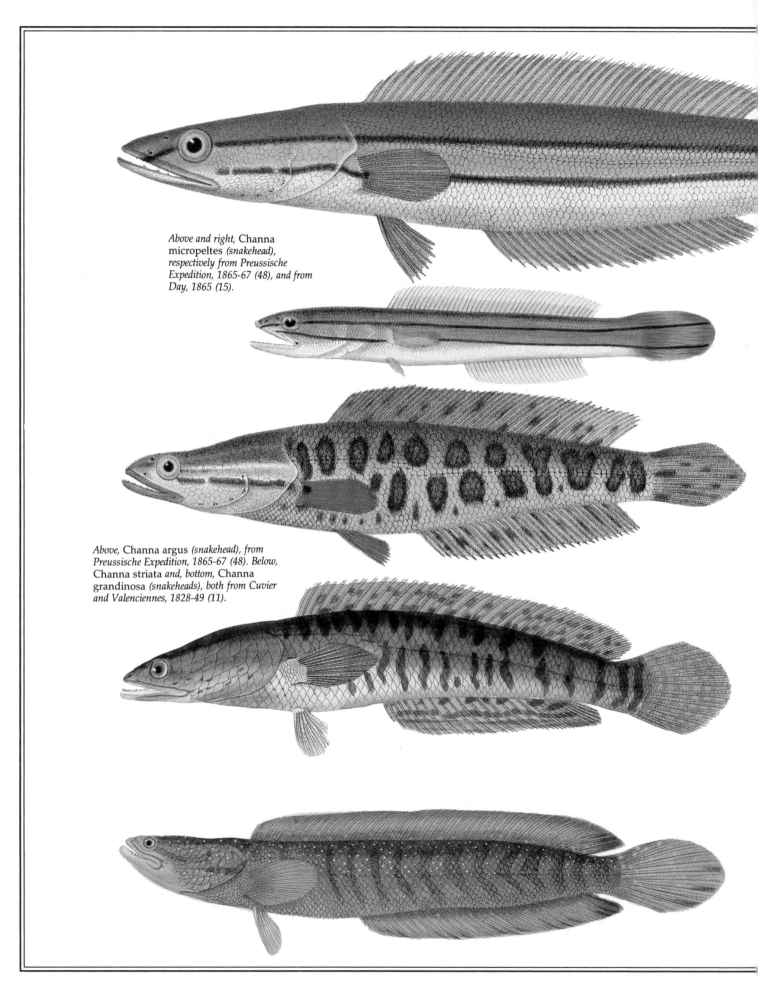

Above and right, Channa
micropeltes *(snakehead),*
respectively from Preussische
Expedition, 1865-67 (48), and from
Day, 1865 (15).

Above, Channa argus *(snakehead), from*
Preussische Expedition, 1865-67 (48). Below,
Channa striata *and, bottom,* Channa
grandinosa *(snakeheads), both from Cuvier*
and Valenciennes, 1828-49 (11).

Top, Helostoma temmincki *(kissing gourami), from Cuvier and Valenciennes, 1828-49 (11); below this,* Channa maculata *(snakehead), from Takagi, 1850 (60). Center, left,* Polyacanthus hasselti *(Belontid) and, right,* Trichogaster trichopterus *(three-spot gourami), both from Cuvier and Valenciennes, 1828-49 (11). On the plate,* Osphronemus goramy *(gourami, or gold strain), from Cuvier and Valenciennes, 1828-49 (11).*

Opposite page, top, Macropodus
operacularis *(paradise fish), from Cuvier and
Valenciennes, 1828-49 (11). Center,*
Luciocephalus pulcher *(pike-head) and*
Mastacembelus favus *(spiny eel), both from
Preussische Expedition, 1865-67 (48), and*
Mastacembelus guentheri *(spiny eel), from
Day, 1865 (15). Bottom,* Mastacembelus
maculatus *(spiny eel), from Cuvier, 19836-49
(13).*

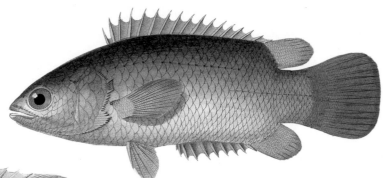

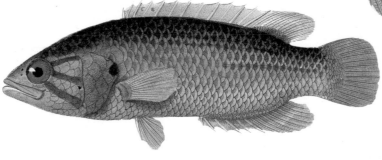

Above, Anabas testudineus *(climbing perch);
left,* Sandelia capensis *(cape curper), both
from Cuvier and Valenciennes, 1828-49 (11).
On the plate below,* Betta splendens *(Siamese
fighting fish), from Ohno, 1937-44 (46).*

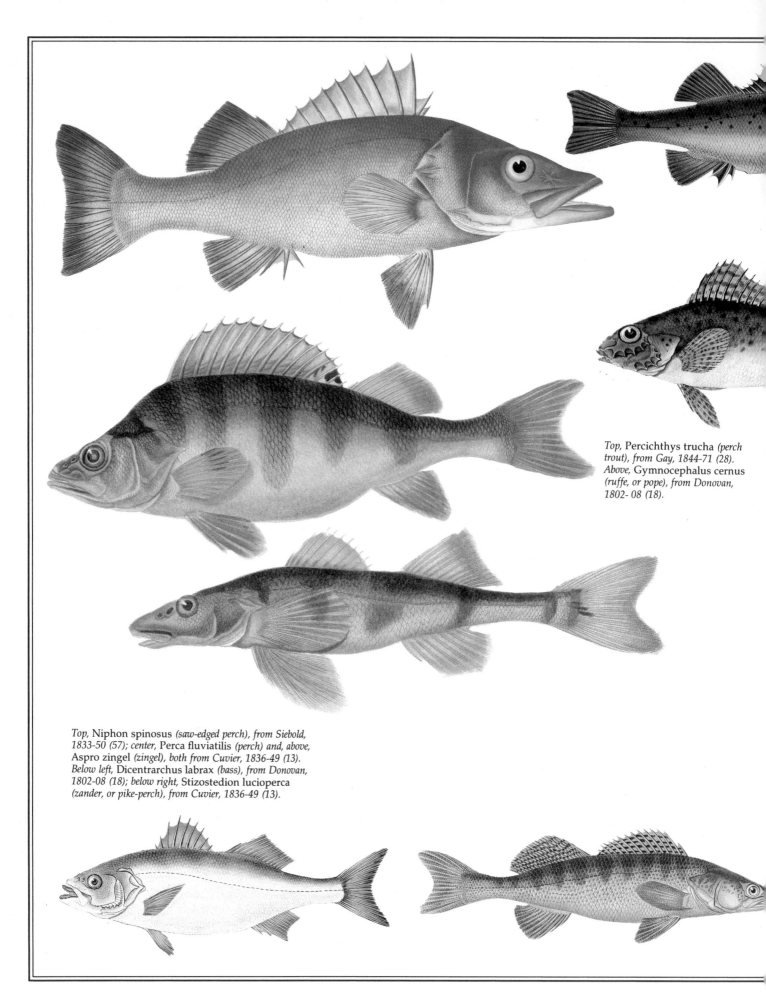

Top, Percichthys trucha *(perch trout), from Gay, 1844-71 (28). Above,* Gymnocephalus cernus *(ruffe, or pope), from Donovan, 1802- 08 (18).*

Top, Niphon spinosus *(saw-edged perch), from Siebold, 1833-50 (57); center,* Perca fluviatilis *(perch) and, above,* Aspro zingel *(zingel), both from Cuvier, 1836-49 (13). Below left,* Dicentrarchus labrax *(bass), from Donovan, 1802-08 (18); below right,* Stizostedion lucioperca *(zander, or pike-perch), from Cuvier, 1836-49 (13).*

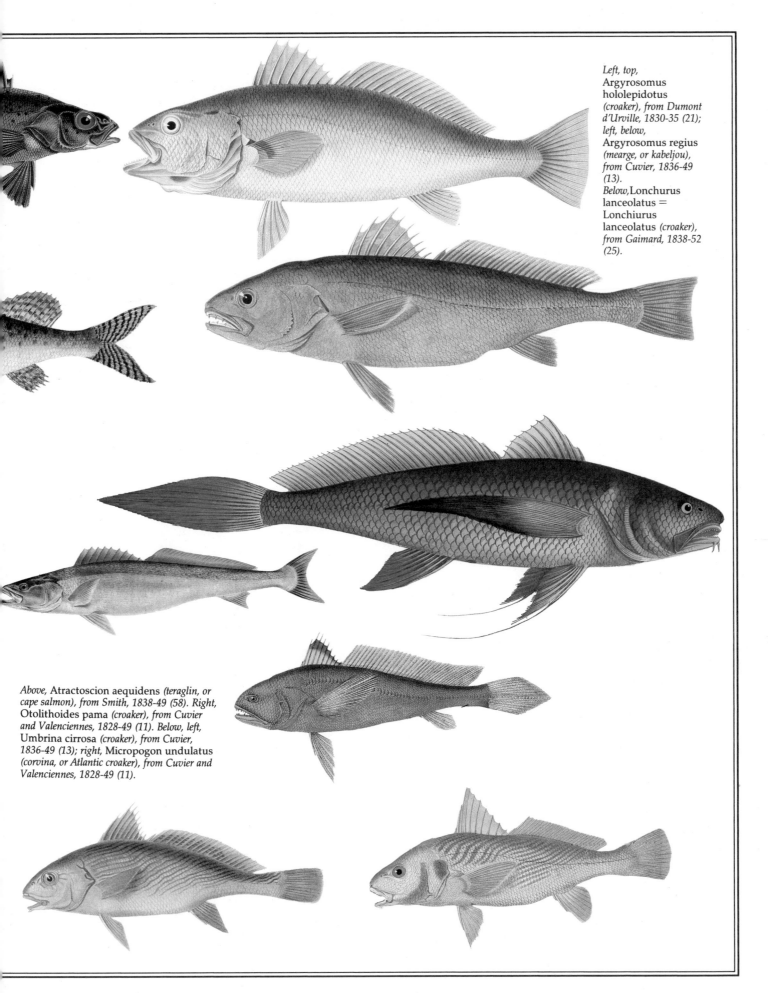

Left, top, Argyrosomus hololepidotus *(croaker), from Dumont d'Urville, 1830-35 (21); left, below,* Argyrosomus regius *(mearge, or kabeljou), from Cuvier, 1836-49 (13). Below,* Lonchurus lanceolatus = Lonchiurus lanceolatus *(croaker), from Gaimard, 1838-52 (25).*

Above, Atractoscion aequidens *(teraglin, or cape salmon), from Smith, 1838-49 (58). Right,* Otolithoides pama *(croaker), from Cuvier and Valenciennes, 1828-49 (11). Below, left,* Umbrina cirrosa *(croaker), from Cuvier, 1836-49 (13); right,* Micropogon undulatus *(corvina, or Atlantic croaker), from Cuvier and Valenciennes, 1828-49 (11).*

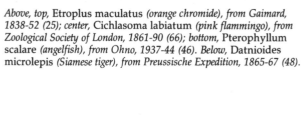

Above, top, Etroplus maculatus *(orange chromide), from Gaimard, 1838-52 (25); center,* Cichlasoma labiatum *(pink flammingo), from Zoological Society of London, 1861-90 (66); bottom,* Pterophyllum scalare *(angelfish), from Ohno, 1937-44 (46).* Below, *Datnioides microlepis (Siamese tiger), from Preussische Expedition, 1865-67 (48).*

Top, Astronotus ocellatus *(oscar, or peacock cichlid), from Schomburgk, 1843 (56). Center, above,* Tilapia sparrmani *(Sparrman's tilapia), from Smith, 1838-49 (58); center, below,* Uaru amphiacanthoides *(triangle cichlid), from Schomburgk, 1843 (56). Bottom,* Acarichthys heckelii *(Thayer's cichlid, or flag cichlid), from Aqualium, 1932-66 (1).*

Above, Cichla temensis *(lukanani, or eyespot cichlid), from Schomburgk, 1843 (56). Right,* Lepomis gibbosus *(pumpkinseed); below,* Pomoxis nigromaculatus *(black-spotted sunfish), both from Cuvier and Valenciennes, 1828-49 (11).*

Right, Micropterus salmoides *(black bass), from Cuvier, 1836-49 (13). Below,* Nandus nandus *(nandus), from Cuvier and Valenciennes, 1838-49 (11).*

Fishes with suitcases

The ichthyofauna of many fresh-water environments appears today to have been deeply modified by the introduction of exotic species. This is an intervention that requires maximum caution if we consider the serious damages — of an economic and above all naturalistic order — that can ensue.

If History with a capital "H" — the History written by the Powerful of the Earth, by their armies and their gold — is only one, the small histories indissolubly connected to it are thousands, entirely unknown to people who do not consider them with any special interest. So the history of English power, of its expansion all over the world, which appeared at one time to be limitless, finds still today a rather special but no doubt still existing resonance in the distribution — much larger than in its native Europe — of a fresh-water fish: the trout. Indeed, if *Salmo trutta* can be found today in all continents, this is mainly a consequence of the fact that the English, wherever they brought their flag and their commerce, did not fail to transplant also a piece of their faraway England, so as to be able to drink good tea, play good cricket, and also — why not — practice some good trout fishing with the "artificial fly." No small matter this, no doubt, considering the fact that some of the colonized lands were exactly at the antipodes of Great Britain and that all ships were only sail ships. Nevertheless, offering a further proof of their proverbial determination and perseverance, since 1852 the English attempted repeatedly to ship some fecundated trout eggs to the faraway lands of the Austral Hemisphere: Australia, New Zealand, Tasmania.

The first expeditions were a complete failure: in fact, long before the long journey came to an end, the ice destined to keep the eggs at a barely tolerable temperature melted, with consequent death of the eggs themselves. However, the attempts were repeated and at last — it was the year 1864 — a small quantity of eggs reached safely those remote lands. Today in Australia the European trout can be found in the rivers of the highlands in the states of Victoria and New South Wales above 600 m of altitude; and in Tasmania it is present practically in all rivers; and the same total success can be noticed in New

Zealand, where it is possible to find, besides river trout populations, also lake trout, as well as migratory trout, that is, trout that mate in fresh water to descend then and live in the sea. The present-day existence of the European trout in the Asian continent and precisely in Pakistan and Northern India (Kashmir, Himachal, Uttar Pradesh) is also connected to the English colonization.

In North America, a land of practically Anglo-Saxon "coinage," and therefore very sensitive to the appeal of "sports fishing," the first imports of European trout eggs took place in 1883, and the newly hatched trout were transferred to a water course in Michigan, the river Père Marquette. Nowadays this fish species is present in 45 states and can also be found in Canada (Alberta, British Columbia, New Brunswick, New Foundland, Nova Scotia, Ontario, and Saskatchewan).

To complete the description, we must mention also the introduction of the European trout in the Southernmost part of South America, where it can be found nowadays in almost all rivers and lakes of Argentinian Patagonia and also in the Chilean fresh waters included approximately between 19° and 55° of latitude South, as well as in some Peruvian waters, above 2,500 m of altitude.

Thanks to its practically worldwide presence, therefore, the adventurous story of the European trout most convincingly demonstrates how deeply and to what extent man can influence the fish population of fresh waters by the introduction of fish not present originally. This activity started in very remote ages. One fish that Europeans consider eminently "theirs," the carp (*Cyprinus carpio*), actually reached Europe — from its native Near East — with the Roman legions; and in Scandinavia the practice of transferring fish from one lake to another is testified to by ancient inscriptions in runic characters. Apart from this, there is no doubt that the introduction of "exotic" or "allochthonous" fish (literally: coming from another land) had become common practice by the middle of the last century, together with the interest in the study of water environments (*Hydrobiology*) and as a consequence of the improvement of the technique for artificial fish reproduction. A history of voyages and successes, as the one — mentioned before — of the European trout would have been unthinkable if at the time it had not become possible to produce fecundated eggs of this fish and other Salmonoids in practically unlimited quantities.

Above all, one event promoted and favored the "ichthyogenic" activities — those meant to increase the presence of fish in the waters — including the introduction of exotic species: the enormous International Fishing Exhibition held in Berlin from April 20 to July 1, 1880. Among the large pavilions lavishly set up by the various countries — the Italian ones, for example, were spread over an area of about twenty thousand sq.m — hydrobiology and ichthyology experts of the whole world were able to meet and discuss; from those meetings and discussions started many of the numerous acclimation experiments carried out in the following years. Thus, Professor Baird from Washington and Dr. Von Behr, a German, united by a mutual enthusiasm that did not fail even in front of the immensity of the ocean, started an intense reciprocal exchange of fish species; and among the several species of North American Salmonoids that arrived in Europe was one, the rainbow trout (*Salmo gairdneri*), destined for a brilliant success, though more as a hatchery fish than a wild fish.

However, little remains of the great majority of those attempts at introduction, because they were obviously not based on a sufficiently deep knowledge of the species that were meant for acclimation. This was certainly not the case of another introduc-

tion also conceived in that climate of enthusiasm and contact among experts in the Berlin exhibition: the introduction of other Salmonoids — whitefishes — south of the Alps, where originally they were absent. In fact, still today the work of the Italian professor Pietro Pavesi, a zoology teacher at the University of Pavia, appears to be an example of enlightened and cautious application of the principles and general knowledge of hydrobiology and ichthyology; and the results he obtained, very efficient still today, are the best proof of it.

This introduction was in fact preceded by a long period of personal research and intense contact with his foreign colleagues, from which it resulted that there is a substantial similarity of environmental conditions in the large deep lakes of glacial origin located respectively north and south of the Alps. He noticed a particularly obvious resemblance of the *zooplancton*, the mass of animal microorganisms that live suspended in the water and are the main source of food of the whitefishes that existed in the lakes of Central Europe but were absent in the Italian lakes. So Pavesi asked himself: if in these years my friend and colleague Professor Leydig has demonstrated that whitefishes feed on zooplancton, and at the same time I have proved that the same zooplancton exists in the north Italian lakes, why not try and introduce into the latter this highly appreciated fish that might constitute an important source of income for our fishermen? So, in the first days of 1855, 500,000 fecundated eggs of *Coregonus wartmanni* left the German hatchery of Hüngen for one near Lake Como, into which — from February 15 to March 5 — the newly hatched trouts were introduced. In the autumn of that same year 43 young whitefishes were caught with nets, demonstrating the full success of the operation, which was therefore successively repeated, with the same result, in the other deep north Italian lakes (Maggiore, Lugano, Iseo,

Orta, Garda) as well as in some lakes of volcanic origin of central Italy. And the joy and gratitude of fishermen for that gift that had come from far away were so great that for many years they called whitefishes "Pavesi's fishes!"

In the same way, by the end of the last century another fish of central Europe reached the south side of the otherwise impassable Alps chain: the pike-perch (*Stizostedion lucioperca*), of the Perciformes family, which, however, acclimatized successfully only in a couple of small Italian lakes. In the meantime, the affluence of North American species toward Europe grew larger and larger with other Salmonoids (the brook trout, *Salvelinus fontinalis*, the lake trout, *Salvelinus namaycush*); two Centrarchidae (pumpkinseed, *Lepomis gibbosus*, or sun fish, and the large mouth black bass, *Micropterus salmoides*, most desired prey of many sports fishermen in the United States); one or more species, it is not known for sure, of Ictaluridae (the catfishes, belonging to the genus *Ictalurus*); gambusia (*Gambusia affinis holbrooki*), of the Pecilidae family, introduced particularly in the Mediterranean area as a means of biological extermination of anopheles, the mosquitoes that transmit malaria.

Other fish crossed the Atlantic in the opposite direction, from Europe to North America. However, with the important exception of the *Salmo trutta*, mentioned before, there were few introductions beyond the redfish (*Carassius gibelio auratus*) and above all the carp. But this Cyprinid, today widely diffused in the United States and Canada, was very soon looked upon unfavorably in its new home, because it was accused of influencing negatively the environment, making water murky and uprooting water plants by its ceaseless rummaging along the bottom in search of food.

In more recent times this tendency toward the introduction of exotic fish in fresh water, far from diminishing, has further expanded and increased, greatly facilitated by air transport and stimulated not only by the desire of acquiring new species of commercial interest destined to merchant fishing but also by the ever increasing need for "novelties" on the part of sports fishermen and by the possibility of exploiting the particular biologic characteristics of a fish. This is precisely the case of the Cyprinid *Ctenopharyngodon idella*, or grass-eating carp, largely introduced into the temperate and warm waters of the whole world — starting from the Eastern Asian regions it originates from — with the purpose of controlling, thanks to its feeding habits, the infestant aquatic vegetation.

Quite often, such introductions have not been the result of intentional introduction to natural water environments, but have involved fishes that themselves, once introduced into a certain geographic area to create hatcheries, escaped from the hatchery ponds to external waters. This has happened many times and in several areas, particularly with the African Cichlids of the genus *Tilapia* — and the like — introduced in numerous tropical and equatorial countries as they represent a highly appreciated source of food, and also with other kinds of fish meant to populate ornamental aquariums. The latter, requiring generally constantly warm waters, will obviously live successfully only in the open waters of countries enjoying suitable climatic conditions; but in this case, their numbers may also rise beyond any expected or desired level.

Florida has turned out to be a true "paradise of escapes": here the climate and the presence of an enormously extended hydrographic network facilitated the acclimation of many exotic ornamental species, especially the Cichlids *Cichlasoma bimaculatus* and *Tilapia aurea*, as well as the Clariidae *Clarias batrachus*, of Asian origin, and of the Pecilidae *Belonesox belizanus*, originating from Central America.

These two, in particular, created remarkable problems: the first one, thanks to its natural capacity to come out of the water and scramble on dry land (hence its common name of walking catfish) can move quickly from one aquatic environment to the next, carrying out a heavy predatory action on the preexisting fish; the second one, called pike killfish, turned out to be a voracious predator of gambusia, seriously counteracting the successfull control of mosquito larvae effected by those small fishes.

Although the intentions behind the introduction of exotic fish are usually good, the results are often exactly the opposite. In the basin of Lake Titicaca, for example, divided between Peru and Bolivia, the introduction of *Salmo trutta, Salvelinus fontinalis, Salvelinus namaycush*, and also of the Silversides *Basilichthys bonariensis*, originating from the southeastern regions of the same subcontinent, should have produced a remarkable nutritional and economical advantage for the local people. Instead, it caused a drastic reduction of the indigenous fish most appreciated and fished by the natives (mostly belonging to the genus *Orestias*), who were also unable to catch, with their rough fishing equipment, the new species. Similarly, in Lake Lanao (Island of Mindanao, Philippines) the voluntary introduction of *Clarias batrachus, Tilapia mossambica*, and the Ophicephalidae *Ophiocephalus striatus*, together with the incidental introduction of the Gobiida *Glossogobius giurus*, brought on the almost total destruction of the native Cyprinids belonging to the genus *Barboides*.

Such cases, and many more in all parts of the world, clearly demonstrate how cautiously the introduction of exotic fish must be dealt with, to prevent the newcomers — with their action of predators or food competitors, including the possible introduction of illnesses or parasites — from damaging sometimes irreparably the original fish population of an aquatic environment. This is a very dangerous risk, that can be eliminated, or at least considerably reduced, only through accurate preliminary research about the species to be introduced, about its original environment, and about the environment that will receive it.

The sources

The color prints of fishes in this book are taken from the following famous ichthyological works. The numbers used in the captions correspond to the numbers above each title. The page numbers indicate the illustrations taken from each work.

1. *Aqualium (The)*, 1932-66. Pp. 223, 246, 254

2. Baien Mouri
Exact Illustrations of Fishes Painted by Syaseisai (Baien Mouri), 1835. P. 55

3. Baien Mouri
Illustrations of Fishes painted by Baien Mouri, date missing. P. 58

4. Bennett, John Whitchurch
A Selection from the most Remarkable and Interesting Fishes found on the Coast of Ceylon. London 1830. Pp. 64, 81, 87, 99, 104, 109, 128, 129, 132, 133, 134, 136, 142, 145, 146, 149, 161, 172, 183, 185, 189

5. Bleeker, M.-Pieter
Atlas Ichthyologique des Indes Orientales Néerlandaises. Amsterdam, 1862-78. Pp. 131, 132, 135, 136, 137, 138, 139, 140, 141, 143, 241, 242, 243, 244

6. Bloch, Marcus Elieser
Ichthyologie 1785-89. Pp. 88, 176, 185, 234

7. Brauer, A.
Die Tiefsee-Fische, Deutsche Tiefsee-Expedition, 1898-99. Pp. 44, 45, 46, 47, 48, 49, 50

8. Bushnan, J.S.
"The Naturalist's Library," vol. XXVII-XXVIII, "The Natural History of Fishes, particularly their structure and economical uses." Edinburgh, 1843. Pp. 184, 186, 187

9. Castelnau, Francis L. de Laporte, comte de
Expédition dans les parties centrales de l'Amérique du Sud. Partie 7. Zoologie, 1855-57. P. 29

10. Cooper, C. Forster

Cephalochorda - I Systematic and Anatomical Account, reprinted from "The Fauna and Geography of the Maldive and Laccadive Archipelagoes," 1906. P. 22

11. Cuvier, Georges-Léopold-Chrétien-Frédéric Dagobert et Valenciennes, Achille
Histoire Naturelle des Poissons. Paris, 1828-49. Pp. 40, 41, 44, 47, 54, 58, 59, 60, 61, 64, 67, 68, 71, 73, 74, 75, 76, 79, 82, 91, 92, 93, 98, 99, 100, 103, 104, 105, 106, 107, 109, 110, 111, 112, 113, 114, 116, 117, 120, 121, 124, 125, 127, 128, 130, 131, 133, 135, 136, 138, 139, 141, 143, 144, 145, 146, 147, 149, 152, 154, 157, 159, 161, 165, 166, 192, 193, 195, 213, 215, 216, 217, 218, 219, 221, 222, 223, 224, 225, 226, 227, 228, 229, 230, 234, 235, 236, 237, 238, 239, 240, 241, 242, 243, 244, 245, 246, 248, 249, 250, 251, 253, 255

12. Cuvier, Georges-Léopold-Chrétien-Frédéric Dagobert
The Animal Kingdom, Arranged According to Its Organization, Serving as a Foundation for the Natural History of Animals, and an Introduction to Comparative Anatomy. London, 1833-37. Pp. 63, 88, 164, 165, 216

13. Cuvier, Georges-Léopold-Chrétien-Frédéric Dagobert
Le Règne Animal distribué d'après son organisation. Paris, 1836-49. Pp. 22, 25, 26, 27, 29, 31, 51, 55, 62, 64, 65, 68, 73, 75, 77, 80, 81, 83, 89, 92, 93, 94, 95, 99, 100, 101, 103, 104, 108, 110, 111, 112, 113, 114, 115, 117, 118, 119, 120, 123, 125, 127, 128, 140, 144, 145, 147, 149, 153, 156, 163, 167, 168, 173, 174, 175, 178, 179, 180, 181, 195, 212, 216, 217, 219, 228, 235, 239, 247, 249, 250, 252, 253, 255

14. Cuvier, Georges-Léopold-Chrétien-Frédéric Dagobert
Histoire Naturelle de Lacépède. Paris 1841. P. 27

15. Day, Francis
The Fishes of Malabar. London, 1865. Pp. 74, 86, 96, 109, 118, 124, 188, 228, 233, 248, 250

16. Dean, Bashford
Chimaeroid Fishes and their Development. Washington, 1906. Pp. 30, 31

17. De Spix, J. and Agassiz, L.
Selecta genera et species Piscium quos in itinere per Brasiliam annis 1817-20 digesit, descripsit et observationibus anatomicis illustravit. Munich, 1829. P. 224

18. Donovan, Edward
The Natural History of British Fishes, including scientific and general descriptions of the most interesting species, and an extensive selection of accurately finished coloured plates. Taken entirely from original drawings. London, 1802-08. Pp. 22, 25, 26, 27, 28, 40, 51, 56, 57, 59, 60, 62, 63, 73, 74, 76, 102, 116, 119, 120, 122, 123, 126, 127, 133, 168, 171, 176, 177, 178, 179, 180, 181, 189, 217, 218, 219, 220, 226, 227, 229, 233, 247, 253

19. Donovan, Edward
The naturalist's repository or miscellany of exotic natural history, exhibiting rare and beautiful specimens of foreign birds, insects, shells, quadrupeds, fishes, and marine productions; more especially such new subjects as have not hitherto been figured, or correctly described. London, 1823-27. Pp. 16, 182, 186

20. D'Orbigny, Alcide Charles Victor Dessalines
Dictionnaire universel d'Histoire naturelle. Paris, 1837. Pp. 51, 60, 62, 70, 77, 100, 103, 107, 129, 229

21. Dumont d'Urville, M. Jules
Voyage de la Corvette L'Astrolabe exécuté pendant les années 1826-29 sous le commandement de M. Jules Dumont d'Urville, Capitaine de Vaisseau. Paris, 1830-35. Pp. 56, 77, 79, 81, 84, 95, 97, 123, 135, 140, 174, 175, 253

22. Du Petit-Thouars, Abel Aubert
Voyage Autour du Monde sur la Frégate La Vénus pendant les années 1836-39. Paris, 1846. Pp. 23, 52, 88, 91, 93, 103, 104, 130, 156, 165, 170, 174

23. *Egypte, Description de l'* 1809-30. P. 108

24. *Fauna Pontica.* Paris, date missing. Pp. 63, 124

25. Gaimard, Joseph Paul
Voyage en Islande et au Groënland exécuté pendant les années 1835 et 1836 sur la Corvette La Recherche comandé par M. Tréhouart, publié par ordre du Roi sous la direction de M. Paul Gaimard. Paris, 1838-52. Pp. 24, 30, 70, 162, 179, 193, 253, 254

26. Garman, Samuel
"Memoirs of the Museum of Comparative Zoology at Harvard College," vol. XXIV, "Reports on an Exploration off the West Coast of Mexico, Central and South America, and off the Galapagos Islands,... by the U.S. Fish Commission Steamer Albatross during 1891"; XXVI, The Fishes. Cambridge, 1899. Pp. 42, 43, 44, 46, 47, 64, 161

27. Garrett, Andrew and Günther, Albert Carl Ludwig Gotthilf
Fische der Südsee. Hamburg, 1873-1910. Pp. 50, 78, 85, 87, 91, 99, 105, 130, 147, 148, 149, 150, 151, 154, 155, 158, 159, 160, 163, 172, 189, 190

28. Gay, Claude
Historia fisica y politica de Chile. Santiago and Paris, 1844-71. Pp. 52, 74, 89, 93, 105, 106, 109, 118, 122, 125, 174, 237, 253

29. Gray, John Edward
Illustrations of Indian zoology chiefly selected from the collection of Maj.-Gen. Hardwicke. London, 1830-34. Pp. 53, 63, 134, 172, 183, 184, 213, 218, 227, 228, 229, 241

30. Hamilton, Robert
"The Naturalist's Library," vol. XXXII-XXXIII, "The Natural History of British Fishes." Edinburgh 1843. Pp. 26, 53, 69

31. Houghton, William
British Freshwater Fishes. London, 1879. P. 226

32. Iinuma, Tansai
Nankai Gyofu, 19th century. P. 191

33. *Illustrations of Fishes,* manuscript from the Meiji period (1868-1912). Pp. 55, 72, 92, 101, 139, 152, 177, 179, 194, 220

34. *Illustrations of many kinds of Fishes*, late 18th century. Pp. 80, 99, 105, 115, 173

35. Jardine, William
"The Naturalist's Library," vol. XXIX, *The Natural History of Fishes of the Perch Family.* Edinburgh, 1843. Pp. 82, 88, 89, 247

36. Kerr, John Graham
The External Features in the Development of Lepidosiren Paradoxa, from "Philosophical Transactions of the Royal Society of London." London, 1900. P. 212.

37. Kruzenshtern, Ivan Fyodorovich
Puteshchestvie vokrug' sveta v' 1803, 4,5 i 1806 godakh'. Po Poveleniyu ego imperatorskago velichestva Aleksandra Pervago, na korablyakh' Nedezhde i Nebe, pod' nachal'sshvom, 1809-10. Pp. 76, 83

38. Lefèvre, MM. T.
Voyage en Abyssinie pendant 1839-43 par une commission scientifique composée de MM. T. Lefèvre... Paris, 1845. P. 187

39. Lesson, René-Primevère
Voyage autour du monde sur la Coquille pendant 1822-25, 1826-30. P. 29

40. Lo Bianco, Salvatore
Fauna e Flora del Golfo di Napoli. Naples, date missing. Pp. 56, 75, 77, 92, 106, 107, 119, 121, 169, 170, 171, 174, 178

41. Matsumori, Taneyasu
Ryou Hakubutsu Zufu, 1881-92. P. 169

42. Meyer, Johann Daniel
Vorstellung allerhand Thiere mit ihren Gerippen Zweiter Teil alle auf das richtigste in Kupfer gebracht der Natur gemasse mit ihren Farben abgebildet und heraus gegeben. Nuremberg, 1752. Pp. 176, 220, 226, 227, 233

43. Müller, Salomon
Verhandelingen over de natuurlijke geschiedenis der Neder-landsche overzeesche bezittingen, door de leden der Natuurkundige Commissie in Indië en andere schrijvers. Uitgegeven door C.J. Temminck. Zoologie. Geredigeerd door J.A. Susanna. Leiden, 1839-44. Pp. 129, 166, 167, 215

44. Museum Godeffroy
Journal des Museum Godeffroy. Hamburg, 1873-1910. Pp. 52, 53, 134, 187, 189, 191

45. National Museum of Tokyo
Illustrations of fishes from the original water-color drawings in the Library of the National Museum of Tokyo, unpublished. Pp. 59, 71, 73, 77, 103, 110, 122, 126, 153, 218, 231, 232

46. Ohno, Bakufu
Illustrations of the Japanese fishes drawn by Bakufu Ohno, 1937-44. Pp. 29, 41, 58, 61, 67, 76, 77, 89, 101, 102, 108, 117, 118, 126, 131, 170, 175, 183, 188, 220, 221, 229, 232, 233, 251, 254

47. Pouchet, F.-A.
Zoologie classique, ou Histoire naturelle du règne animal. Paris, 1841. Pp. 168, 178

48. Preussische Expedition
Die Preussische Expedition nach Ost-Asien. Nach amtlichen Quellen. Berlin, 1865-67. Pp. 75, 240, 244, 248, 250, 254

49. Renard, Louis
Poissons, Ecrevisses et Crabes. Que l'on trouvé autour des isles Moluque, et sur les côtés des Térres Australes. Amsterdam, 1754. Pp. 27, 62, 94, 97, 99, 137, 146, 150, 151, 152, 154, 155, 157, 159, 162, 163, 165, 167, 178, 185, 186

50. Richardson, John
Icones Piscium or Plates of Rare Fishes. London, 1843. Pp. 54, 94, 95, 96, 126, 137, 182

51. Risyun, Goto
Exact Illustrations of Nature occasionally observed by Risyun Goto. 1771. Pp. 51, 182, 193

52. Rüppell, Wilhelm Peter Eduard Simon
Atlas zu der Reise im nördlichen Afrika Erste Abteilung:
Zoologie. Frankfurt-am-Main, 1826. Pp. 29, 53, 65, 79,
85, 86, 95, 98, 109, 119, 121, 128, 129, 134, 141, 142, 146,
149, 155, 162, 164, 166, 169, 187, 190, 245

53. Rüppell, Wilhelm Peter Eduard Simon
Neue Wirbeltiere, zu der Fauna von Abyssinien gehörig.
Frankfurt-am-Main, 1835-40. Pp. 75, 90, 93, 97, 102,
108, 113, 116, 120, 137, 142, 150, 155, 184, 185, 190

54. Ryokuiken
Illustrations of Animals painted by Ryokuiken. Late Edo
period, (1830-44) P. 27

55. Schlosser, Johannes Albertus - Boddaert, Pieter
Musaeum Schlosserianum. Amsterdam, 1768-72. Pp.
145, 159

56. Schomburgk, Robert Hermann
"The Naturalist's Library," vol. XXX-XXXI, *The Natural*
History of the Fishes of Guiana. Edinburgh, 1843. Pp.
214, 223, 224, 225, 234, 254, 255

57. Siebold, Philipp Franz von
Fauna Japonica, sive descriptio animalum, quae in itinere
per Japoniam... 1823-30, etc. Leiden, 1835-50. Pp. 8, 81,
82, 83, 88, 90, 96, 104, 119, 252

58. Smith, Andrew
Illustrations of the Zoology of South Africa. London,
1838-49. Pp. 23, 24, 26, 40, 53, 56, 82, 102, 107, 174, 186,
187, 231, 253, 254

59. Syuntei
Illustrations of Fishes, manuscript of the Meiji period,
(1868-1912). Pp. 82, 158, 190

60. Takagi, Shunzan
Illustrated Natural History, Edo period (1830-44). Pp.
25, 66, 111, 146, 173, 178, 195, 232, 249

61. Tanaka, Shigeho
Japanese Fishes in life colour, 1952. P. 219

62. Tansyu, Kurimoto
Senchufu, 1811. P. 192

63. Tansyu, Kurimoto
Illustrations of Fishes from the originals by Rissi (Tansyu
Kurimoto), 1819. Pp. 69, 71, 107, 122, 124, 132, 168, 181,
216, 232, 244, 245

64. Tansyu, Kurimoto
Illustrations of Fishes from the originals by Tansyu,
undated manuscript. P. 65

65. Yamamoto, Keigu
Exact Illustrations of Animals and Plants, date missing.
Pp. 144, 158, 247

66. Zoological Society of London
Proceedings of the Scientific Meetings, London, 1861-90.
Pp. 23, 25, 62, 90, 124, 136, 144, 145, 212, 218, 219, 220,
254

Latin names of the species

English names of the species